Collins

Tea

Maths Frameworking

3rd edition

Rob Ellis, Kevin Evans,
Keith Gordon, Chris Pearce,
Trevor Senior, Brian Speed,
Sandra Wharton

William Collins's dream of knowledge for all began with the publication of his first book in 1819. A self-educated mill worker, he not only enriched millions of lives, but also founded a flourishing publishing house. Today, staying true to this spirit, Collins books are packed with inspiration, innovation and practical expertise. They place you at the centre of a world of possibility and give you exactly what you need to explore it.

Collins. Freedom to teach.

Published by Collins
An imprint of HarperCollins*Publishers*
The News Building
1 London Bridge Street
London
SE1 9GF

Browse the complete Collins catalogue at
www.collins.co.uk

British Library Cataloguing in Publication Data
A Catalogue record for this publication is available from the British Library.

Written by Rob Ellis, Kevin Evans, Keith Gordon, Chris Pearce Trevor Senior, Brian Speed and Sandra Wharton
Commissioned by Katie Sergeant
Project managed by Elektra Media Ltd
Development edited and copy-edited by Gudrun Kaiser
Edited by Helen Marsden
Proofread by Grace Glendinning
Illustrations by Jerry Fowler and Ann Paganuzzi
Typeset by Elektra Media Ltd
Cover design by Angela English
Production by Emma Roberts

Printed and bound in Great Britain by Martins the Printers

Acknowledgements
The publishers wish to thank the following for permission to reproduce photographs. Every effort has been made to trace copyright holders and to obtain their permission for the use of copyright materials. The publishers will gladly receive any information enabling them to rectify any error or omission at the first opportunity.

Cover Nikonaft/Shutterstock.

Contents

17 Ratio

Introduction

Maths Frameworking has been fully revised and updated in line with the 2014 Programme of study for Key Stage 3 Mathematics. This third edition provides complete coverage of the subject content of the new curriculum, as well as ample material to support pupils in fulfilling its three overarching aims: developing mathematical fluency, mathematical reasoning, and problem-solving skills.

Maths Frameworking 3rd edition components

- **Pupil Books:** three per year, catering for different levels of ability.
- **Teacher Packs:** one to accompany each Pupil Book.
- **Homework Books:** one per year, encompassing practice material, which is graduated in difficulty and suitable for all ability levels.
- **Intervention Workbooks:** five workbooks of increasing difficulty level (levels 3–7 of the previous national curriculum), designed for targeted one-to-one intervention to help pupils achieve the expected level of progress.
- **Digital resources on Collins Connect:** Collins Connect is an online platform which includes interactive versions of the Pupil Books, with interactive classroom and homework activities, assessments, tools and videos that have been specially developed to help pupils improve their mathematics skills.

Features of this Teacher Pack

This Teacher Pack accompanies *Maths Frameworking 3rd edition Pupil Book 1.1* and caters for lower-tier pupils (working at roughly Levels 3–5 of the previous curriculum). Middle-tier pupils (working at roughly Levels 4–6) are catered for by Pupil Book 1.2 and the accompanying Teacher Pack 1.2, and higher-tier pupils (Levels 5–6) are catered for by Pupil Book 1.3 and Teacher Pack 1.3. The topics and their sequence are the same across all three books but are handled at different levels, allowing for sensitive differentiation in mixed-ability classes.

We have produced around 100 one-hour lessons to cover all the material you need in order to deliver the new Programme of study. These lessons should provide the flexibility to include tests, extended activities and revision classes in the teaching programme, and allow for the normal events that may disrupt teaching time. For further help when mapping lessons and producing your scheme of work, please consult the Contents pages and the Programme of study matching chart provided in this book.

Chapter overview

Pupil Book chapters are categorised according to the sections of the Programme of study to which they relate, and are colour-coded as follows:

- Number – pink
- Algebra – green
- Ratio, proportion and rates of change – lilac
- Geometry and measures – orange
- Probability – navy
- Statistics – teal

Each chapter of this Teacher Pack starts with an outline of the content covered in the chapter, explaining clearly how the lesson plans cover the National Curriculum and providing context for the topics covered. Its features are listed below.

- **Learning objectives** identify the key learning outcomes.
- **Prior knowledge** highlights the underpinning mathematics that pupils will draw on in the chapter, taking into account the coverage of the new Programme of study for Key Stage 2.
- **Context** provides some real-life or historical background for the key mathematical ideas explored in the chapter and gives suggestions on how to use the corresponding chapter opener in the Pupil Book.
- **Discussion points** provide some ideas for warm-up questions to introduce pupils to the topic.
- **Associated Collins ICT resources** provide an overview of the digital resources related to the chapter, which are available on the Collins Connect online platform.
- **Curriculum references** show how the materials meet the requirements of the new curriculum with references to the 2014 Programme of study.
- **Fast-track for classes following a 2-year scheme of work** provides suggestions for parts of the chapter that can be omitted if the class is following a condensed Key Stage 3.

Lesson plans

A lesson plan is provided for each topic in the Pupil Book. Every plan follows the same format, making it easy to prepare for and use. Its features are listed below.

- **Learning objectives** identify the key learning outcomes of the lesson.
- **Links to other subjects** highlight the topics' cross-curricular links, encouraging pupils to relate what they are learning in mathematics to what they are learning in other subjects.
- **Resources** list the content relating to the lesson that is available in other components of the scheme.
- **Homework activities** provide references to the related activities in the Homework Book and on the Collins Connect online platform.
- **Key words** provide a list of the key terms that pupils need to understand and use to talk about this topic. The words match the key words in the Pupil Book.
- **Problem solving, reasoning and financial skills help** details how the topic relates to the overarching aims of the Programme of study and, where appropriate, how it helps pupils to develop their financial skills.
- **Common misconceptions and remediation** pinpoints typical problems that pupils may have in getting to grips with the topic, and gives advice on how pupils can overcome these problems.
- **Probing questions** are designed to bring out important aspects of the topic and to link these aspects to pupils' prior knowledge.
- **Part 1** of the lesson plan is an engaging oral and mental starter involving the whole class; it has been designed to require minimal specialised equipment.
- **Part 2** is a main lesson activity, which helps you to lead pupils into the exercise questions.
- **Part 3** is a plenary designed to round off the three-part lesson.
- **Answers** are provided at the end of each lesson plan. Answers for the review questions and the activity are at the end of each chapter.

Answers for other course components

Answers to the Homework Book and Intervention Workbook questions can be found at this website link: **www.collins.co.uk/mathsframeworkinganswers**.

Scheme of work

A flexible 2-year and 3-year scheme of work is provided at the back of the book and in editable Word and Excel format on the CD-ROM accompanying this book. It shows two routes through the content, which are suitable for schools following a 2- or 3-year programme for Key Stage 3.

Teacher Pack CD-ROM

The CD-ROM in the front cover of this book contains:
- all the lesson plans in Word format for you to customise as you wish
- the 2- and 3-year schemes of work in Word and Excel format
- a printable version of the progression checklists for each chapter of the Pupil Book, which may be copied and distributed to the class for self-assessment, and for pupils to gauge their progress and learn how to improve
- skills maps for fluency, mathematical reasoning and problem solving
- a letter describing the philosophy and features of *Maths Frameworking 3rd edition* that can be customised and distributed to parents.

Digital resources available on Collins Connect

A variety of engaging resources are available on Collins Connect to support and enhance your teaching.

- **Classroom presentation resources** include:
  - an interactive version of the three Pupil Books for each year
  - interactive activities, including matching pairs and drag-and-drops, that can be used as starters and plenaries to improve fluency or stimulate group discussion
  - engaging video clips that develop pupils' conceptual understanding of key topics
  - 'Maths Man' videos that use rhythm and music to help pupils remember essential maths facts
  - exciting real-life videos and images, with accompanying teacher notes, that bring to life the awe and wonder of mathematics and encourage open conversations involving mathematics
  - audio-worked examples that model how to approach a variety of question types – including problem solving – and demonstrate best practice.
- Innovative **skills-building interactives** that enable pupils to explore and discover confidentially in order to build their conceptual understanding of, and skills in, proportional reasoning and equations.
- A **digital version of the Pupil Book glossary**, complete with recordings of all the key words – ideal for supporting literacy.
- **Automarked homework** tasks to accompany each lesson. Differentiated homeworks are provided for in the different Pupil Books.
- **Automarked assessments with diagnostic feedback**, including a diagnostic assessment for the start of the course, half-term assessments covering the main

Collins Connect also provides invaluable tools to aid in tracking pupils' progress:

- **Synchronisation with SIMS**, enabling you to set up individual pupil accounts quickly and easily.
- **Task assignment** functionality, which lets you set any part of the interactive Pupil Book to a pupil or class as an assignment. As with the interactive homework tasks, you can set pupils a deadline for completion.
- **Results overviews** show the marks achieved by your classes in the homework tasks and tests you have set for them. Results can be displayed by a pupil, an assignment or a class, so that you can pinpoint areas for intervention easily.

Find out more at **www.collins.co.uk/connect**.

Maths Frameworking and the 2014 Key Stage 3 Programme of study for mathematics

Rationale

Following the publication of the Schools White Paper, 'The Importance of Teaching' (DfE, November 2010), the UK government instigated a review into the national curriculum in mathematics. The stated aim of the review was to benchmark expectations for pupils in this country against the expectations of the most successful nations in the world, and to draw on this information to design a new curriculum that would put English pupils on a par with pupils in the highest performing countries. In February 2013, the DfE began an extensive consultation process involving the mathematics community. In September 2013, this process resulted in the publication of a revised Programme of study for Key Stage 3 mathematics. The new curriculum became statutory in September 2014.

The 2014 Programme of study for mathematics

Subject content

The subject content of both the new Key Stage 2 and Key Stage 3 programmes of study has changed with respect to the former curriculum. Probability has been removed from the Key Stage 2 curriculum, in favour of greater emphasis on the foundations of algebra and on skills in number (for example, multiplication tables up to 12×12 and long multiplication and division). This means that the expectations of the prior knowledge that pupils bring with them at the start of Key Stage 3 will also change. Although there has been some reduction of content, in other areas the expectation in Key Stage 2 is very demanding as it includes some topics that were at level 6 in the old Programme of study. This third edition of *Maths Frameworking* considers these new expectations and creates a framework for progression from this new starting point.

At Key Stage 3, the Programme of study is divided into six strands. Within these, some of the content requirements have been more fully described. One example is a deeper exploration of the properties of prime numbers than before. There is also increased precision in the areas of algebra and of geometry and measures. 'Ratio, proportion and rates of change' now stands alone as a strand in its own right, emphasising the links between fractions, ratios, proportion and percentages. Probability and Statistics are now also treated as separate strands. Some of the material that was at level 8 in the old Programme of study has been removed. Trigonometry is an example. The intention is that pupils who grasp concepts rapidly should be challenged with more demanding problems on the same subject matter rather than being accelerated through new content in preparation for GCSE. The structure and coverage of the *Maths Frameworking* Pupil Books has been reworked comprehensively to reflect these changes.

Overarching aims

A key difference in the new Programme of study for mathematics is the introduction of three overarching aims, which are presented as integral to study of the subject content. The aims are to ensure that all pupils:

- become fluent in the fundamentals of mathematics, including through varied and frequent practice with increasingly complex problems over time, so that pupils develop conceptual understanding and the ability to recall and apply knowledge rapidly and accurately.
- reason mathematically by following a line of enquiry, conjecturing relationships and generalisations, and developing an argument, justification or proof using mathematical language.
- can solve problems by applying their mathematics to a variety of routine and non-routine problems with increasing sophistication, including breaking down problems into a series of simpler steps and persevering in seeking solutions.

The Key Stage 2 and Key Stage 3 programmes of study share the same overarching aims, and these aims form the basis for the assessment objectives in the new mathematics GCSE for first teaching in September 2015. The intention of the DfE is to ensure smooth progression through the three Key Stages, with the Key Stage 3 Programme of study consolidating and building on understanding from Key Stage 2 in order to form solid foundations for further study at GCSE and beyond.

The aims of the national curriculum are intended to be developed and applied across the mathematical content of the Programme of study, and their treatment in *Maths Frameworking 3rd edition* reflects this. For example, pupils develop fluency by using algebra to consolidate their understanding from Key Stage 2 and generalise the structure of arithmetic. They reason mathematically and extend their understanding of the number system by making connections between number relationships and their algebraic and graphical representations. They solve problems by selecting appropriate concepts, methods and techniques to apply to unfamiliar and non-routine problems.

Fluency and linking

Fluency in mathematics has two important facets: familiarity and recollection. Familiarity is important because it means that, when faced with a calculation, pupils can recognise the steps required to complete it by drawing on prior experience of completing other similar calculations. The ability to recollect pertinent mathematics facts and techniques further enhances pupils' ability to complete calculations rapidly, as they access, for example, their knowledge of times tables and mental mathematics techniques to reach an answer without needing to use a calculator.

Fundamental to fostering both of these aspects of mathematical fluency, is ensuring that pupils gain extensive practice. Rich and varied practice lies at the heart of *Maths*

Frameworking. At the start of each lesson plan in this Teacher Pack, we suggest a series of probing questions, which are designed to encourage pupils to recall previously learnt mathematics facts and skills that are of relevance to the topic. The exercises within every topic offer a wide range of questions of increasing complexity to which pupils can apply these skills and knowledge. The Homework Books and auto-marked homework activities on Collins Connect offer further opportunities for practice.

In addition to ensuring plentiful practice, the *Maths Frameworking* scheme ensures that the practice encourages in pupils the understanding and mastery that are the hallmarks of true fluency by providing opportunities for practice across different mathematical and cross-curricular contexts.

In Ofsted's paper, 'Mathematics: Understanding the Score' (Ofsted, September 2008), Ofsted identified that the majority of pupils had too few opportunities to use and apply mathematics and to make connections across different areas of the subject. In the 2014 national curriculum, mathematical topics figure in a wide variety of curricular subjects. For example, Design and technology pupils need to be comfortable when working with 2D and 3D plans, while data-handling skills are required in Geography, Science and Computing. The 2014 national curriculum also places renewed emphasis on financial education, with a focus within the new mathematics Programme of study on solving problems involving percentage increases and decreases, simple interest and repeated growth. This has clear links to the Programme of study for Citizenship, which requires pupils to learn the functions and uses of money, the importance and practice of budgeting, and managing risk.

Maths Frameworking draws out these intra- and cross-curricular links in order to help pupils to become adept at making connections. Throughout the books, questions are presented in varied contexts taken both from real life and from the subject areas mentioned previously, plus other subject areas. In the 'Review' questions at the end of each chapter, as well as checking pupils' grasp of the mathematics topics covered within it, other parts of mathematics are also brought into play. Questions are posed, which require pupils to combine learning across different topics in order to answer them. Furthermore, each chapter begins with an opening page that presents real-life applications of the topic covered, giving pupils a window onto why it is important and useful outside of the classroom. This helps pupils to make links between the mathematics they are studying in different parts of the curriculum, to the relevance in real life, rather than learning only the mathematics. These Pupil Book features are supported by accompanying guidance in this Teacher Pack: the 'Context' section at the start of each chapter provides background information for teachers, while the 'Links to other subjects' section of each lesson plan highlights cross-curricular links in each topic.

Problem solving and reasoning

The ability to solve problems within mathematics and in other subjects is a key skill, which consultations have shown that employers require across different industries and economic sectors. In the specifications for the new mathematics GCSE for first teaching in September 2015, problem solving is to become one of the three assessment objectives, together with using and applying standard techniques and reasoning mathematically. Teaching at Key Stage 3 needs to build pupils' problem-solving skills in preparation for study at GCSE level. Crucial to this is equipping pupils with strategies that will help them to see the 'big picture' and nurture mathematical independence, allowing time for thinking, and encouraging discussion in the classroom. The lesson plans in this book provide a wide variety of suggestions on how teachers can do this, and offer varied opportunities for probing pupils' understanding and encouraging reflection.

The first step in problem solving in mathematics at this level is often identifying 'where the maths is' and what mathematical techniques can be applied to answer a question. The problem-solving questions in *Maths Frameworking*, especially the extended double-page problem-solving spreads, guide pupils through this process, equipping them with techniques to decipher word problems and 'translate' descriptions into mathematics. Making conjectures and trying different approaches to solve problems is also an important reflex that *Maths Frameworking* develops by providing guided questions in which pupils can experiment and are encouraged to question and reflect. Across the varied problem-solving questions in *Maths Frameworking*, pupils are also encouraged to develop visual representation techniques by using graphs, charts or diagrams to help them get to grips with a word problem or identify a pattern.

Mathematical reasoning is another key skill that has been embedded in this third edition of *Maths Frameworking*. Pupils are reasoning mathematically when they follow a line of enquiry, conjecture a relationship or generalisation, and develop an argument, justification or proof using mathematical language. Reasoning questions and extended double-page reasoning spreads, give pupils opportunities to do this, encouraging them to develop the skill set needed in order to investigate, prove and explain. Developing good habits for showing working and justifying answers will stand pupils in good stead for the second new assessment objective at GCSE level, for which they will need to demonstrate their ability to: make deductions, inferences and draw conclusions from mathematical information, construct chains of reasoning to achieve a given result, interpret and communicate information accurately, present arguments and proofs and assess the validity of an argument and critically evaluate a given way of presenting information. Giving pupils the opportunity to improve the quality of their reasoning is also important in developing their abilities in this area. The 'Common misconceptions and remediation' section of each lesson plan aims to guide teachers in helping pupils to improve.

Providing opportunities for extended responses builds mathematical resilience in pupils, and is a necessary skill for problem solving and reasoning. In the Pupil Book, particular types of question are flagged so that teachers and pupils can find them easily and see which skills are being worked on:

 indicates questions that require pupils to solve problems

 indicates questions that require pupils to reason mathematically

 indicates questions that help to develop pupils' financial skills and financial awareness.

Approach to progression

In the 2014 curriculum, the system of levels formerly used to report pupils' attainment and progress has been removed. The reason given for this by the DfE was that the over-emphasis on levelling in schools encouraged teachers to focus too tightly on 'hitting the numbers' rather than forming a more holistic view of each pupil's progress in terms of conceptual understanding. Ofsted subject-specific exemplification states that the 'development of all pupils' conceptual understanding [...] and progression within each lesson and over time' is one of the hallmarks of outstanding mathematical teaching. In keeping with this, the new Programme of study sets out what subject knowledge should be acquired by the end of Key Stage 3, but gives schools the freedom to develop their own scheme of work for covering it, and their own system for tracking pupils' progress.

The scheme of work and lesson plans in *Maths Frameworking* offer schools a framework structured to ensure progression both over time and within every lesson. The scheme of work has been developed to ensure that all pupils meet expectations in relation to the aims and content of the Key Stage 3 Programme of study, and that they have the opportunity to progress through the curriculum in a way that supports understanding and challenge. We appreciate that giving pupils the *appropriate degree* of challenge for their current level of ability and knowledge is crucial to their making progress, and the three different tiers of the *Maths Frameworking* scheme enable us to achieve this by creating differentiated progression pathways for pupils according to their different starting points. Pupil Book 1.1 covers levels 3–5 of the former national curriculum; Pupil Book 1.2 covers levels 4–6, and Pupil Book 1.3 covers levels 4–6, with a greater proportion of level 5 and 6 materials. We have consulted with mathematics teachers and experts on how material should be presented and structured within the different tiers in order to ensure smooth progression for different pupils. The result is materials that are tailored to pupils' differential prior knowledge, skills and understanding, which gradually build on these to foster and support progress.

Progression is built into every exercise in the scheme. Exercises start with straightforward questions to consolidate skills and understanding; then move on to more varied and demanding material, and end with extension tasks that are designed to challenge and stretch pupils at the level that is appropriate to their learning abilities. At the end of each chapter of the Pupil Book, pupils are encouraged to reflect on what they have learned and what they need to do to progress by self-assessing using the 'Ready to progress?' checklist (also available in printable format on the CD-ROM accompanying this book).

To enable schools and teachers to check that pupils are on track to meet expectations, we have developed a system of colour-coded icons to show the level of difficulty of each question in the Pupil Books. Teachers and pupils can see at a glance whether they are working in line with expected progress for each learning pathway and year of study. We appreciate that, during the first stages of implementing the new curriculum, many schools will continue to monitor pupils' progression in terms of the levels used in the former curriculum. To facilitate this, and aid in the transition between this system and the new system, which is based on expectations of progress, we have based our system of icons on the former level descriptors. The table below shows the approximate correlation between the progress indicators used in *Maths Frameworking* and the levels used in the previous national curriculum:

	Less than expected progress	Expected progress	More than expected progress
Pupil Book 1.1	≤ Level 3	Level 4	≥ Level 5
Pupil Book 1.2	≤ Level 4	Level 5	≥ Level 6
Pupil Book 1.3	≤ Level 4	Level 5	≥ Level 6
Pupil Book 2.1	≤ Level 4	Level 5	≥ Level 6
Pupil Book 2.2	≤ Level 5	Level 6	≥ Level 7
Pupil Book 2.3	≤ Level 5	Level 6	≥ Level 7
Pupil Book 3.1	≤ Level 4	Level 5	≥ Level 6
Pupil Book 3.2	≤ Level 5	Level 6	≥ Level 7
Pupil Book 3.3	≤ Level 6	Level 7	≥ Level 8

Another aspect of progression that has been emphasised in recent studies on mathematics pedagogy is the CPA, or concrete-pictorial-abstract, sequence. Research suggests that progression in mathematical thinking rests on transitioning from the physical manipulation of concrete materials (an important feature of practice at primary level) to pictorial representations, and finally to written representations in mathematical notation. Developing connections between these three types of experiences, and thereby transitioning through the three stages of understanding, is foremost for making solid progress and becoming mathematically confident and fluent. *Maths Frameworking* aids pupils in building on their experiences in Key Stage 2 and progressing to pictorial and abstract representations by drawing on a variety of different media, for example, pictures, diagrams and charts, as well as correct mathematical notation, in order to explain concepts. Where appropriate, for concepts that are being introduced for the first time, the lesson plans in this Teacher Pack provide suggestions for guidance to use in class.

Approach to assessment

In its paper, 'Mathematics: Understanding the Score', Ofsted identified the need for teachers to place greater emphasis on developing pupils' understanding and on checking it throughout lessons. Ofsted advocated that schools should ensure that pupils have a wide range of opportunities to use and apply mathematics, and that these should be underpinned by thorough assessment, recording and reporting. Regular assessment is known to be a motivating factor for pupils, as gaining awareness of the progress they are making helps to build their confidence, thereby laying the foundations for further achievement. The abolition of levels in the 2014 national curriculum will see a phase shift in how schools approach assessment; *Maths Frameworking* offers a range of tools to support schools in making this transition.

Under the new curriculum, it is the intention of the DfE that assessment should be built into and become integral to the school curriculum, thus allowing schools to check what pupils have learned and whether they are on track to meet expectations at the end of the Key Stage ('Assessing Without Levels', DfE, June 2013). This means creating opportunities for formal, periodic assessment and building informal assessment into daily classroom practices through, for example, the effective use of probing questions to assess progress and identify and tackle misconceptions.

Maths Frameworking supports schools' own approaches to formative assessment by providing a suite of resources that will enable them to track and offer evidence of each pupil's progress through the Key Stage, however and whenever they desire.

- Discussion points are suggested at the start of each chapter of this Teacher Pack, to enable teachers to detect prior knowledge before starting work on a topic.
- Probing questions are provided in each lesson plan to support informal assessment during the course of normal lessons.
- In order to facilitate regular monitoring of pupils' progress, at the end of each chapter of the Pupil Book, synoptic review questions are provided so that pupils and teachers have an opportunity to assess understanding of the topic covered.
- The 'Ready to progress' chart at the end of each chapter provides an opportunity for self-assessment, and for pupils to see what they need to do next in order to improve.
- Auto-marked homework tasks on the Collins Connect platform provide opportunities for formative assessment for each topic in the Pupil Books. Diagnostic feedback enables pupils to identify areas that they need to strengthen and directs them to resources that will help them. Results overviews help you to identify pupils' strengths and any areas where you might need to intervene.
- Tailor-made assessments are also provided for each tier of the *Maths Frameworking* scheme on the Collins Connect platform. A diagnostic assessment is available to evaluate pupils' starting points at the beginning of the first year of Key Stage 3 and to help you to decide how to set them. Thereafter, differentiated half-term tests are provided for each strand of the scheme, each one covering roughly five to six chapters of material. These tests evaluate pupils' progress against the stated objectives for each topic and again provide diagnostic feedback to identify pupils' strengths and areas for improvement.

Maths Frameworking and the new mathematics GCSE

In the new national curriculum, there is greater continuity between the Key Stage 3 Programme of study and the subject content of the new maths GCSE for first teaching in September 2015. The same six thematic strands are used in both Key Stages 3 and 4, and there are a number of examples where the wording used is exactly the same in the subject content for both levels. This means that pupils who have a secure understanding of the material in the Key Stage 3 Programme of study will be very well prepared for the study of mathematics at Key Stage 4.

The assessment objectives for the new mathematics GCSE also build on and formalise the overarching aims of the Programme of study for Key Stages 1, 2 and 3, thereby forming a unified pathway for mathematics across primary and secondary. The Key Stage 3 Programme of study makes it clear, however, that there is no expectation that teaching of content from previous Key Stages should be repeated. Instead, pupils should be given the opportunity in Key Stage 4 to make choices and decisions about the mathematics they use, drawing on a well-developed toolkit to interpret and communicate mathematics for different audiences and purposes. It is this well-developed toolkit – a secure grounding in both content and process skills – that *Maths Frameworking 3rd edition* provides, thus creating the firm foundations that should enable every pupil to progress to GCSE and succeed at it.

Programme of study matching chart

This chart matches the subject content of the 2014 Programme of study for Key Stage 3 mathematics to specific lesson plans contained in this Teacher Pack.

Working mathematically Through the mathematics content, pupils should be taught to:	Chapter title	Lesson number and title
Number		
Understand and use place value for decimals, measures and integers of any size	1 Using numbers 4 Decimal numbers	1.1 The calendar 1.2 The 12-hour and 24-hour clocks 1.3 Managing money 1.4 Positive and negative numbers 1.5 Adding negative numbers 1.6 Subtracting negative numbers 4.1 Multiplying and dividing by 10, 100 and 1000 4.2 Ordering decimals 4.4 Adding and subtracting decimals 4.5 Multiplying and dividing decimals
Order positive and negative integers, decimals and fractions; use the number line as a model for ordering of the real numbers; use the symbols =, ≠, <, >, ≤, ≥	1 Using numbers 4 Decimal numbers 8 Fractions	1.4 Positive and negative numbers 1.5 Adding negative numbers 1.6 Subtracting negative numbers 4.2 Ordering decimals 8.2 Comparing fractions
Use the concepts and vocabulary of prime numbers, factors (or divisors), multiples, common factors, common multiples, highest common factor, lowest common multiple, prime factorisation, including using product notation and the unique factorisation property	Covered in Year 8	
Use the four operations, including formal written methods, applied to integers, decimals, proper and improper fractions, and mixed numbers, all both positive and negative	1 Using numbers	1.1 The calendar 1.2 The 12-hour and 24-hour clocks 1.4 Positive and negative numbers 1.5 Adding negative numbers 1.6 Subtracting negative numbers

	4 Decimal numbers	4.1 Multiplying and dividing by 10, 100 and 1000 4.4 Adding and subtracting decimals 4.5 Multiplying and dividing decimals
	5 Working with numbers	5.1 Square numbers 5.3 Order of operations 5.4 Long and short multiplication 5.5 Long and short division 5.6 Calculating with measurements
	8 Fractions	8.1 Equivalent fractions 8.2 Comparing fractions 8.3 Adding and subtracting fractions 8.4 Mixed numbers and improper fractions 8.5 Calculations with mixed numbers
Use conventional notation for the priority of operations, including brackets, powers, roots and reciprocals	5 Working with numbers	5.1 Square numbers 5.3 Order of operations
Recognise and use relationships between operations including inverse operations	14 Equations	14.3 Solving more complex equations
Use integer powers and associated real roots (square, cube and higher), recognise powers of 2, 3, 4, 5 and distinguish between exact representations of roots and their decimal approximations	5 Working with numbers	5.1 Square numbers 5.3 Order of operations
Interpret and compare numbers in standard form $A \times 10^n$ $1 \le A < 10$, where n is a positive or negative integer or zero	Covered in Year 8 Covered in Year 9	
Work interchangeably with terminating decimals and their corresponding fractions (such as 3.5 and $\frac{7}{2}$)	Covered in Year 8	
Define percentage as 'number of parts per hundred', interpret percentages and percentage changes as a fraction or a decimal, interpret these multiplicatively, express one quantity as a percentage of another, compare two	11 Percentages	11.1 Fractions and percentages

quantities using percentages, and work with percentages greater than 100%		
Interpret fractions and percentages as operators	11 Percentages	11.2 Fractions of a quantity 11.3 Percentages of a quantity
Use standard units of mass, length, time, money and other measures, including with decimal quantities	1 Using numbers 5 Working with numbers	1.1 The calendar 1.2 The 12-hour and 24-hour clocks 1.3 Managing money 5.6 Calculations with measurements
Round numbers and measures to an appropriate degree of accuracy [for example, to a number of decimal places or significant figures]	5 Working with numbers	5.2 Rounding
Use approximation through rounding to estimate answers and calculate possible resulting errors expressed using inequality notation $a < x \le b$	4 Decimal numbers	4.3 Estimates
Use a calculator and other technologies to calculate results accurately and then interpret them appropriately	5 Working with numbers 11 Percentages	5.1 Square numbers 5.3 Order of operations 11.4 Percentages with a calculator
Appreciate the infinite nature of the sets of integers, real and rational numbers	Covered in Year 8	
Algebra		
Use and interpret algebraic notation, including: ab in place of $a \times b$ $3y$ in place of $y + y + y$ and $3 \times y$ a^2 in place of $a \times a$, a^3 in place of $a \times a \times a$; a^2b in place of $a \times a \times b$ $\dfrac{a}{b}$ in place of $a \div b$ coefficients written as fractions rather than as decimals brackets	2 Sequences 7 Algebra 14 Equations	2.1 To use function machines to generate inputs and outputs 2.5 To introduce the sequence of triangular numbers 7.1 Expressions and substitution 7.2 Simplifying expressions 7.3 Using formulae 7.4 Writing formulae 14.1 Finding unknown numbers 14.2 Solving equations 14.3 Solving more complex equations 14.4 Setting up and solving equations
Substitute numerical values into formulae and expressions, including scientific formulae	7 Algebra	7.1 Expressions and substitution 7.3 Using formulae

		7.4 Writing formulae
Understand and use the concepts and vocabulary of expressions, equations, inequalities, terms and factors	7 Algebra 14 Equations	7.1 Expressions and substitution 7.2 Simplifying expressions 14.1 Finding unknown numbers 14.2 Solving equations
Simplify and manipulate algebraic expressions to maintain equivalence by: collecting like terms multiplying a single term over a bracket taking out common factors expanding products of two or more binomials.	7 Algebra 14 Equations	7.2 Simplifying expressions 14.2 Solving equations 14.3 Solving more complex equations
Understand and use standard mathematical formulae; rearrange formulae to change the subject	7 Algebra	7.3 Using formulae 7.4 Writing formulae
Model situations or procedures by translating them into algebraic expressions or formulae and by using graphs	Covered in Year 9	
Use algebraic methods to solve linear equations in one variable (including all forms that require rearrangement)	14 Equations	14.2 Solving equations 14.3 Solving more complex equations 14.4 Setting up and solving equations
Work with coordinates in all four quadrants	Covered in Year 8 Covered in Year 9	
Recognise, sketch and produce graphs of linear and quadratic functions of one variable with appropriate scaling, using equations in x and y and the Cartesian plane	10 Coordinates and graphs	10.2 From mappings to graphs 10.3 Naming graphs
Interpret mathematical relationships both algebraically and graphically	2 Sequences 10 Coordinates and graphs	2.1 Function machines 2.5 The triangular numbers 10.2 From mappings to graphs 10.4 Graphs from the real world
Reduce a given linear equation in two variables to the standard form $y = mx + c$; calculate and interpret gradients and intercepts of graphs of such linear equations numerically, graphically and algebraically	Covered in Year 8 Covered in Year 9	
Use linear and quadratic graphs to estimate values of y for given values of x and vice versa and to find	Covered in Year 8 Covered in Year 9	

approximate solutions of simultaneous linear equations		
Find approximate solutions to contextual problems from given graphs of a variety of functions, including piece-wise linear, exponential and reciprocal graphs	Covered in Year 9	
Generate terms of a sequence from either a term-to-term or a position-to-term rule	2 Sequences	2.1 Function machines 2.2 Sequences and rules 2.3 Finding terms in patterns
Recognise arithmetic sequences and find the *n*th term	2 Sequences	2.2 Sequences and rules 2.3 Finding terms in patterns
Recognise geometric sequences and appreciate other sequences that arise	2 Sequences	2.2 Sequences and rules 2.4 The square numbers 2.5 The triangular numbers
Ratio, proportion and rates of change		
Change freely between related standard units [for example time, length, area, volume/capacity, mass]	1 Using numbers	1.2 The 12-hour and 24-hour clocks
Use scale factors, scale diagrams and maps	Covered in Year 8	
Express one quantity as a fraction of another, where the fraction is less than 1 and greater than 1	17 Ratio	17.3 Ratios and sharing 17.4 Ratios and fractions
Use ratio notation, including reduction to simplest form	17 Ratio	17.1 Introduction to ratios 17.2 Simplifying ratios 17.3 Ratios and sharing 17.4 Solving problems
Divide a given quantity into two parts in a given part : part or part : whole ratio; express the division of a quantity into two parts as a ratio	17 Ratio	17.2 Simplifying ratios 17.3 Ratios and sharing 17.4 Ratios and fractions
Understand that a multiplicative relationship between two quantities can be expressed as a ratio or a fraction	Covered in Year 8	
Relate the language of ratios and the associated calculations to the arithmetic of fractions and to linear functions	17 Ratio	17.3 Ratios and sharing 17.4 Ratios and fractions
Solve problems involving percentage change, including: percentage increase, decrease and original value problems and simple interest in financial mathematics	11 Percentages	11.5 Percentage increases and decreases
Solve problems involving direct and inverse proportion, including graphical and algebraic representations	Covered in Year 8	
Use compound units such as speed,	Covered in Year 9	

unit pricing and density to solve problems.		
Geometry and measures		
Derive and apply formulae to calculate and solve problems involving: perimeter and area of triangles, parallelograms, trapezia, volume of cuboids (including cubes) and other prisms (including cylinders)	3 Perimeter and area	3.3 Perimeter and area of rectangles
Calculate and solve problems involving: perimeters of 2D shapes (including circles), areas of circles and composite shapes	3 Perimeter and area	3.1 Length and perimeter 3.3 Perimeter and area of rectangles
Draw and measure line segments and angles in geometric figures, including interpreting scale drawings	3 Perimeter and area 9 Angles	3.1 Length and perimeter 9.2 Measuring angles 9.3 Drawing angles
Derive and use the standard ruler and compass constructions (perpendicular bisector of a line segment, constructing a perpendicular to a given line from/at a given point, bisecting a given angle); recognise and use the perpendicular distance from a point to a line as the shortest distance to the line	Covered in Year 8	
Describe, sketch and draw using conventional terms and notations: points, lines, parallel lines, perpendicular lines, right angles, regular polygons, and other polygons that are reflectively and rotationally symmetric	9 Angles	9.5 Properties of triangles and quadrilaterals
Use the standard conventions for labelling the sides and angles of triangle ABC, and know and use the criteria for congruence of triangles	9 Angles	9.5 Properties of triangles and quadrilaterals
Derive and illustrate properties of triangles, quadrilaterals, circles, and other plane figures [for example, equal lengths and angles] using appropriate language and technologies	9 Angles	9.5 Properties of triangles and quadrilaterals
Identify properties of, and describe the results of, translations, rotations and reflections applied to given figures	13 Symmetry	13.1 Line symmetry 13.2 Rotational symmetry 13.3 Reflections
Identify and construct congruent triangles, and construct similar	Covered in Year 8	

shapes by enlargement, with and without coordinate grids		
Apply the properties of angles at a point, angles at a point on a straight line, vertically opposite angles	9 Angles	9.4 Calculating angles
Understand and use the relationship between parallel lines and alternate and corresponding angles	Covered in Year 8	
Derive and use the sum of angles in a triangle and use it to deduce the angle sum in any polygon, and to derive properties of regular polygons	Covered in Year 9	
Apply angle facts, triangle congruence, similarity and properties of quadrilaterals to derive results about angles and sides, including Pythagoras' Theorem, and use known results to obtain simple proofs	Covered in Year 8 Covered in Year 9	
Use Pythagoras' Theorem and trigonometric ratios in similar triangles to solve problems involving right-angled triangles	Covered in Year 9	
Use the properties of faces, surfaces, edges and vertices of cubes, cuboids, prisms, cylinders, pyramids, cones and spheres to solve problems in 3D	16 3D shapes	16.1 3D shapes and nets 16.2 Using nets to construct 3D shapes 16.3 3D investigations
Interpret mathematical relationships both algebraically and geometrically		
Probability		
Record, describe and analyse the frequency of outcomes of simple probability experiments involving randomness, fairness, equally and unequally likely outcomes, using appropriate language and the 0–1 probability scale	12 Probability	12.1 Probability words 12.2 Probability scales 12.3 Experimental probability
Understand that the probabilities of all possible outcomes sum to 1	12 Probability	12.1 Probability words
Enumerate sets and unions/intersections of sets systematically, using tables, grids and Venn diagrams	Covered in Year 8	
Generate theoretical sample spaces for single and combined events with equally likely, mutually exclusive outcomes and use these to calculate theoretical probabilities	Covered in Year 8	
Statistics		
Describe, interpret and compare	6 Statistics	6.1 Mode, median and range

observed distributions of a single variable through: appropriate graphical representation involving discrete, continuous and grouped data; and appropriate measures of central tendency (mean, mode, median) and spread (range, consideration of outliers)	15 Interpreting data	6.4 Using data 6.5 Grouped frequency 6.6 Data collection 15.2 Comparing data by median and range 15.3 Statistical surveys
Construct and interpret appropriate tables, charts, and diagrams, including frequency tables, bar charts, pie charts, and pictograms for categorical data, and vertical line (or bar) charts for ungrouped and grouped numerical data	6 Statistics 15 Interpreting data	6.2 Reading data from tables and charts 6.3 Using a tally chart 6.4 Using data 6.5 Grouped frequency 6.6 Data collection 15.1 Pie charts
Describe simple mathematical relationships between two variables (bivariate data) in observational and experimental contexts and illustrate using scatter graphs	Covered in Year 8	

1 Using numbers

Learning objectives

- How to use number skills in real life
- How to use number in everyday money problems
- How to use a number line to understand negative whole numbers
- How to use a number line to calculate with negative whole numbers
- How to add negative numbers
- How to subtract negative numbers

Prior knowledge

- How to write and read whole numbers. By Year 6, pupils read, write, order and compare numbers up to 10 000 000 and determine the value of each digit.
- How to add and subtract positive numbers. In KS2, pupils perform increasingly complex calculations using a range of mental methods; and more formal written algorithms.
- Multiplication tables up to 12 × 12. By Year 5, pupils frequently apply the multiplication tables and related division facts, commit them to memory and use them confidently to make larger calculations. During Year 6, pupils continue to use these skills to maintain their fluency.
- How to use a calculator to do simple calculations. Calculators are introduced near the end of KS2 (if pupils' written and mental arithmetic are secure), in order to support pupils' conceptual understanding and exploration of more complex number problems.

Context

- Questions to activate prior knowledge and exercise mathematical 'fluency', that is, the ability to manipulate mathematical language and concepts and apply them in different contexts.
- Tables and charts appear everywhere. It is important for pupils to be confident in their ability to extract and use information from these, in increasingly unfamiliar and complex situations.
- Pupils should also be confident in setting up their own charts and tables to help them solve problems both in mathematics and across a range of subjects. Pupils should be able to assess what types of charts and tables help to clarify problems, and to identify when the representation used may be less helpful.
- The first reference to negative numbers can be found in China in 200 BCE. Introduce the history of negative numbers with this unusual statement of the rules for negative numbers by an Indian mathematician named Brahmagupta (598–670).

  A debt minus zero is a debt. A fortune minus zero is a fortune.
  Zero minus zero is a zero. A debt subtracted from zero is a fortune.
  A fortune subtracted from zero is a debt.
  The product of zero multiplied by a debt or fortune is zero.
  The product of zero multiplied by zero is zero.
  The product or quotient of two fortunes is one fortune.
  The product or quotient of two debts is one fortune.
  The product or quotient of a debt and a fortune is a debt.
  The product or quotient of a fortune and a debt is a debt.

- Find information on the internet by doing a search for: history of negative numbers.

- Money problems are everywhere in life and pupils need to realise how important their ability to interpret these problems and identify the mathematics involved is to their future financial wellbeing. This chapter provides plenty of financial skills (**FS**) questions for practice.

Discussion points

- If someone has forgotten the 7× multiplication table, what tips would you give the person so that he or she can work it out?
- What tips would you give someone to be able to work out the 9× multiplication table?
- What other links between tables are useful?

Associated Collins ICT resources

- Chapter 1 interactive activities on Collins Connect online platform
- *Subtracting negative numbers* video on Collins Connect online platform
- *Escape* Wonder of Maths on Collins Connect online platform

Discussion points

Number

- Understand and use place value for decimals, measures and integers of any size
- Order positive and negative integers, decimals and fractions; use the number line as a model for ordering of the real numbers; use the symbols =, ≠, <, >, ≤, ≥
- Use the four operations, including formal written methods, applied to integers, decimals, proper and improper fractions, and mixed numbers, all both positive and negative
- Use standard units of mass, length, time, money and other measures, including with decimal quantities

Solve problems

- Develop their mathematical knowledge, in part through solving problems and evaluating the outcomes, including multi-step problems
- Develop their use of formal mathematical knowledge to interpret and solve problems, including in financial mathematics
- Begin to model situations mathematically and express the results using a range of formal mathematical representations

Fast-track for classes following a 2-year scheme of work

- If pupils are familiar with the material in lessons 1.1 and 1.2 from KS2, they can leave out Exercise 1A and 1B, and jump straight to the **PS** questions at the end of each exercise.
- Ensure that pupils understand all the rules that they are applying throughout the chapter.

Lesson 1.1 The calendar

Learning objective
- To read and use calendars

Resources and homework
- Pupil Book 1.1, pages 7–9
- Online homework 1.1, questions 1–10

Links to other subjects
- **Science** – to use information given in tables and charts
- **History** – to extract chronological information provided in tables and charts
- **Physical education** – to compare results given in tables and charts

Key word
- calendar

Problem solving and reasoning help
- Most questions in this section are **PS** although they are not marked as such. Pupils may not see right away how the mathematical techniques they are learning apply to some questions, so ensure that pupils read the questions carefully and talk about the mathematics involved. Encourage them to use the content of the lesson to help them solve the problem more efficiently and experiment with different ways of representing the information provided.

Common misconceptions and remediation
- Pupils forget that they are working in a different base when working with time, for example: interpreting $7\frac{1}{4}$ hours as 7 hours and 25 minutes instead of 7 hours and 15 minutes; or tackling 7:55 to 8:10 as a standard decimal calculation (55 minutes instead of 15 minutes).

Probing questions
- Present pupils with a chart or table and ask them to design a question for it. Encourage **more able** pupils to design easy and hard questions, and to identify the criteria for each.
- *Number of days = seven times the number of weeks.* Ask pupils to write as many sentences as they can like this, using time. Encourage **more able** pupils to recognise fractional relationships and the link to inverse relationships – a good link to algebraic relationships.

Part 1
- Write the number 60 on the board. (Pupils can write the answers on the board.)
- Ask for 'fractions' of 60, for example: $\frac{1}{2}$ (30), $\frac{1}{4}$ (15), $\frac{1}{3}$ (20), $\frac{1}{6}$ (10), $\frac{3}{4}$ (45).
- Now ask for multiples, or times, of 60, for example: 2× (120), 3× (180) …. Or, ask the class to chant the 60× multiplication table. If necessary ask them to chant the 6× table first.
- Now ask for the remainder when 60 is divided into, for example: 90 (30), 130 (10), 200 (20).
- Write 24 on the board. Ask for 'fractions' of 24 such as $\frac{1}{2}$ (12), $\frac{1}{4}$ (6), $\frac{1}{3}$ (8), $\frac{1}{6}$ (4), $\frac{3}{4}$ (18).
- Ask for multiples, or times, of 24 such as 2× (48), 3× (72). Or, they can chant the 24× table.

Literacy activity
- *'Write a short paragraph to explain how to work out the number of days in a year.'*

Part 2

- Ask pupils for 'time' facts: number of days of the week, number of months in the year, ...
- Establish that there are 60 seconds in a minute, 60 minutes in an hour, 24 hours in a day, 7 days in a week, 4 weeks (approximately) in a month, 12 months in a year, 365 days in a year (366 in a leap year). Also make sure pupils know the number of days in each month.
- Ask for the number of seconds in, for example, 2 minutes; the number of days in 3 weeks.
- Ask pupils what is used to help with, for example, appointments, keeping track of events.
- Distribute, or have on the board, a calendar. Discuss how to interpret the calendar.
- Ask questions such as 'What day of the week is ...?', 'How many Mondays are in ...?', 'Which month has five Wednesdays?', 'What date is the second Sunday in ...?'.
- Ask pupils how many days are between two dates – say, 4 April and 22 April. (17)
- Ask: 'If these were holiday dates, how many nights away is this?' (17)
- **Pupils can now do Exercise 1A from Pupil Book 1.1.**

Part 3

- Ask pupils if they can relate the names of the months to any common shapes. Prompt them with September, October, November and December. These have the same stem as Septagon, Octagon .... But, they are not the 7th, 8th, 9th and 10th months.
- Explain that originally, there were only 10 months in the Roman calendar; this was altered to 12 months in about 700 BC. The current calendar was introduced in about 46 BC.
- Explain that leap year came about because a year (the time it takes for the Earth to rotate round the Sun) is 365.25 days, so every fourth year an extra day is inserted to stop the seasons getting out of line. However, years ending in '00' are not leap years unless they divide by 400. Hence 2000 was a leap year but 2100 will not be a leap year.
- Encourage pupils to look up facts about the calendar on the internet.

Answers
Exercise 1A
1   a 21   b 84   c 364
2   a 96   b 168   c 744
3   a 120   b 300   c 1440
4   a 300   b 1440 c 3600
5   a 2 b 5
6   a 3 h 20 min   b 5 h 50 min
7   2020
8   92
9   32
10 a Tuesday   b 16th August   c 14   d 12th June   e 40

Learning objectives

- To read and use 12-hour and 24-hour clocks
- To convert between the 12-hour and 24-hour systems

Links to other subjects

- **Food technology** – to calculate cooking time

Resources and homework

- Pupil Book 1.1, pages 9–13
- Intervention Workbook 1, pages 49–51
- Online homework 1.2, questions 1–10

Key words

- 12-hour clock
- analogue
- 24-hour clock
- digital

Problem solving and reasoning help

- **PS** and **MR** questions 8 and 9 use everyday applications of time. Pairs should discuss the questions first. Ask **more able** pupils to design some problems using a real timetable.

Common misconceptions and remediation

- Make sure pupils understand the difference between 12 am and 12 pm (this often causes confusion), and that they do not confuse the hour and minute hands on analogue clocks.

Probing questions

- If you are born at midnight on 8 April, is this the start or the end of the day?
- Why do airlines and the military use the 24-hour clock?
- Is there a quick way to convert between the 12- and 24-hour clock formats?

Part 1

- Use a target board like the one shown here. Point to a number and ask pupils to give the difference between the number and, for example, 60; the number and 80, and so on.

48	32	15	38
52	74	22	25
39	14	82	30
68	92	9	17

Literacy activity

- Ask pupils to write a short paragraph, detailing their journey to school using the 24-hour clock time format. (Peer mark this for S.P.A.G. – spelling, punctuation and grammar.)

Part 2

- Ask pupils what time they get up and/or go to bed.
- If they answer in am/pm times, ask if they can express these values in the 24-hour clock.
- Write some times on the board in am/pm times, for example: 6:45 am, 7:25 pm.
- Discuss am and pm: ante meridian/post meridian or ante midday/post midday.
- Now explain, or ask pupils to explain, how to convert these to the 24-hour clock.
- Put some 24-hour clock times on the board, for example: 14:32 or 09:17.
- Explain how to convert these to the 12-hour clock. Be careful with times between 12 midday and 1 pm; these are pm times but stay the same in 12-hour and 24-hour clock notation. Times after midnight and before 1 am start at 00.

- Ask a pupil what time she/he arrived at school and what time school started. Calculate the interval between these times. Repeat with other pairs of times.
- Introduce a timeline where the number of minutes to the next hour is counted on, then the hours, then the minutes after the hour. To get the final time interval, total these values. For example, 08:40 to 18:52 is: 20 minutes (m) + 9 hours (h) + 52 m = 10 h 12 m.

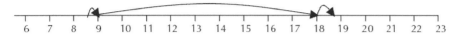

- Ask pupils what fraction of an hour is 15 minutes. What is this as a decimal?
- Point out that when using a calculator, certain minutes must be converted to a decimal.
- Put a timetable on the board, or distribute copies. Check that pupils can read the timetable by asking questions such as, 'What time does the first train/bus leave from ...?', 'What is the first train after ... from ...?', 'How long does the ... take to get from ... to ...?'
- **Pupils can now do Exercise 1B from Pupil Book 1.1.**

Part 3

- Draw or put up a diagram of a clock on the board. It should show the hours for the 12- and 24-hour clocks around a regular clock face: 12/00:00; 1/13:00; 2/14:00; 3/15:00 and so on.
- Ask a pupil to start at 00:00; join the multiples of 5 (or 7); keep going once reaching 20:00 by counting on five spaces, until the pattern returns to 00:00. This will produce a star pattern.
- Ask pupils if they know the prime numbers and if they can identify them on the diagram. (The prime numbers are all in pairs (1, 13), (5, 17), (7, 19) (11, 23) on the same points.)
- Ask pupils to research why there are 24 hours in a day. (No generally accepted reason)

Answers
Exercise 1B

1 a 05:00 b 17:00   c 11:20   d 12:00   e 17:15   f 23:05   g 10:45
   h 00:00

2 a 6 pm b 7 am   c 12:15 pm d 00:25 am e 4:20 pm   f 10:30 pm g 11:07 am
   h 7:25 pm

3 a 4 hrs   b 2 h 30 min c 4 h 10 min d 3 h 11 min e 8 h 45 min f 12 h 16 min

4 35 min

5 10:20

6 a 09:43 b 50 minutes   c 12:32

7 a $2\frac{1}{4}$, 2.25   b $3\frac{3}{4}$, 3.75   c $1\frac{1}{3}$, 1.33   d $\frac{1}{2}$, 3.5   e $1\frac{2}{3}$, 1.67   f $2\frac{3}{10}$, 2.3

8 a 13:35 b 21:55   c 11:15   d 30 mins

9 06:56

10 a i 50p   ii £1.25   b 5 minutes

Problem solving: Times

A 4 h 55 min
B 17 mins
C 12 mins
D 1 h 4 mins
E 10:17
F 35 mins

Lesson 1.3 Managing money

Learning objectives
- To work out everyday money problems

Resources and homework
- Pupil Book 1.1, pages 13–15
- Online homework 1.3, questions 1–10

Links to other subjects
- **Business and economics** – to manage finances

Key words
- No new key words for this topic

Problem solving and reasoning help
- The problems in Exercise 1C are all either **FS**, **PS** or **MR** questions. Make certain pupils have a good understanding of the UK monetary system before starting the exercise.

Common misconceptions and remediation
- Pupils should read carefully to decide whether to use addition, subtraction, multiplication or division. If some prices are in pence and some are in pounds, they should change them so that the prices are all in pounds or all in pence, making sure that the answer is in the format requested. Remind pupils to put the decimal point and pound symbol £ in the right place.

Probing questions
- Why is it important to understand the values of coins?
- Can you represent the same amount of money using various different coins and notes?
- When should you estimate amounts of money?

Part 1
- You will need a box to act as a money box and sets of coins (five to 10, including: 1p, 2p, 5p, 10p, and so on.
- Explain that you will drop some coins into the money box.
- The challenge is to work out how much money you have in the box: Start with 1p and work upwards so that pupils must do some mental addition or use their times tables.
  Then remove coins from the box and ask pupils how much money you have left in the box.

Literacy activity
- Ask pupils to compose two sentences in their head to explain what they have learnt during the lesson and how they have learnt it. Ask pupils to say their sentences out loud.

Part 2
- Discuss the coins in circulation (see the Pupil Book): 1p, 2p, 5p, 10p, 20p, 50p, £1, £2. Say: '*There are 100 pence in £1. How many ways can you use the coins to make: £1 and £2?*'
- Discuss the four notes in circulation (see the Pupil Book): £5, £10, £20, £50.
- Explain that if you use a note to pay for things that cost less than the note's value, you get money back as *change*. For example, if you were to buy a game that costs £3 with a £10 note, you would get £7 back in change. Change can be given in a variety of coins.
- Ask pupils how much change would you get from a £20 note if you spent £12.50 on a magazine. Ask pupils for different ways of receiving the change
- **Pupils can now do Exercise 1C from Pupil Book 1.1.**

Part 3

- Convert these amounts of pence into pounds and pence: 1235p, 156p, 1045p
- Convert the following amounts in Pounds and pence into pence: £0.59, £34.12, £5

Answers
Exercise 1C
1 1p, 1p, 1p, 1p; 1p, 1p, 2p; 2p, 2p
2 2p, 2p, 2p, 2p, 2p, 2p; 2p, 5p, 5p
3 50p, 10p, 10p, 5p
4 Zara gives 41p back to Ali.
5 5
6 Don has 2 × 5p and Donna has 5 × 2p or Don has 2 × 50p and Donna has 5 × 20p.
7 9
8 nine × 20p and three × 1p
9 three 1p coins x, three 2p coins x, 3 × 5p = 15p (no 3p coin), 3 × 10p = 30p (no 6p coin), 3 × 20p = 60p (no 12p coin), 3 × 50p = 150p (no 30p coin)
10 20p, 20p, 5p, 1p
11 20p, 5p, 1p
12 20p, 10p, 5p, 2p
Problem solving: USA money
A 7 pennies, 14 nickels, 3 dimes, 1 quarter
B 7 nickels, 12 dimes, 16 quarters

Lesson 1.4 Positive and negative numbers

Learning objectives

- To use a number line to order positive and negative whole numbers
- To solve problems involving negative temperatures

Resources and homework

- Pupil Book 1.1, pages 16–18
- Intervention Workbook 3, pages 20–21
- Homework Book, section 1.2
- Online homework 1.4 and 1.4a, questions 1–10

Links to other subjects

- **Geography** – to compare temperature when doing country evaluations

Key words

- negative number
- positive number
- temperature

Problem solving and reasoning help

- Most questions in this section focus on temperature as the context, and the use of negative numbers to describe temperatures below zero. This section also uses the concept of difference to introduce negative numbers as an operator, and as a point on the number line.
- Challenge pupils to explain how they can transfer their understanding to different contexts. Encourage them to explain that while the context may be different, the mathematics they need to apply is the same. A suitable example would be the use of negative numbers to describe credit and debt situations. You could find suitable support material at: **http://www.pfeg.org/resources**.

Common misconceptions and remediation

- Pupils often confuse the operation of subtraction and negative numbers as numbers on a number line, especially as the sign is the same for both. Encourage pupils to visualise the number line when making calculations so that they will see the place of negative numbers, the effect of subtracting positive and negative numbers, and to discuss the difference.

Probing questions

- Explain whether the following are true or false: –8 is less than –6; –36 is greater than –34.

Part 1

- This is best done using a number hoop, but can also be done using a number line marked with 10 segments drawn on the board, or a counting stick marked with 10 segments.
- Point to one marker and say, '*This is 20.*' Point to the next marker and say, '*This is 18.*' The class, or individuals, should then count down in twos until someone get it wrong.
- Repeat with different starting numbers and different jumps, but always count into the negative integers.

Literacy activity

- Write down any new words and their meanings in mathematics. (Check spellings in pairs.)

Part 2

- On the board, draw (horizontally or vertically) a number line and mark 20 segments on it. Starting the mid-point, number the right half of the line: 0 to 10; the left half: –1 to –10.
- Show pupils the method for ordering numbers by reading them off from left to right. Demonstrate this method with: –5, 4, 6, 8, –2, –4, –9, 10.

- Ask how we could use the number line to work out the difference between 7 and –3.
- Establish that we start at zero and move first in the positive direction for 7, and then in the negative direction for –3. Mark the number line as below.

- Repeat with similar examples, making sure that pupils obtain positive answers.
- **Pupils can now do Exercise 1D from Pupil Book 1.1.**

Part 3

- Order the following places from coldest to warmest:
  - o   Moscow, Russia: –45 °C
  - o   Yakutsk, Russia: –71 °C
  - o   Barrow, Alaska, USA: –21 °C
  - o   Vostok station, Antarctica: –89 °C
  - o   North Ice, Greenland: –66 °C
  - o   Snag, Yukon, Canada: –58 °C.
- Ask pupils to use the internet to find the five hottest cities in the world.

Answers

Exercise 1D

1 **a** 5 °C, –6 °C   **b** 6 °C, –10 °C   **c** –5 °C, –15 °C

2 **a** 12 degrees   **b** 10 degrees   **c** 13 degrees

3 0 °C

4 **a** 0, 2, 5, 7, 9   **b** –5, 2, 3, 7, 9   **c** –8, –6, 0, 4, 12   **d** –15, –9, –1, 1, 8
   e –12, –9, –5, –3, 1   **f** –9, –8, –3, 4, 5

5 **a** T   **b** T   **c** F   **d** F   **e** F   **f** T   **g** F   **h** T

6 16, 10, –5, –6, –10

7 **a** –3   **b** –5   **c** –6

Challenge: Temperatures on the Moon

A 270 degrees

B the lowest

Lesson 1.5 Adding negative numbers

Learning objectives

- To carry out additions and subtractions involving negative numbers
- To use a number line to calculate with negative numbers

Links to other subjects

- **Geography** – to work with weather, climate and temperatures
- **Chemistry** – to work with properties of substances below zero

Resources and homework

- Pupil Book 1.1, pages 18–21
- Intervention Workbook 3, pages 20–21
- Homework Book, section 1.3
- Online homework 1.5, questions 1–10

Key word

- bracket

Problem solving and reasoning help

- MR/PS question 8 of Exercise 1E is a simple application of negative numbers to bank accounts.
- Encourage pupils to discuss the meaning of the question with a partner before doing the calculation. The magic square is a type of problem that pupils will have met before.

Common misconceptions and remediation

- Pupils often learn rules without understanding the reasoning behind them. They need a visual image such as the number line and/or an understanding of the patterns that lead directly to the rules, in this case how we use the four operations with both positive and negative numbers. This will ensure that when in stressful situations, such as examinations, they can fall back on these images to provide backup in the case of uncertainty.

Probing questions

- The answer to a calculation is –8. Make up some addition calculations to give this answer.
- The answer on your calculator is –156. What keys did you enter to get this answer?

Part 1

- *Addition makes numbers bigger.* When is this statement true, and when is it false?
- *Subtraction makes numbers smaller.* When is this statement true, and when is it false?

Literacy activity

- Write down three true and three false statements based on the lesson objectives. Then share some of these with the class, asking if the statements are true or false.

Part 2

- Write the following pattern on the board. Working in pairs, ask pupils to complete the pattern.

$$5 + +1 = 6$$
$$5 + 0 = 5$$
$$5 + -1 = 4$$
$$5 + -2 = \ldots$$
$$5 + \ldots = \ldots$$
$$5 + \ldots = \ldots$$

- Encourage pupils to place the examples in context so that they start to appreciate what is happening. Ask **less able** pupils to visualise the examples on a number line.
- Pupils could repeat the pattern with a different starting number.
- Ask **more able** pupils to complete the sentence: Adding a negative number gives the same result ….
- Using mini whiteboards, put a couple of example on the board, for example, 6 + 7 + (–9). Encourage pupils to see how brackets can help them, for example: 5 + 6 + (–8).
- Pupils are now ready for Exercise 1E. After going through some simple examples, ask **more able** pupils to focus on questions 6–9. Provide extension work by asking pupils if they can design their own 3 × 3 magic square using negative numbers. Give the starting point of –2 and say that the sum of the rows will be three times this. Find further guidance with 'magic sums and products' at: **http://nrich.maths.org/1376**.
- **Pupils can now do Exercise 1E from Pupil Book 1.1.**

Part 3

- Ask pupils to work in pairs to design a test question based on the work they have done in this section and the last section.
- Encourage **more able** pupils to review what makes questions about negative numbers easy or hard and to design multi-step problems. They could include a mark scheme.
- Choose pairs to present their questions. The class could assess them according to an agreed set of criteria, for example, choice of context, accuracy and complexity.

Answers

Exercise 1E

1	a 4	b 5	c –4	d 12	e –3	f 0	g 6	h –5
	i –6	j 7	k –10	l –2	m –1	n –2	o –10	p –3
2	a 6	b 4	c 3	d 8	e –9			
3	a –2	b 3	c 1	d 4	e –6	f –4	g 6	h –8
	i 6	j –8	k 3	l 0	m –1	n –10	o –4	p –11
4	a 5	b –15	c –60	d –20	e 10	f 0		
	g –5	h –100	i 5	j –190	k –30	l –20		
5	a 1	b 8	c 5	d 8	e 6	f –2		
6	a 12	b 15	c –4					

7 a

8	1	6
3	5	7
4	9	2

b

6	–1	4
1	3	5
2	7	0

c

1	–6	–1
–4	–2	0
–3	2	–5

Challenge: Number squares

A

–8	–1	1	6
3	4	–6	–3
–2	–7	7	0
5	2	–4	–5

B

10	–4	–3	7
–1	5	4	2
3	1	0	6
–2	8	9	–5

Lesson 1.6 Subtracting negative numbers

Learning objective
- To carry out subtractions involving negative numbers

Resources and homework
- Pupil Book 1.1, pages 21–23
- Intervention Workbook 3, pages 20–21
- Homework Book, section 1.4
- Online homework 1.6, questions 1–10

Links to other subjects
- **Business and economics** – to work with bank statements, credit and debt, profit loss accounts
- **Geography** – to work with temperature comparisons when doing country evaluations

Key words
- No new key words for this topic

Problem solving and reasoning help
- Ask pupils to design their own contextualised problem, similar that in **MR** question 10 of Exercise 1F. Challenge them to write the same type of question, n a different context. Pupils should see how important it is to identify different types of questions in different contexts.

Common misconceptions and remediation
- Pupils often learn mathematical rules without understanding the reasoning. They need a visual image such as the number line and/or an understanding of the patterns that lead directly to the rules; here, how we use the four operations with positive numbers and negative numbers. Thus, during examinations, pupils can use these images as reminders.

Probing questions
- The answer to a calculation is –23. Can you make up some subtraction calculations?
- The answer on your calculator is –148. What keys could you have pressed for this answer?

Part 1
- On the board (horizontally or vertically), draw a number line, and mark 20 segments on it. Starting at the mid-point, number the right half of the line from 0 to 10.
- In pairs, ask pupils to explain to each other how they would use a number line to calculate 7 – 3. Then they should do the same to find the answer to 3 – 7. Challenge pupils to provide constructive feedback. They can challenge each other if they think an explanation is inaccurate or not strong enough. More able pupils can adapt the number line to use a wider range of numbers and include calculations with more than one step such as: 10 – 12 + 6.
- Encourage pairs to share their explanations. Establish that we start at 0 and move first in the positive direction for 7, and then in the negative direction for –3 and the same for 3 – 7; but this time we move back through 0 to negative numbers. This activity revisits ideas that pupils will have met when learning how to place numbers on the number line and to add and subtract positive and negative numbers. The activity also prepares pupils for the next stage.

Literacy activity
- '*Write three top tips for both adding negative numbers and subtracting negative numbers.*'

Part 2

- Building on the work in the last section, write the following pattern on the board, and ask pupils to complete it in pairs:

  $-3 - +1 = -4$ $\qquad$ $-3 - -2 = \ldots$

  $-3 - 0 = -3$ $\qquad$ $-3 - \ldots = \ldots$

  $-3 - -1 = -2$ $\qquad$ $-3 - \ldots = \ldots$

- Encourage pupils to place the examples in context. They could repeat the pattern with a different starting number. Ask **less able** pupils to visualise the pattern on a number line.
- Ask **more able** pupils to complete the sentence:
  '*Subtracting a negative number gives the same result as ...*'
- Use mini whiteboards to write a couple of examples on the board, for example: $-6 -7 - (-9)$. Encourage pupils to see how brackets can help them: $5 + 6 + (-8)$.
- **Pupils can now do Exercise 1D from Pupil Book 1.1.** Pupils who are **more able** could extend the work on the magic square, which they started in the last section.

Part 3

- **Problem 1:** Before Sarah was paid, her bank balance was $-£275.34$, showing an overdrawn account. After Sarah was paid, her bank balance was $£1752.48$. How much was she paid?
- **Problem 2:** The lowest winter temperature in a city in Norway was $-20\,°C$. The highest summer temperature was $49°$ higher. What was the summer temperature?
- Ask pupils to work in pairs on these two problems, and then to present their solution to one problem, with an explanation, to another pair, who should provide constructive feedback.
- The second pair should then present their solution to the second problem and then they should repeat the process. **More able** pupils who finish this quickly can design a similar question but in a different context, and present it in groups of four, as outlined above.

Answers

Exercise 1F

1   **a** 10   **b** 15   **c** 30   **d** −10   **e** 0

2   **a** 10   **b** 9   **c** 0   **d** 12   **e** −2   **f** 9   **g** 5   **h** −7   **i** 12   **j** −6   **k** 0   **l** 0
   m −6 **n** 10   **o** 10 **p** 4

3   **a** 18 **b** 0   **c** 30 **d** −10 **e** 37   **f** 60   **g** −5   **h** −60 **i** 27   **j** −50 **k** 34   **l** 8

4   **a** 21 **b** −4   **c** 20 **d** 49   **e** 2   **f** 6

5   biggest $32 - -9 = 41$, smallest $-9 - 32 = -41$

6   **a** −4 **b** −5   **c** 16 **d** −12

7   **a** 3; −3, 2; −4, 1   **b** −1; −3, 0; −4, 1   **c** 3; −3, 3; −1, −4, 3

8   **a** 3 **b** 0   **c** 13 **d** −8   **e** 7   **f** −2   **g** 0   **h** 13   **i** −4   **j** −12 **k** −1   **l** 15
   m −2 **n** −2   **o** −7

9   5, −11, 5, 4, −3, 5

10   35 m

Challenge: Marking a maths test

A   **a i** 20   **ii** 40   **iii** 12   **iv** 8   **b** the 2 times table

B   **i** 10   **ii** 35   **iii** 0   **iv** −5

Review questions (Pupil Book pages 24–25)

- The review questions will help to determine pupils' abilities with regard to the material within Chapter 1.

Problem solving – Where in the UK?
(Pupil Book pages 26–27)

- This activity is designed to use both the **MR** and **PS** outcomes covered in this chapter in a series of real-life problems.
- Pupils will need to apply their learning from Chapter 1 in order to answer the questions. Model some examples from section 1.4 from the pupil book for **less able pupils** before they start this task.
- Part B involves using timetables. Using timetables is a common everyday problem, but not a context that pupils have met explicitly in the unit. Pupils often make mistakes with timetables. A discussion about the units of seconds and minutes may be useful, as the use of these different units of time often confuses **less able** pupils.
- Ask pupils further questions as a warm-up to start working on the questions in the Pupil Book, for example:

  What do you know temperatures in the UK during a calendar year?
  Where do you think will have the coldest temperature and when? Why?
  Where do you think will have the warmest temperature and when? Why?

- Pupils can now work on the questions individually or in groups.
- You could ask **more able** pupils to develop this topic further by using the internet to research other negative numbers or more complex timetables.

Answers to Review questions

1 20:30
2 12
3 **a** 4 hours   **b** 06:00   **c** €250
4 30 m
5 15th
6 **a** £40   **b** £5
7 22
8 £40, –£20, –£30, £50
9 **a** 20 km   **b** 2 km
10 **a** £30, £30, –£10, £125, –£20
   b £10, £25, £55, £190, £40
   c blue team won by £60 (40 – –20)

Answers to Problem solving – Where in the UK?

A **1** –2 °C   **2** –3 °C   **3** Norwich   **4** Aberdeen   **5** 6 degrees
   6 2 degrees   **7** Edinburgh   **8** Belfast   **9** Belfast
B 08:00 from London, returning by any of 16:30, 17:00 or 17:30 from Edinburgh or
   09:00 from London returning by 17:30 from Edinburgh

2 Sequences

Learning objectives

- How to use function machines
- How to describe some simple number patterns
- How to generate and describe some simple whole-number sequences
- How to use the special sequence called the sequence of square numbers
- How to use the special sequence called the sequence of triangular numbers

Prior knowledge

- Odd and even numbers
- Multiplication tables up to 12 × 12. By Year 5, pupils frequently apply the multiplication tables and related division facts, commit them to memory and use them confidently to make larger calculations. During Year 6, pupils continue to use these skills to maintain their fluency.
- How to apply the four rules of number. Year 6 pupils are expected to be able to solve problems involving addition, subtraction, multiplication and division. They will also have explored the order of operations.

Context

- The ability to generalise is crucial in a complex modern society. Being able to identify and generate number sequences is the first step towards progressing from the particular to the general in mathematics. Mathematics is all about the ability to see patterns, to hypothesise about these patterns and then seek to prove the hypothesis from first principles. With KS3 pupils, explore the following concept by looking at 'Generic examples: Seeing through from the particular to the general' at the following link **http://nrich.maths.org/7831.**

Discussion points

- Two numbers multiplied together give an answer of 30. Make up some questions. How are these different questions linked?
- Two numbers divided give an answer of 6. Make up some questions. How did you make up these questions?

Associated Collins ICT resources

- Chapter 2 interactive activities on Collins Connect online platform
- *Describing and generating simple sequences* video on Collins Connect online platform
- *Function machines* and *Other sequences* Worked solutions on Collins Connect online platform

Curriculum references

- Algebra
- Read and interpret algebraic notation
- Interpret mathematical relationships algebraically
- Generate terms of a sequence from a term-to-term rule

- Recognise arithmetic sequences
- Begin to model simple contextual and subject-based problems algebraically
- Appreciate other sequences that arise
- Solve problems
- Begin to model situations mathematically and express the results using a range of formal mathematical representations

Fast-track for classes following a 2-year scheme of work

- For **more able** pupils, put greater emphasis on inverse functions.
- Make sure pupils realise that there is a range of types of sequences, and that within this range, specific examples often follow specific patterns. Provide opportunities for pupils to become fluent in identifying types of sequences.
- Increase the emphasis on being able to explain and justify the patterns spotted, using the structure of the problem. This will start to make the link between pattern spotting and mathematical proof.

Lesson 2.1 Function machines

Learning objectives

- To use function machines to generate inputs and outputs

Resources and homework

- Pupil Book 1.1, pages 29–33
- Homework Book 1, section 2.1
- Online homework 2.1, questions 1–10

Links to other subjects

- **ICT** – to link directly to programming/coding
- **Science** – to electronics inputs and outputs from integrated circuits

Key words

- double function machine
- input
- function machine
- inverse operation
- output

Problem solving and reasoning help

- **PS** question 8 of Exercise 2A requires an understanding of inverse operations. This concept is introduced in question 1 and will need careful explanation. Most questions on this exercise can be solved by **less able** pupils using a trial and error method.

Common misconceptions and remediation

- One of the biggest challenges to pupils' understanding of algebra is the inability to see that letters represent variables. Exploring a range of function machines creatively gives pupils a visual image of how to enter different values into the same formula, for a range of outcomes.

Probing questions

- Give pupils a function, for example: $x \rightarrow +2 \rightarrow \div 3$. Ask what values of x will give a whole number answer.
- Ask pupils to design three number machines that will give an output of 15 when 3 is the input. Ask **more able** pupils to design similar questions.

Part 1

- Tell the story: '*Last week I went shopping at …. A shop that was closing down was having a half-price sale. They were selling shirts that usually cost £8 at the new price of …?*' (£4) Continue with other examples such as suits at £60, trainers at £24, books at £4.
- These were easy to do, but what about some pictures at £7? What is half of that? Continue with a few similar problems, for example: MP3 downloads at £8, DVDs at £21.
- Discuss strategy with the class. How did they work out half of £21? (Probably: half of £20 added to half of £1, which is £10 + 50p = £10.50)
- Ask for some more halves, for example, half of: £27, £45, £89.
- What about half of £38? How do we work this out? (Be ready for many different strategies.) We could work out half of £30 (= £15), and add it to half of £8 (= £4), to give £19.
- Try a few more halves, for example, half of: £32, £54, £56, £94. You could extend this to half of amounts such as £37. (Half of £30 + half of £7 = £15 + £3.50)

Literacy activity

- Ask pupils to list three things they have learned today.

Part 2

- On the board, show the following rule: → +3 →
- Explain that today we are looking at functions. A function is a rule that gives a unique result for each different starting number or input.
- We can think of this as a machine, a function machine, which has an input and an output.
- If the input is 2, then 2 goes into the machine. What comes out is 2 + 3 = the output of 5.
- Show this on the diagram, so that it looks like this: input 2 → +3 → 5 output.
- Ask for the outputs from some other input numbers and add them to the diagram. Create a list under 'Input' and 'Output'.
- Demonstrate that we can go backwards. Ask: '*What input is needed to get 12 as the output?*' Extend the function diagram, illustrating that we can work from either side.
- Then show a *combined function*. For example: → × 2 → + 3 →
- Go through the input to the output with, say, {2, 3, 4 and 5} to get this diagram:
  - 2 → 2 × 2 + 3 → 7
  - 4 → 4 × 2 + 3 → 11
  - 3 → 3 × 2 + 3 → 9
  - 5 → 5 × 2 + 3 → 13
- **Pupils can now do Exercise 2A. Less able** pupils should start at the beginning. **More able** pupils could start with question 4.

Part 3

- On the board, write, and then ask: '*Can someone tell me a simple function? 'Can someone give me an input? And an output? What is the output? What is the input?*'
- Then ask what would be the function that took outputs and created inputs?
- Tell the class that this is called the *inverse function*.

Answers

Exercise 2A
1. **a** output 6, 7, 10, 13   **b** output 1, 2, 5; input 12   **c** output 16, 20, 44; input 10
   d output 10, 8, 7; input 25
2. **a** add 4   **b** multiply by 5   **c** divide by 4   **d** multiply by 9
3. **a** output 3, 5, 9; input 19 **b** output 3, 6, 9; input 20   **c** output 12, 16; input 5, 10
   d output 32; input 1, 3, 10
4. check answers for the following function machines
   a add 1   **b** multiply by 10   **c** subtract 3
   d halve   **e** add 11   **f** subtract 20
5. **a** 9, 11, 13, 15   **b** 7, 13, 19, 25   **c** 9, 12, 15, 18   **d** 18, 20, 22, 24
6. check answers for the following double function machines
   a multiply by 3, subtract 2   **b** multiply by 5, subtract 4   **c** subtract 3, multiply by 10
   d double, add 8
7. **a** multiply by 2 or double; output 18, 20   **b** subtract 1; output 14, 17
   c multiply by 4; output 15, 19   **d** add 3; input 7, 8
8. **a** 2, 5, 8, 11   **b** 4, 5, 7, 10   **c** 4, 6, 10, 11
9. **a** add 4   **b** subtract 7   **c** multiply by 3   **d** divide by 8

Challenge: Functions with two operations
A   multiply by 2 → add 1
B   multiply by 3 → subtract 1
C   multiply by 5 → add 2
D   add 3 → multiply by 2 or multiply by 2 → add 6
E   add 1 → multiply by 3 or multiply by 3 → add 3
F   add 2 → multiply by 5 or multiply by 5 → add 10

Lesson 2.2 Sequences and rules

Learning objectives

- To recognise, describe and write down sequences that are based on a simple rule

Resources and homework

- Pupil Book 1.1, pages 34–36
- Intervention Book 1, pages 33–34
- Intervention Book 3, pages 29–30
- Homework Book 1, section 2.2
- Online homework 2.2–3, questions 1–10

Links to other subjects

- **Music** – to generate sequences by beats and rhythms

Key words

- first term
- sequence
- term-to-term
- rule
- term

Problem solving and reasoning help

- The **PS** questions in Exercise 2B involve rules other than basic addition sequences and touch on the concept of a geometric progression, which is beyond the scope of this book. Question 8 requires pupils to create a sequence based on a rule.

Common misconceptions and remediation

- Pupils find it reasonably easy to generate term-to-term rules, but more difficult to extend this to position-to-term rules. Extend **more able** pupils by introducing position-to-term rules.

Probing questions

- I have a number sequence in my head. How many questions would you need to ask me to be sure you know my number sequence? What are the questions?

Part 1

- Start with, for example, 105. Ask which integers (whole numbers) divide exactly into this number (5). Say that numbers ending in 5 or 0 will divide exactly by 5; '... *divisible by 5*'.
- Ask which other number divides exactly into 105. Lead pupils to 3. Ask if anyone can tell from the digits that 105 is divisible by 3 (1 + 5 = 6, which is divisible by 3).
- Write down more numbers that are divisible by 3. Ask what is common. Lead pupils to see that adding the digits results in a number that is divisible by 3. Say that this is a useful way to test for divisibility. Ask if 78 can be divided by 3. (Yes: 7 + 8 = 15; 15 is divisible by 3.)
- To finish, hold up number cards while asking which numbers are divisible by 5, or 3, or both.

Literacy activity

- Ask pupils to write down the new words they have learned and their meanings.

Part 2

- Ask the class for the next numbers in this sequence (write it on the board): 2, 5, 8, 11, 14, ...
- You should get some correct answers of, for example: 17, 20, 23 ....
- Draw the idea of a rule here: add 3 each time. Introduce the term *difference*. Ask if this rule always gives the same sequence. (No, changing the start number changes the sequence.)
- Ask someone to suggest a rule. Keep it simple, accepting only *add* or *multiply*. Leave subtraction and division until later (unless you feel like introducing the idea here).

- Using the same rule, ask for some different starting points and encourage the class to tell you the different sequences. Choose a variety of additions and multiplications, keeping the numbers within the scope of the class. Write 1 and 2 on the board. Ask: '*What comes next?*'
- Ask for answers and rules, or prompt pupils. For example: 1, 2, 3, 4, … add 1 each time; 1, 2, 4, 8, … double the number each time; 1, 2, 4, 7, … add 1, then 2, then 3, ….
- Starting with the same numbers can lead to different sequences with different rules.
- Write 1, …, 10 on the board and ask: '*What sequence of numbers can go in between?*'
- Ask for answers and rules from the class, or prompt pupils, for example: 1, 5, 10, … add 4, then 5; 1, 2, 3, 4, 5, 6, 7, 8, 9, 10, … add 1 each time; 1, 4, 7, 10, … add 3 each time.
- **Pupils can now do Exercise 2B from Pupil Book 1.1.**

Part 3

- Ask for the next terms in these sequences:
  1, 3, 6, 10, 15, 21, … (28, 36, …); 1, 4, 9, 16, 25, 36, … (49, 64, …)
- For each, ask for the term-to-term rule. Discuss the differences in these sequences and those in Exercise 2B. Name the sequences: triangle numbers and square numbers.

Answers

Exercise 2B

1 **a** 2, 5, 8, 11   **b** 1, 3, 9, 27   **c** 4, 9, 14, 19   **d** 3, 30, 300, 3000
   e 6, 15, 24, 33   **f** 2, 10, 50, 250 **g** 3, 10, 17, 24   **h** 5, 10, 20, 40
2 **a** 21, 18, 15, 12 **b** 31, 26, 21, 16 **c** 250, 50, 10, 2   **d** 32, 16, 8, 4
   e 36, 28, 20, 12 **f** 64, 16, 4, 1   **g** 8, 4, 2, 1   **h** 45, 36, 27, 18
3 **a** add 2; 12, 14   **b** add 5; 20, 25   **c** multiply by 10; 2000, 20 000
   d multiply by 4; 64, 256   **e** add 7; 23, 30   **f** subtract 7; 9, 2
   g multiply by 2; 40, 80   **h** add 22; 77, 99
4 **a** add 3; 2, 5, 8, 11, 14, 17   **b** add 5; 1, 6, 11, 16, 21, 26
   c add 2; 5, 7, 9, 11, 13, 15   **d** add 5; 9, 14, 19, 24, 29, 34
5 **a** multiply by 10; 1, 10, 100, 1000, 10 000   **b** multiply by 2; 3, 6, 12, 24, 48, 96
   c multiply by 2; 2, 4, 8, 16, 32, 64   **d** multiply by 3; 4, 12, 36, 108, 324
6 **a** subtract 7; 52, 45, 38, 31, 24, 17   **b** subtract 5; 31, 26, 21, 16, 11, 6
   c subtract 10; 45, 35, 25, 15, 5   **d** subtract 6; 50, 44, 38, 32, 26, 20
7 **a** divide by 2; 80, 40, 20, 10, 5   **b** divide by 3; 81, 27, 9, 3, 1
   c divide by 2; 32, 16, 8, 4, 2, 1   **d** divide by 5; 1250, 250, 50, 10, 2
8 **a** 2, 4, 6, 8, 10   **b** 2, 8, 32, 128, 512   **c** 2, 7, 12, 17, 22
   d 2, 20, 200, 2000, 20 000   **e** 2, 10, 18, 26, 34   **f** 2, 10, 50, 250, 1250
   g 2, 5, 8, 11, 14   **h** 2, 4, 8, 16, 32
9 **a** 10 and 160   **b** 96, 6 and 3

Challenge: Rules for sequences

A **a** add 2; 5, 7 and multiply by 3; 9, 27   **b** add 6; 14, 20 and multiply by 4; 32, 128
   c add 5; 15, 20 and multiply by 2; 20, 40 **d** add 4; 9, 13 and multiply by 5; 25, 125
   e add 10; 30, 40 and multiply by 2; 40, 80   **f** add 9; 21, 30 and multiply by 4; 48, 192
B **a** add 3; 1, 4, 7, 10   **b** add 5; 1, 6, 11, 16, 21   **c** add 5; 15, 20, 25, 30
   d add 3; 6, 9, 12, 15   **e** add 10; 5, 15, 25, 35   **f** add 2; 18, 20, 22, 24

Lesson 2.3 Finding terms in patterns

Learning objective
- To work out missing terms in a sequence

Resources and homework
- Pupil Book 1.1, pages 37–39
- Intervention Book 1, pages 33–34
- Intervention Book 2, pages 24–25
- Intervention Book 3, pages 29–30
- Homework Book 1, section 2.3
- Online homework 2.2–3, questions 1–10

Links to other subjects
- Design and technology – to work out the material required for a given product

Key word
- differences

Problem solving and reasoning help
- Encourage pupils to explain their rules based on the structure of the problem.

Common misconceptions and remediation
- Pupils often find it difficult to understand why spotting patterns in numbers is not an end in itself and why they need to provide justification. The examples in this lesson enable pupils to understand how to link the basic structure of the problem to the rule, in order to explain and justify the patterns they have spotted. This introduces the basic concept of mathematical proof. 'Train Spotters' Paradise' at this link may be of interest: **http://nrich.maths.org/9071**.

Probing questions
- The term-to-term rule for a sequence is +5. What other information do you need to be able to generate the first terms in the sequence?
- The term-to-term rule is +3. The first term is 2; the fourth is 12. How would you respond?

Part 1
- Say: '*When I was on holiday in Tango Land, to work out the price of things in pence, I had to double their dollar prices.*' For example, an ice cream costs $24. What is the price in pence?
- Give examples of easy doubles such as: chocolate $32, muffin $25, cola $43.
- Give a more difficult question such as: An ice cream costs $37. What is the price in pence?
- Show a possible strategy on the board: Double $37 = 2 \times 30 + 2 \times 7 = 60 + 14 = 74$.
- Ask pupils to share other strategies for doubling such numbers and give more examples.
- Extend this to the hundreds, asking pupils to concentrate on the doubling techniques.
- Move this on to ×4 by doubling and doubling again. Give some examples and ask for answers. Extend this for **more able** pupils to multiplying by 8 or even 16.

Literacy activity
- Ask pupils to write three questions of their own based on the learning objective of the lesson.
- The local park is having a new path laid with 50 black slabs. How many white slabs are needed to go with the black slabs to complete the pattern? Let us break down the pattern.

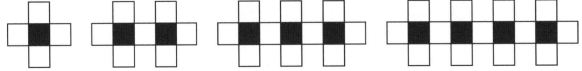

Number of black slabs: 1, 2, 3, 4; Number of white slabs: 4, 7, 10, 13

- Look at the *differences*. We add three white slabs each time. The number of 3s we add, are:
  - For 2 black slabs, we add 1 three. For 3 black slabs, we add 2 threes.
  - For 4 black slabs, we add 3 threes, and so on.
- Hence, for 50 black slabs, we add $(50 - 1)$ threes = 49 threes. So, the number of white slabs to go with 50 black slabs is: $4 + (50 - 1) \times 3 = 4 + 147 = 151$
- If we have a sequence such as: 7, 12, 17, 22, …, how do we find the 50th term?
- Talk about the terms: first term is 7, second term is 12, third term is 17, and so on.
- Again, we look at the differences: it is 5 each time. To get to the 50th term, we will need to add $(50 - 1)$ 5s to the first term of 7. This gives: $49 \times 5 + 7 = 245 + 7 = 252$.
- **Pupils can now do Exercise 2C from Pupil Book 1.1.**

Part 3

- Ask the class to explain the words: *term*, *difference*.
- Remind the class that they have been looking at simple sequences, but there are many other sequences. Write a sequence on the board, for example: 8, 10, 12, 14, ….
- Ask: *'What is the 10th term? What is the 21st term? What is the 51st term? What is the 100th term, the 101st term, …?'*

Answers

Exercise 2C

1	**a** pattern 5 drawn	**b** 4, 7, 10, 13, 16	**c i** 31 matches	**ii** 61 matches
2	**a** pattern 5 drawn	**b** 6, 11, 16, 21, 26	**c i** 51 matches	**ii** 101 matches
3	**a** pattern 5 drawn	**b** 5, 8, 11, 14, 17	**c i** 32 matches	**ii** 62 matches
4	**a** pattern 5 drawn	**b** 5, 9, 13, 17, 21	**c i** 41 matches	**ii** 81 matches
5	**a** pattern 5 drawn	**b** 6, 10, 14, 18, 22	**c i** 42 matches	**ii** 82 matches
6	**a i** add 2 **ii** 20	**b i** add 5 **ii** 48	**c i** add 6 **ii** 58	
	d i add 4 **i** 40	**e i** add 3 **ii** 34	**f i** add 8 **ii** 73	

Challenge: Dot patterns

A	**a** 25	**b** 100
B	**a** 15	**b** 55
C	**a** 30	**b** 110

Lesson 2.4 The square numbers

Learning objective
- To introduce the sequence of square numbers

Resources and homework
- Pupil Book 1.1, pages 39–41
- Intervention Book 2, pages 28–30
- Intervention Book 3, pages 31–33
- Online homework 2.4–5, questions 1–10

Links to other subjects
- **Design and technology** – to work out the area of a square for design purposes

Key words
- squaring
- square numbers

Problem solving and reasoning help
- **PS** question 5 of Exercise 2D will help pupils to understand how square numbers are generated. Relating each sum to a diagram will help pupils' understanding.

Common misconceptions and remediation
- The most common error when squaring a number is to multiply it by 2. Check pupils' understanding of how to square a number correctly and reinforce this throughout the lesson.

Probing questions
- How would you work out the 15th square number or the 24th square number?
- Why do square numbers have an odd number of factors?

Part 1
- The sum of consecutive odd numbers can be represented as square arrays, as shown in the diagram. The sum of the first four consecutive numbers is: 1 + 3 + 5 + 7 = ….
- Ask pupils to use the diagram to work out the answer without adding all the numbers. Then ask them to explain how they have done this.
- Use grouping to support **less able** and/or challenge **more able** pupils.

Literacy activity
- Ask pupils to explain orally why 64 is a square number and 24 is not a square number. Then ask pupils to write this in a sentence.

Part 2
- Write the first few square numbers on the board: 1, 4, 9, 16, 25, ….
- What are the next two numbers in the sequence? Ask pupils to explain how they worked out the numbers, and the rule they used. Tell pupils that these are called square numbers.
- Thinking about the images they used in the starter, challenge pupils to draw a square to illustrate each square number.
- **Pupils can now do Exercise 2D from Pupil Book 1.1.**

Part 3
- Write the first few square numbers on the board:
    - 1, 4, 9, 16, 25, 36, 49, …
- Along with this, write: '*Adding an even and an odd number makes an odd number.*'

- Ask pupils to write any observations they have about the list of square numbers.
- Can they use the statement to provide a mathematical justification for any of these statements?

Answers

Exercise 2D

1

8 × 8	9 × 9	10 × 10
8^2	9^2	10^2
64	81	100

2 121, 144, 169, 196, 225

3 **a** 324 **b** 441 **c** 625
   d 1600 **e** 1225 **f** 1764

4 **c** $13 = 4 + 9$ **d** $17 = 1 + 16$ **e** $20 = 4 + 16$ **f** $25 = 9 + 16$

5 **a** $1 + 3 + 5 + 7 = 16 = 4^2$
   $1 + 3 + 5 + 7 + 9 = 25 = 5^2$
   b they are all square numbers
   c i 36 **ii** 64

Challenge: Triples of squares

A $6^2 + 8^2 = 36 + 64 = 100 = 10^2$
B $5^2 + 12^2 = 25 + 144 = 169 = 13^2$
C $7^2 + 24^2 = 49 + 576 = 625 = 25^2$
D $10^2 + 24^2 = 100 + 576 = 676 = 26^2$
E $8^2 + 15^2 = 64 + 225 = 289 = 17^2$
F $9^2 + 12^2 = 81 + 144 = 225 = 15^2$

Lesson 2.5 The triangular numbers

Learning objective
- To introduce the sequence of triangular numbers

Links to other subjects
- **Physical education** – to prepare for a tournament that uses a round robin grouping strategy; the number of matches played between *n* teams will be the *n*–1 triangular number

Resources and homework
- Pupil Book 1.1, pages 41–43
- Online homework 2.4–5, questions 1–10

Key word
- triangular number

Problem solving and reasoning help
- **PS** question 5 of Exercise 2E will help to embed pupils' understanding of triangular numbers. Ask pupils to draw a diagram to represent each sum.

Common misconceptions and remediation
- Pupils need to have a good understanding of how to generate triangular numbers, as they can be difficult to remember. Always relate them to the diagrams, which explain why they are called triangular numbers.

Probing questions
- Trinni is fascinated by triangular numbers (1, 3, 6, 10, 15, 21, …). Recently she found that she could rearrange the 12 numbers on a clock 1, 2, 3, ..., 12 around the face so that each adjacent pair added up to a triangular number. She left the 12 in place. What number did she put where the 6 would usually be? Refer to this problem at: **http://nrich.maths.org/5684.**

Part 1
- If a group of people all shake hands with each other, the total number of handshakes will always be a triangular number. Try this with five pupils to give a triangular number of 10.
- Can pupils make the first 10 triangular numbers using this method?

Literacy activity
- Ask pupils to design a word search that includes all the new words in this chapter. Pupils can then solve each other's word searches.

Part 2
- Write the first few triangular numbers on the board: 1, 3, 6, 10, 15 ….
- What are the next two numbers in the sequence? Ask pupils to explain how they worked out the numbers, and to explain the rule they used.
- Tell pupils that these are called triangular numbers.
- Thinking about the images they used in the starter, challenge them to draw a 'triangular' to illustrate each triangular number.
- **Pupils can now do Exercise 2E from Pupil Book 1.1.**

Part 3

- Write the first few triangular numbers on the board: 1, 3, 6, 10, 15, 21, 28, 36, 45, 55 ….
  Along with this, write: *'Adding an even and an odd number makes an odd number'*.
- Ask pupils to write any observations they have about the list of triangular numbers. Ask if they can use the statement to provide a mathematical justification for any of the statements.

Answers

Exercise 2E

1

28 + 8	36 + 9	45 + 10
36	45	55

2 66, 78, 91, 105, 120

3 **c** 9 = 3 + 6   **d** 11 = 1 + 10   **e** 13 = 3 + 10   **f** 16 = 6 + 10 or 16 = 1 + 15

4 1 and 36

5 **a** 1 + 2 + 3 + 4 = 10
$\qquad$ 1 + 2 + 3 + 4 + 5 = 15
$\qquad$ **b** each line is a sequence of consecutive whole numbers
$\qquad$ **c** it is a sequence of triangular numbers
$\qquad$ **d i** 21   **ii** 36

6 **a** 4, 9, 16, 25, 36   **b** they form a sequence of square numbers

Challenge: Triangular numbers

A The 5th term is 15. This can be worked out from $0.5 \times 5 \times 6 = 15$.
$\qquad$ The 6th term is 21. This can be worked out from $0.5 \times 6 \times 7 = 21$.
$\qquad$ The 7th term is 28. This can be worked out from $0.5 \times 7 \times 8 = 28$.

B work out 0.5 × the term number × the term number + 1

C **a** 55   **b** 210   **c** 1275   **d** 5050

Investigation: A function machine problem

A 7

B 9

C 9

D it repeats itself

E it also repeats itself

F it starts to repeat itself

G it also starts to repeat itself

H **a** 9   **b** 9, $5 \times 6 = 6 \times 5 = 30$

- The review questions will help to determine pupils' abilities with regard to the material within Chapter 2.
- These questions also draw on the maths covered in earlier chapters of the book to encourage pupils to make links between different topics.

Mathematical reasoning – Valencia Planetarium

- Look at the key and examples on the Valencia Planetarium activity using ladders and grids on page 38 of Pupil Book 1.2.
- Draw some ladders and grids on the board and set up the algebraic expressions with pupils' help. Grids do not have to be rectangular. You can use the examples below.

$$(4L + 4R, \quad 4L + 8T + 3X + 22R, \quad 5L + 2T + X + 10R)$$

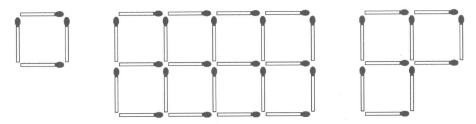

- Draw some ladders that increase in size consecutively. Set up the algebraic expressions.
- Put these in the form of a table or write them under each other. Discuss with pupils if they can see any patterns in the number of L and T links and the R rods. Predict the next number in the table then draw the ladder to check.
- Use the patterns in the table to set up algebraic expressions.
- Encourage pupils to suggest possible questions. They could do these in small groups or individually, then present these to the class for others to answer.
- Once they have done this, the class can work through the questions on pages 38–39.
- Ask pupils to draw a grid to fit: 6L + 2T + 2X + 13R. Do the same with: 8L + 4X + 16R.
- Ask pupils what is the biggest ladder they could make with 5L links, 10T links and 20R rods. (Answer: a ladder with six squares)
- If there is time, investigate the patterns in 'crosses'.

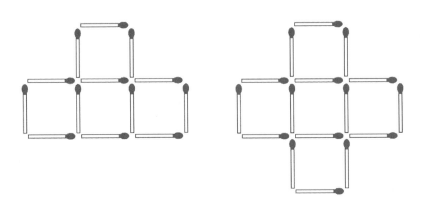

Answers to Review questions

1 **a** output 0, 1, 4; input 15   **b** output 12, 15, 24; input 10
2 **a** 24   **b** 48   **c** 90   **d** 6
3 **b** add 3   **c** multiply by 8   **d** multiply by 3
4 **a i** 16, 22   **ii** 16, 64   **iii** 25, 53   **b** −2
5 **a i** £40   **ii** £160

    b

Week	1	2	3	4	5	6	7	8
Amount saved	£9	£11	£13	£15	£17	£19	£21	£23
Total amount saved	£25	£36	£49	£64	£81	£100	£121	£144

    c i Jeni   **ii** £16
6 **a** 1, 3, 6, 10, 15   **b** 0, 1, 3, 6, 10   **c** 21 + 28   **d** 45 + 55

Answers to Mathematical reasoning – Valencia Planetarium

1 **a**

Grid	'L' links	'T' links	'R' rods
1	4	0	4
2	4	2	7
3	4	4	10

    b

Grid	'L' links	'T' links	'R' rods
1	4	0	4
2	4	2	7
3	4	4	10
4	4	6	13
5	4	8	16
6	4	10	19

    c 'L' links = 4, 'T' links = grid number × 2 – 2, 'R' rods = grid number × 3 + 1

2 **a**

Grid	'L' links	'T' links	'X' links	'R' rods
1	4	2	0	7
2	4	4	1	12
3	4	6	2	17
4	4	8	3	21

    b 'L' links = 4, 'T' links = grid number × 2, 'X' links = grid number × 1 – 1,
    'R' rods = grid number × 5 + 2

3 **a**

Grid	'L' links	'T' links	'X' links	'R' rods
1	4	4	0	10
2	4	6	2	17
3	4	8	4	24
4	4	10	6	31

    b 'L' links = 4, 'T' links = grid number × 2 + 2, 'X' links = grid number × 2 – 2,
    'R' rods = grid number × 7 + 3

3 Perimeter and area

Learning objectives

- How to measure and draw lines
- How to work out the perimeter of 2D shapes
- How to work out the area of 2D shapes by counting squares
- How to work out the perimeter of a square and a rectangle by using a rule
- How to work out the area of a square and a rectangle by using a rule

Prior knowledge

- The metric units of length
- How to recognise triangles, squares and rectangles
- That the perimeter of a 2D shape is the distance around its edges
- That the area of a 2D shape is the space inside it
- By the end of KS2, pupils can recognise that shapes with the same areas can have different perimeters and vice versa.

Context

- Remind pupils that measurement, perimeter and area are used widely in many jobs and professions, from farming to astronomy. Encourage pupils to talk to family and relatives to see if anyone uses these skills in their work or to explore specific jobs on the internet. A good example is the building industry, which is totally dependent on workers being able to measure lengths and calculate areas.
- Pupils could also talk to family and relatives about how they might use area and perimeter in projects such as laying carpets and flooring, and decorating, to estimate how much carpet, flooring or wallpaper is needed.

Discussion points

- How are the perimeter and the area of a shape different?
- Do you have any tips for remember which is which?

Associated Collins ICT resources

- Chapter 3 interactive activities on Collins Connect online platform
- *Understanding the volume of a cuboid* video on Collins Connect online platform
- *Milk bottles* Wonder of Maths on Collins Connect online platform
- *Perimeter and area of rectangles* and *Other sequences* Worked solutions on Collins Connect online platform

Curriculum references

Geometry and measures

- Derive and apply formulae to calculate and solve problems involving: perimeter and area
- Calculate and solve problems involving: perimeter of 2D shapes
- Draw and measure line segments

Develop fluency

- Use language and properties precisely

Solve problems

- Apply elementary knowledge to multi-step and increasingly sophisticated problems

Fast-track for classes following a 2-year scheme of work

- Leave out Exercises 3.1 and 3.2 in the Pupil Book if you are happy that the class is familiar with this material from KS2.
- Most pupils will have met the basic concepts in this chapter. If they can demonstrate that they are confident and fluent with these basic concepts they can move on to the activity, challenge or investigation questions at the end of each exercise.

Lesson 3.1 Length and perimeter

Learning objectives

- To measure and draw lines
- To work out the perimeter of a shape

Resources and homework

- Pupil Book 1.1, pages 49–53
- Intervention Workbook 2, pages 62–64
- Intervention Workbook 3, pages 57–60
- Homework Book 1, section 3.1
- Online homework 3.1, questions 1–10

Links to other subjects

- **Physical education** – to calculate the distance around a running track or the area of a sports field
- **Geography** – to calculate the perimeter and area on town planning maps

Key words

- perimeter
- millimetre
- centimetre
- metric units

Problem solving and reasoning help

- Question 7 of Exercise 3A requires pupils to understand that regular shapes have sides of the same length. They need to apply this knowledge by multiplying the length of one side by the number of sides. Pupils who work out relationships using their own prior knowledge are more likely to understand these relationships and be able to apply these confidently in less familiar contexts.

Common misconceptions and remediation

- It is important for pupils to know how to measure correctly using a ruler.
- Common mistakes are:
  - starting at the end of the ruler rather than where the scale starts on the ruler
  - using the inches scale when attempting to measure in centimetres or millimetres.

Probing questions

- What mistakes could you make when reading from a ruler? How would you avoid these mistakes?
- How would you measure 4.6 cm if the zero end of your ruler was broken, for example, at 1 cm, 1.5 cm or 2.3 cm?

Part 1

- Show the class a metre rule.
- Ask: '*How many centimetres are there in 1 metre, 2 metres, 3 metres, ...?*'
- Then invite pupils to estimate heights and lengths, in metres, of various objects. For example, the classroom, a desk, the school hall, a double-decker bus, a football pitch.

Literacy activity

- Ask pupils to incorporate the new words they have learned this lesson into sentences or a short paragraph.

Part 2

- Working in pairs or groups, ask the class to write down all the different units they know to measure length.
- Divide the board into two sections – metric and imperial.
- Write all pupils' responses in the correct sections.
- Discuss the different units used and get suggestions for when each might be appropriate.
- *Metric units in common use:* millimetre, centimetre, metre and kilometre.
- Divide the class into groups and give them a variety of objects to measure, for example: a book, a pen, a hand-span.
- Explain ways to measure length, for example: 7.2 cm, 7 cm 2 mm, or 72 mm. (Explain that millimetres are used mainly in subjects such as Technology and Science.)
- Draw a large rectangle divided into unit squares.
- Explain how to find the perimeter of the rectangle: the distance around the rectangle.
- Show the class how to find the perimeter of a shape, as shown in the following diagram:

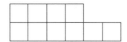

- Pupils can now do Exercise 3A in Pupil Book 1.1.

Part 3

- Using squared paper, ask pupils to draw as many rectangles as they can with a perimeter of 24 cm and whole number dimensions.

Answers

Exercise 3A
1	**a** 40 mm	**b** 100 mm	**c** 75 mm	**d** 89 mm	**e** 124 mm
2	**a** 7 cm	**b** 14 cm	**c** 6.5 cm	**d** 3.2 cm	**e** 11.6cm
3	**a** 2 cm ´	**b** 5 cm	**c** 8 cm	**d** 10 cm	**e** 12 cm
4	**a** 40 mm	**b** 55 mm	**c** 71 mm	**d** 80 mm	**e** 118 mm
6	**a** 12 cm	**b** 16 cm	**c** 18 cm	**d** 22 cm	**e** 20 cm
7	**a i** 15 cm	**ii** 16 cm	**iii** 15 cm	**iv** 12 cm	

    b the length of each side by the number of sides

8   2 cm, 2.6 cm, 1.8 cm, 2.4 cm, 2.2 cm

Activity: Guess the length
Pupils' own answers

Lesson 3.2 Area

Learning objective
- To work out the area of a shape by counting squares

Resources and homework
- Pupil Book 1.3, pages 53–55
- Intervention Workbook 2, pages 62–64
- Intervention Workbook 3, pages 57–60
- Homework Book 1, section 3.1
- Online homework 3.2, questions 1–10

Links to other subjects
- **Geography** – to calculate area on ordnance survey (OS) maps by counting squares

Key words
- area
- square centimetre

Problem solving and reasoning help
- When **more able** pupils tackle the challenge question at the end of Exercise 3B, they could solve it by estimating fractions of areas and summing them to get a more accurate estimate of the total area. Provide support for **less able** pupils with this technique.

Common misconceptions and remediation
- It is important for pupils to understand the units in which they are working when solving these problems. Difficulties may arise when the squares are not 1 cm^2, for example, half-cm squares that are found in some exercise books. Pupils will often copy the diagram blindly onto the half-cm squares and give an incorrect answer for the drawn shape.

Probing questions
- In what way are the perimeter of a shape and the area of a shape different?
- How can you remember the differences? Or, in which objects area can be measured in cm²?

Part 1
- Hand out squared paper and ask pupils to draw a shape with using 10 square units.
- Encourage pupils to be creative, and to incorporate half-squares into different shapes.
- Remind pupils that two half-square units are equal to one square unit.
- Repeat the activity with 20 square units or 50 square units.

Literacy activity
- Ask pupils to write down where they could use what they have learned today. This could be in other lessons or in real life.

Part 2
- Area and perimeter may confuse some pupils, so review them: area is the measurement of the space inside a shape; perimeter is the total distance around a shape. If necessary, explain the differences further. Ask pupils why knowing the area of something is helpful. Encourage pupils to come up with the following ideas: that we calculate area to figure out the size of a room, how much carpet we might need to cover a floor, or how much wallpaper, tile, or paint we might need to cover a wall. Brainstorm other uses for area as a class.

- Next, place a 1 cm² sheet of paper under a visualiser. Say that it is 1 cm on each side, or 1 cm². Then place three more squares in a row next to it. Ask pupils how much of the surface the paper is covering. (The amount of surface covered by the paper is 4 cm².)
- Then add another row of paper squares below the first row. Have pupils count the squares. (There are eight squares, so the area is 8 cm².)
- On cm² paper, draw a shape that includes half squares. Ask pupils to work out the cm² area.
- **Pupils can now do Exercise 3B from Pupil Book 1.1.**

Part 3

- Ask each pupil to draw an outline of their hand on cm² paper. Now ask them to calculate the area of their hand by counting the squares.
- What is the area of the largest hand? What is the area of the smallest hand?

Answers
Exercise 3B

1	**a** 3 cm²	**b** 4 cm²	**c** 6 cm²	**d** 6 cm²
2	**a** 9 cm²	**b** 12 cm²	**c** 10 cm²	
3	**a** 14 cm²	**b** 11 cm²	**c** 18 cm²	**d** 25 cm²
4	**a** 6½ cm²	**b** 9 cm²	**c** 5½ cm²	**d** 2 cm²

5 for example:

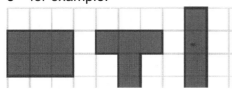

6 4 by 4 square drawn.

Challenge: More difficult shapes

A approximately 14 cm²

B approximately 15 cm²

Lesson 3.3 Perimeter and area of rectangles

Learning objectives
- To work out the perimeter of a rectangle
- To work out the area of a rectangle

Resources and homework
- Pupil Book 1.3, pages 56–59
- Intervention Workbook 2, pages 62–64
- Intervention Workbook 3, pages 57–59
- Homework Book 1, section 3.2
- Online homework 3.3, questions 1–10

Links to other subjects
- **Design and technology** – to make the best use of materials to reduce wastage

Key words
- length
- rectangle
- square metre
- metre
- square
- width

Problem solving and reasoning help
- When working on the investigation at the end of Exercise 3C, pupils need to make the link between the theoretical and applied parts of the question. Use guided group work to support **less able** pupils. Encourage pupils to be methodical when working through the question.

Common misconceptions and remediation
- Pupils are often taught rules without being given the opportunity to explore the origins of these rules and how they are derived. This means they tend to confuse them when under pressure and do not know how to check if they have remembered them correctly. It also means they struggle to apply the rules in new situations.

Probing questions
- Is this statement always, sometimes or never true: If a rectangle has a larger perimeter than another rectangle, it will also have a larger area.

Part 1
- On the board, draw various squares and rectangles.
- Ask pupils if they can explain how they would find the area and perimeter of each shape.
- Ask pupils to write down the different metric units that are used to measure length and area.

Literacy activity
- Give pupils an answer, for example, 40 cm^2 and ask them to write a question.

Part 2
- Draw four different rectangles on a square grid on the board. Ask pupils which one has the greatest perimeter and which one has the greatest area. Explain how to find the area and perimeter of a rectangle when we know the measurements.
- On the board, write the following for pupils. To find the perimeter of a rectangle:
  Perimeter = 2 × *length* + 2 × *width*
  The formula is: $P = 2l + 2w$
- To find the area of a rectangle:
  Area = *length* × *width*
  The formula is: $A = l \times w$ OR $A = lw$
- **Pupils can now do Exercise 3C from Pupil Book 1.1.**

Part 3

- On the board, draw various squares and rectangles.
- Ask pupils to explain how they would find the area and perimeter of each shape. (They should know the formula for each.)
- Ask the class to make a list of the different metric units for measuring length and area.

Answers

Exercise 3C

1   **a** 4 cm   **b** 16 cm   **c** 28 cm   **d** 40 cm

2   **a** 14 cm   **b** 18 cm   **c** 30 m   **d** 54 m

3   **a** 30 m   **b** 10

4   48 cm

5   280 m

6   **a** 1 cm^2 **b** 16 cm^2 **c** 49 cm^2 **d** 100 cm^2

7   **a** 10 cm^2 **b** 18 cm^2 **c** 56 m^2 **d** 180 m^2 **e** 88 m^2
     f 24 cm^2 **g** 32 cm^2 **h** 60 cm^2

8   9

9   **a** 12 cm, 8 cm^2 **b** 22 cm, 30 cm^2 **c** 24 cm, 32 cm^2
     d 38 cm, 90 cm^2 **e** 18 cm, 8 cm^2 **f** 18 cm, 14 cm^2

Investigation: Different rectangles, same perimeter

A   1 cm by 9 cm, 2 cm by 8 cm, 3 cm by 7 cm, 4 cm by 6 cm, 5 cm by 5 cm

B   9 cm^2, 16 cm^2, 21 cm^2, 24 cm^2, 25 cm^2

C   the square with an area of 25 cm^2

Review questions (Pupil Book pages 60–61)

- The review questions will help to determine pupils' abilities with regard to the material within Chapter 3.
- These questions also draw on the maths covered in earlier chapters of the book to encourage pupils to make links between different topics.

Problem solving – Design a bedroom (Pupil Book pages 62–63)

This activity is designed to show pupils an everyday situation that involves area and perimeter.
- Pupils will need 1-centimetre squared paper and thin card for cut-outs for the furniture challenge. Pupils may use a calculator.
- Catalogues from furniture stores or access to the Internet would also be useful.
- Pupils could work on the task individually or in small groups.

Bedroom plan
- Pupils often confuse perimeter with area, and some revision work may be appropriate. It is hoped that this practical approach will help pupils to understand the concepts of perimeter and area. Drawing a sketch of the room may also help.
- Note: The door is not considered when finding the perimeter.

Posters
- If a calculator is used to perform the division, it is useful to discuss the decimal display, as pupils may consider that the decimal part of the answer is the amount left over. Encourage pupils to write the calculation for the amount left over as, for example: $50 - (6 \times 7.5)$

Painting the bedroom
- To help pupils find the area of each wall, they could draw a sketch or scale drawing on squared paper. This involves finding the area of walls with a window and a door, so it is worth finding the area of each first. Remind pupils that they will need to do some subtractions (subtract window and door from total area). Pupils may not understand what 'minimum' means in this context. Suggest that it may be worth buying an extra tin of paint. Pupils can then explain the reasons for this.

Furniture challenge
- You may need to tell pupils that the dimensions given for each piece of furniture is for the floor space covered and that they must also take the height of each piece of furniture into account, since some pieces could be placed under the windows. Explain that the scale could also be given as: 1 metre is represented by 2 centimetres. It might be worth considering that chairs, stools and other pieces of furniture are required in the bedroom. Allow pupils to discuss their plans with other groups.

Answers to Review questions

| 1 | **a** 20 mm | **b** 45 mm | **c** 6 cm | **d** 7.2 cm |
| 2 | **a** 4 cm | **b** 6 cm | **c** 7.5 cm | **d** 8.3 cm |

4   arrows at $3\frac{1}{2}$ cm and $12\frac{1}{2}$ cm

| 5 | **a** 12 cm | **b** 20 cm | **c** 20 m | |
| 6 | **a** 12 cm and 5 cm^2 | | **b** shape with an area of 8 cm^2 | |

    c correct perimeter for their shape

| 7 | **a** 6 cm^2 | **b** 15 cm^2 | **c** 72 m^2 | **d** 14 m^2 |
| 8 | **a** 36 | **b** 9 | **c** 4 | |

Answers to Problem solving – Design a bedroom

1   **a** perimeter = 18 m

    b area = 20 m^2

    c cost of carpet = £130

2   **a** 6 posters

    b £2 is left over

3   **a** $5 \times 3 = 15$ m^2, $2 \times 1 = 2$ m^2, $15 - 2 = 13$ m^2

    b short window wall = 11 m^2, long window wall = 14 m^2, plain wall = 12 m^2

    c total area of walls = 50 m^2

    d 6 tins of paint

4 Decimal numbers

Learning objectives

- How to order decimal numbers by size
- How to multiply and divide decimal numbers by 10, 100 and 1000
- How to use estimation to check your answers
- How to solve problems using decimals, with and without a calculator
- How to add and subtract decimal numbers
- How to multiply and divide decimals by whole numbers

Prior knowledge

- How to write and read whole numbers and decimals
- How to write tenths and hundredths as decimals. By the end of KS2, pupils can read, write, order and compare numbers up to 10 000 000.
- Times tables up to 12 × 12. By Year 5, pupils apply all the multiplication tables and related division facts frequently, commit them to memory and use them confidently to make larger calculations. During Year 6, pupils continue to use these to maintain their fluency.
- How to use a calculator to do simple calculations. Calculators are introduced near the end of KS2 to support pupils' conceptual understanding and exploration of more complex number problems, only if pupils' written and mental arithmetic are secure.

Context

- Pupils will be aware of decimals all around them, for example, in the shops, at petrol stations, on television and in magazines. Pupils should know that in prices, the decimal point separates the pounds from the pence. In weights, the decimal point separates the kilograms from the grams. In distances, the decimal point separates the kilometres from metres. For pupils to convert between pounds and pence when solving money problems, they need to draw on their financial skills abilities and be aware of the impact of incorrect conversions.
- Pupils should also be aware that in top sports events athletes may set new records by only a tiny part of a second, and that this is shown as a decimal. Sports stars can win or lose by the smallest of decimal numbers.

Discussion point

- Ask pupils for a number between two other decimal numbers, for example, between 0.24 and 0.28.
- Ask: 'To which of the two numbers is it closer? How do you know?'

Associated Collins ICT resources

- Chapter 4 interactive activities on Collins Connect online platform
- *Estimating height, weight and capacity* and *Maths Man gets the point* videos on Collins Connect online platform
- *Why ten?* Wonder of Maths on Collins Connect online platform
- *Multiplying and dividing by 10, 100 and 1000*, *Ordering decimals* and *Multiplying and dividing decimals* Worked solutions on Collins Connect online platform

Curriculum references

Develop fluency

- Consolidate their numerical and mathematical capability from key stage 2 and extend their understanding of the number system and place value to include decimals

Number

- Order decimals; use the symbols < and >
- Understand and use place value for decimals
- Use the four operations, including formal written methods, applied to decimals

Fast-track for classes following a 2-year scheme of work

- You could leave out Lesson 4.1 if you are confident that your class is familiar with this material from KS2.
- Most pupils will have met the basic concepts in this chapter, although they may not have applied them to decimals. If pupils can demonstrate their ability to transfer this understanding efficiently, they can move on to the activities in the boxes at the end of each exercise in this chapter of the Pupil Book.

Lesson 4.1 Multiplying and dividing by 10, 100 and 1000

Learning objective
- To multiply and divide decimal numbers by 10, 100 and 1000

Resources and homework
- Pupil Book 1.1, pages 65–68
- Intervention Workbook 3, pages 6–8
- Homework Book 1, section 4.1
- Online homework 4.1, questions 1–10

Links to other subjects
- **History** – to use timelines, for example, number of years in two decades or three centuries
- **Science** – to convert standard measurements, for example, metres to centimetres

Key word
- decimal

Problem solving and reasoning help
- The focus of the questions in this lesson is pupils' ability to communicate their mathematical understanding. Pupils could work in threes, taking turns at: providing the explanation; asking questions; and making notes and providing formative feedback on the explanations.

Common misconceptions and remediation
- Pupils need to see that working with decimals is just an extension of the place value work they developed in KS2. Most pupils will grasp that each column to the left of another is 10 times greater. Extend this so that pupils know that each column to the right is 10 times smaller. The zeros may cause confusion, for example, comparing 1.1 and 1.10 and ordering 2, 2.02, 2.22, 0.02, 0.2. Pupils will need practice in giving values to each digit. Remind pupils that they will need their financial skills abilities to convert between pounds and pence. Pupils also need to be aware of the impact of correct conversions when solving money problems.

Probing questions
- How would you explain that 0.72 is greater than 0.072?
- Why do 62 ÷ 10 and 620 ÷ 100 give the same answer?

Part 1
- Draw a number line or use a counting stick marked with 10 segments. Mark 0 at one end and 1 at the other end. Goal: to identify the middle number, then fill in the other numbers.
- Do some counting-on activities with the class. For example, start at 0 and count on in steps of 0.2. Point out the positions until you reach 1. Ask pupils to continue without prompts.
- Start at 1, counting down in steps of 0.1. Repeat, using the 10-segment line, ending at 0.5.
- Continue for as long as possible, making the interval smaller each time. Discuss what each decimal place means, using the terms tenths, hundredths and thousandths.

Literacy activity
- Ask pupils to explain their reasoning for questions 9 and 10 of Exercise 4A in the Pupil Book.
- Write down some incorrect answers and ask pupils to explain *why* these are incorrect.

Part 2
- Pupils can work in groups or individually. They will need calculators.

- Ask one pupil to choose a number, or start with, for example: 52. Write it in the middle of the board. Ask for the answers, or ask one pupil to work them out using a calculator. Use a spider diagram to show what happens when you multiply or divide by 1, 10, 100 and 1000.
- Now ask pupils, working alone or in groups, to repeat the activity in their books or on sheets with the following numbers (or similar numbers): 7; 78; 0.2; 341; 203; 0.056
- After pupils have done this, ask for the rules when multiplying or dividing by: 1, 10, 100 and 1000. (Note that 1 has been included as it is an important concept that is often missed.)

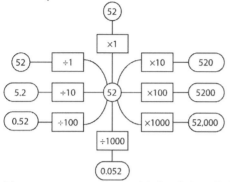

Thousands	Hundreds	Tens	Units	Tenths	Hundredths	Thousandths
		5	2			
			0	0	5	2
	5	2	0			

- Encourage pupils to think of the digits moving left or right. The chart will prove helpful in Exercise 4A. (52 ÷ 1000; 52 × 10).
- **Pupils can now do Exercise 4A from Pupil Book 1.1**.

Part 3

- Use prepared cards or write numbers on the board such as 0.72 and 72, 34 and 3400, 0.005 and 50. Ask pupils to match them with a multiplier or divisor. For example: 34 × 100 = 3400
- Make sure that pupils identify both the multiplier and divisor, and ask if they can explain the connection. Make it clear that multiplication is the inverse operation of division.

Answers
Exercise 4A
1   40, 20, 50, 110, 10, 500, 370, 690
2   800, 1200, 600, 6200, 300, 4000, 1000, 250 000
3   a 140   b 890   c 700   d 4100   e 3   f 890   g 70   h 40   i 580
    j 9000   k 44   l 640
4   a 40   b 900   c 700   d 4000   e 0.3   f 0.08   g 0.02   h 0.005   i 0.008
    j 100   k 0.4   l 600
5   a 540   b 7900   c 8700   d 24 000   e 1.4   f 0.39   g 0.73   h 0.065   i 0.051
    j 1700   k 3.4   l 8500
6   a 1240   b 36 900   c 59 700   d 654 000   e 11.4   f 2.89   g 1.07   h 0.235   i 0.143
    j 71 400   k 97.4   l 72 900
7   a 34   b 89   c 97   d 1400   e 0.34   f 0.89   g 0.07   h 0.0075   i 0.0583
    j 7140   k 0.074   l 1890
8   a 30   b 100   c 0.3   d 100
9   a 560   b 90   c 670   d 7   e 350   f 80   g 0.013   h 0.004   i 0.042
    j 0.0001   k 0.069   l 0.0003   m 0.0624   n 398.1   o 0.17   p 781
10 a 4500   b 870   c 7600   d 30   e 6400   f 820   g 0.0046   h 0.0005
    i 0.0024   j 0.000 03   k 0.0097   l 0.000 02   m 0.0031
    n 8200   o 8200   p 0.023   q 8700
11 £40, £32, £7.50; total = £79.50
12 move digits 6 places
13 Buy at 1p each, it will cost £20. The boxes would cost £28 and the packets £30.
Activity: Billions and billions
A   UK billion was 1 000 000 000 000 USA billion was and still is 1 000 000 000
B   USA move digits 9 places, UK move digits 12 places

Learning objective

- To order decimal numbers according to size

Resources and homework

- Pupil Book 1.1, pages 68–70
- Intervention Workbook 2, pages 8–10
- Intervention Workbook 3, pages 13–14
- Homework Book 1, section 4.2
- Online homework 4.2, questions 1–10

Links to other subjects

- **Food technology** – to compare the nutritional content of different foods

Key words

- decimal point
- order
- place value

Problem solving and reasoning help

- The investigation on page 68 of the Pupil Book uses reciprocals as the context. Encourage **more able** pupils to state hypotheses of what might happen. Then they can assess the validity of their hypotheses. Extension: state a hypothesis and work in the opposite direction to explore the reciprocals of five consecutive decimal numbers to a given decimal place.

Common misconceptions and remediation

- The magnitude of numbers can be confusing. For example, when ordering a set of decimals such as 5.1, 0.3412, 2.45, 13.6, from smallest to largest, pupils give 5.1, 13.6, 2.45, 0.3412. This shows no real understanding of the value of each digit. Pupils look at the digits, ignoring the impact that the decimal point has on the size of the number. Pupils need time to discuss the value of each digit in the numbers. Create a starting point by discussing, for example, whether 5.1 is bigger than 1 and whether 0.2112 is less than 1.

Probing questions

- Describe the key steps to think about when putting a set of decimals in order of size.

Part 1

- Provide pupils with a set of cards with decimal numbers on them.
- Line up pupils. Say that while talking only with the person in front or behind them, they should place themselves in order from smallest to largest.
- Ask pupils to hold up their number. At this point, they can challenge the place of other pupils but they need to be able to justify the challenge. Other pupils can take part in any challenge using the stem of: '*I agree with [name] because …*' or '*I disagree with [name] because …*'

Literacy activity

- In pairs, ask pupils to draw the key words for their partner to guess (as in Pictionary).

Part 2

- Draw the table below on the board, or on an overhead transparency (OHT).
- On the board, write the following, or similar, numbers: 320; 0.7; 0.04; 0.78; 0.4; 4; 32.5. Ask individuals to select a number and put it in a table using the appropriate place-value columns. Or, ask each pupil to select the biggest (or smallest) number, fill it in on the top line, and continue to select the next biggest (or smallest), as appropriate. Then discuss how to decide which number is biggest.
- When comparing numbers, ensure that pupils understand the concept of working from left to right until they encounter the largest digit.

- Repeat the exercise using: 0.345; 0.342; 0.35; 0.3; 0.039; 0.307; 0.38
- Introduce the symbols < and > and discuss what they mean.
- Which symbol should come between 0.35 and 0.347?
- Which symbol should come between 4.111 and 4.118?
- How can we tell, easily? Discuss decimal places. Some pupils find it easier to add zeros to make each number have the same number of decimal places. At this level, there will never be more than three zeros.
- What does this mathematical expression mean: 3.182 < 3.25 < 3.4? It can be read as: 3.182 is less than 3.25, which is less than 3.4; or as: 3.25 is *between* 3.182 and 3.4.
- **Pupils can now do Exercise 4B from Pupil Book 1.1.**

Thousands	Hundreds	Tens	Units	Tenths	Hundredths	Thousandths

Part 3

- Write numbers on the board (or use prepared cards), for example, 3.4 and 3.45, 0.72 and 0.7, 0.005, 0.045. Ask pupils to use greater than or less than signs. For example: 3.4 < 3.45
- Write on the board (or use prepared cards) four sets of numbers, for example:

| 3 kg | 300 g | 0.33 kg; | 52 cm | 5 m | 2.97 m |
| £2.56 | 47 p | £0.07; | 4 h 30 min | 59 min | 3.75 hours |

- Ask pupils to put the sets of numbers in order. Discuss the importance of using the same units. Some pupils might find metric units difficult, but they should know money and time.

Answers

Exercise 4B

1 a

Thousands	Hundreds	Tens	Units	Tenths	Hundredths	Thousandths
	4	5	7			
		4	5			
4	0	5	7			
			4			
	4	5	0			
5	4	0	5			

   b 4, 45, 450, 457, 4057, 5405

2 **a** 29, 47, 69, 70, 75   **b** 92, 98, 203, 302, 907

3 **a** 450, 403, 400, 54, 45   **b** 2531, 513, 315, 153, 135

4 Edinburgh

5 Fort William

6 **a** Nottingham   **b** 5 miles

7 **b** 3.04, 3.4, 3.46, 34, 34.6

8 **a** 0.6, 0.62, 6.02, 6.2   **b** 0.5, 0.54, 5.12, 5.4   **c** 2.03, 2.31, 2.35, 21
   d 1.8, 1.85, 1.88, 12.3   **e** 0.75, 7.5, 7.55, 75   **f** 0.018, 0.1, 0.18, 0.8

9 **a** £0.03, £0.30, 32p, 130p, £1.32   **b** €0.05, €0.55, €1.05, €5, €15

10 half an hour, 35 minutes, 1 h 20 mins, 1 and a half hours

11 **a** <   **b** >   **c** <   **d** >   **e** <   **f** <

12 **a** 1.5 is less than 1.55   **b** 32 pence is greater than 22 pence
   c 3.7 is less than 4.7   **d** 50 pence is greater than 5 pence
   e 3.5 is less than 3.55, which is less than 3.6
   f 12 pence is less than 22 pence, which is less than 32 pence
   g 3.7 is less than 3.75, which is less than 3.8
   h 5 pence is less than 15 pence, which is less than 50 pence

13 **a** tallest is Brian at 158.3 cm   **b** smallest is Malcolm at 157.6 cm

Investigation: Reciprocals

E the bigger the number, the smaller the reciprocal

Learning objective
- To estimate calculations in order to spot possible errors

Resources and homework
- Pupil Book 1.1, pages 71–75
- Intervention Workbook 3, pages 22–23
- Homework Book 1, section 4.3
- Online homework 4.3, questions 1–10

Links to other subjects
- **English** – to estimate how long you will need to deliver a presentation and whether it will meet guidelines

Key words
- approximation
- inverse operation
- estimate
- round

Problem solving and reasoning help

- Exercise 4C of the Pupil Book has many **MR** and **PS** questions. Pupils need to decode the questions and explain their thinking. Make sure they grasp that a useful estimate is one that simplifies the question and gives them a calculation, which they can do mentally. The challenge (rugby) question demonstrates how we use estimates in an everyday context.

Common misconceptions and remediation

- Pupils often do not understand the real purpose of estimation, so when asked to estimate an answer, they think that giving the full calculation will be better. Pupils may also lack the ability to see how to simplify a calculation in order to complete it mentally. Give pupils plenty of practice with mental calculation and opportunities to assess how best to approach different types of calculations. Also provide real-life examples of when the ability to estimate would be useful. You could ask pupils to role-play scenarios.

Probing questions

- Explain how you know that this calculation cannot be correct.
- Give me an example of when estimating would be useful to you?
- Why is being able to estimate useful even if you have a calculator available?
- What is your estimation? Is the accurate answer bigger or smaller? How do you know?

Part 1

- Using a target board like the one shown here, point to a number and ask a pupil to give the complement to 100. For example, point to 63; answer is: 37 (this is the complement to 100).
- After pupils have exhausted all numbers on the target board, carry on giving numbers verbally.
- Repeat with complements to 50. (Note: some answers will be negative.)

25	37	7	61	73
81	19	54	26	45
29	63	76	92	18
32	15	62	75	84

Literacy activity

- Write the following calculations on the board. Ask pupils to write a sentence for each one explaining why they must be wrong: $56 \times 36 = 2061$; $38 \times 42 = 5196$; $430 \div 6 = 55$

Part 2

- Ask pupils to use an OHP calculator to find the answers to a variety of multiplication problems, or they could work out the answers. For example:
  $12 \times 46 = 552$; $13 \times 23 = 299$; $15 \times 24 = 360$; $19 \times 38 = 722$.
- Ask pupils if they can spot a way to check that the answers are correct. For example, why *must* this be wrong: $26 \times 37 = 926$?
  Rule: answer must end in the same digit as that in the product of the original: $6 \times 7 = 42$.

- Some pupils may suggest estimating an answer, for example, $12 \times 46 \approx 10 \times 50 = 500$. (Introduce the notation $\approx$ is approximately equal to.)
- Obtain approximate answers to, for example: 13×23. Example answer: 10×20; 10×23; 10×25. Which is better? Establish that there is no definite way to estimate. Pupils should choose numbers that they can deal with mentally. This will depend on their individual skills.
- Establish rules for dealing with 'halfway' values: Should we go 'one up and one down'?
  For example: $40.8 - 29.7$ can be $40 - 30$ or $41 - 30$, and 8.76×4.79 can be 10×5 or 9×5
- How can we check if $510 \div 30 = 17$ is correct or not? Introduce inverse operations (for example: $510 = 30 \times 17$), which pupils can check mentally.
- Similarly, $237 - 43 = 214$. Check if $237 = 214 + 43$. Answer: not correct.
- Addition is the inverse of subtraction and is usually easier to work out.
- Multiplication is the inverse of division and is almost always easier to work out.
- Use a scale with 10 divisions to estimate the value of a given point when the end values are known. For example:
- Key points: Establish the value of each division. Count on (or back) from one end.
- **Pupils can now do Exercise 4C from Pupil Book 1.1.**

Part 3

- Write the following calculations on the board. Ask why they *must* be wrong.
  a $56 \times 36 = 2061$ **b** $38 \times 42 = 5196$ **c** $430 \div 6 = 55$
- Pupils should know how to check the last digit, estimate and check using inverse operations.
- Write the following calculations on the board:
  a $\dfrac{39 + 47}{17}$ **b** $169.3 \div 26.4$ **c** 27.8×12.7 **d** $(58.4)2 + (21.3)2$
- Ask for an estimate of each. Discuss the 'best' way of approximating. For example:
  a could be $90 \div 15$, $100 \div 20$ or $90 \div 20$ **b** could be $175 \div 25$ or $180 \div 30$
  c could be 30×10, 28×10 or 25×12 **d** is clearly $602 + 202 = 4000$
- Tell pupils that there is not always a best approximation. They should choose values either for mental calculation or to avoid lengthy calculation.

Answers

Exercise 4C

1

Name	Aiden	Ben	Carl	Dan	Emma	Freya	George	Helen	Iain	Jemma
Age	11	16	18	2	6	1	9	15	7	12
Age (to nearest 10 years)	10	20	20	0	10	0	10	20	10	10

2 _5 − _9 = _6, so £344 must be wrong

3 _2 − _5 = _7 so £138 must be wrong

4 _7 ÷ 2 = _3.50 so £237 must be wrong

5 Rounding each value to the nearest 1000 and adding gives 162 000, which is more than 160 000.

6   **a** _1 × 7 = _7
    b _2 × 5 = _0
    c _2 × 4 = _8
    d _5 × 5 = _5
    e _9 × 9 = _1
    f _7 × 7 = _9

7   **a** _5 × _2 = _0

    b _6 × _4 = _4
    c _1 × _8 = _8
    d _4 × _7 = _8
    e _3 × _7 = _1
    f _8 × _7 = _6

8   **a** 107 + 96 = 203 – correct
    b 285 + 30 = 315 – correct
    c 350 + 61 = 411 – wrong
    d 148 + 59 = 207 – wrong
    e 446 + 58 = 504 – wrong
    f 682 + 37 = 719 – correct

9   **a** 50 × 9 = 450 – correct
    b 58 × 3 = 174 – wrong
    c 35 × 6 = 210 – correct
    d 92 × 5 = 460 – wrong
    e 5 × 100 = 500 – wrong
    f 5 × 45 = 225 – correct

10   **a** must end in 0

    b 40 × 20 = 800
    c 40 + 60 = 100
    d 6 × 25 = 150
    e 250 – 50 = 200
    f 450 ÷ 10 = 45

11 $400

12   **a** 600   **b** 2000   **c** 5   **d** 900
     e 50 000   **f** 5   **g** 900   **h** 10

13 5 × 50p = £2.50

14 No, 6 × 50p = £3 but cakes cost more than 50p

15   **a** £120   **b** 30 × 60 = 1800   **c** 15 minutes

Challenge: Rugby
B 7000, 27, 2, 32 – 3, 12, 23, 23, 10, 17, 6, 3.10, 3.80
C For example, the scores have to be given accurately.

Lesson 4.4 Adding and subtracting decimals

Learning objective

- To add and subtract decimal numbers

Links to other subjects

- **Food technology** – to calculate the nutritional value of a meal; adding the cost of ingredients for a meal

Resources and homework

- Pupil Book 1.1, pages 75–77
- Homework Book 1, section 4.4
- Online homework 4.4, questions 1–10

Key words

- No new key words for this topic

Problem solving and reasoning help

- Questions 5 to 9 in Exercise 4D in the Pupil Book enable pupils to improve their fluency and confidence, and extend and apply the mathematical techniques they have learnt.

Common misconceptions and remediation

- Pupils need to have a good understanding of place value when completing any numerical calculation. Errors may be ignored as careless mistakes, when in fact pupils do not actually understand place value. Check pupils' decimal points when they add and subtract decimals.

Probing questions

- Give pupils some examples of work with errors. Ask them to check these and to provide formative feedback on what the error is and how to avoid making the error next time.

Part 1

- On the board (or use an OHT), draw the diagram, as shown.
- Explain the key, which indicates the values to subtract in each direction.
- Point to various cells and ask pupils to give the value of the cell, taken in order, or picked at random.

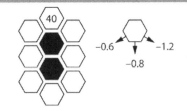

Literacy activity

- Ask pupils to write a short bullet-pointed guide on how to add and subtract decimals.

Part 2

- This is mostly a revision lesson on adding and subtracting decimals. The main procedure to emphasise is to align the decimal points.
- Depending on ability, start by using examples where both numbers have the same number of digits before and after the decimal point, for example: 3.6 + 4.7 or 2.34 + 6.12 or 8.9 – 1.2
- In a whole number, the point comes at the end (after the units digit).
  Make up missing place values using zeros. For example: 6 + 0.72 + 1.28 – 3.47
- Align the points and add zeros as appropriate:

$$
\begin{array}{r}
6.00 \\
0.72 \\
+1.28 \\
\hline
8.00
\end{array}
\qquad
\begin{array}{r}
{}^{7}\!8.{}^{9}\!0\,{}^{1}0 \\
-3.47 \\
\hline
4.53
\end{array}
$$

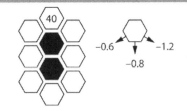

- Extend this to calculations with mixed units, for example: Subtract 378 grams from 3 kilograms. The calculation needs to be in the same units (kilograms), giving:

$$\begin{array}{r} ^2\cancel{3}.^9\cancel{0}\,^9\cancel{0}\,^1 0 \\ -\ 0.\ 3\ \ 7\ \ 8 \\ \hline 2.\ 6\ \ 2\ \ 2 \end{array}$$ Answer: 2.622 kilograms

- Here is another example: Add together 4 litres, 232 millilitres and 72 centilitres. Convert everything to litres, giving: 4000 +0.232 + 0.720 = 4.952
- **Pupils can now do Exercise 4D from Pupil Book 1.1.**

Part 3

- Write numbers on the board (or have prepared cards available), for example:
  - 4, 5, 6 and 0.78, 0.65, 0.92, 0.18
- Match pairs of numbers and ask pupils to give you their differences.
- Discuss the easy way to do this by taking complements of 9 and 10.
- Compare with the standard method of 'borrowing' when using the column method.

Answers

Exercise 4D

1	a 513	b 483	c 1137	d 1032	e 599	f 824	g 809	h 11 390
2	a 229	b 169	c 219	d 892	e 467	f 392	g 5	h 10 174
3	a 5.9	b 11.1	c 6.2	d 9.1	e 2.7	f 2.5	g 3.5	h 0.8
4	a 1.3	b 4.1	c 5.6	d 8.3	e 4.2	f 9.4	g 11.7	h 0.1
5	a £6.50	b £2.01	c £4.86	d £6.25	e £7.17	f £9.70		
6	£7.00							
7	a 5.59	b 10.41	c 8.59	d 5.89	e 5.42	f 10.71	g 15.42	h 10.21
	i 2.51	j 5.15	k 6.21	l 2.11	m 2.15	n 3.18	o 4.92	p 2.29
8	a 2.73	b 5.18	c 5.44	d 9.39	e 5.27	f 10.46	g 10.29	h 2.16
9	1.66 litres							
10	2.63 m							
11	7.5 km							

Lesson 4.5 Multiplying and dividing decimals

Learning objective
- To be able to multiply and divide decimal numbers by any whole number

Resources and homework
- Pupil Book 1.1, pages 77–79
- Homework Book 1, section 4.5
- Online homework 4.5, questions 1–10

Links to other subjects
- **Science** – many aspects of science require you to multiply and divide decimals accurately

Key words
- No new key words in this lesson

Problem solving and reasoning help
- The **PS** questions in Exercise 4E of the Pupil Book enable pupils to improve their fluency and confidence and extend and apply the mathematical techniques they have learnt.

Common misconceptions and remediation
- Pupils who believe that multiplying always makes a number bigger and that division always makes a number smaller will struggle with multiplying and dividing by decimals. Visual representations and comparing decimals to equivalent fractions may help pupils to overcome this misconception, as will contextual problems such as using money.

Probing questions
- How could you help someone who is struggling to understand that $0.6 \times 5 = 3$?
- What other calculations could you do based on this calculation?
- Pupils will also need to use their financial skills abilities to solve money problems such as: If a mobile phone costs £35.60 a month, how much will it cost in a year?

Part 1
- Write or place a set of calculations on the board, for example:
  - 0.6×5
  - $1.6 \div 4$
  - $4.6 \div 10$
  - 1.5×10
  - 0.47×1.2
  - $0.16 \div 0.25$
- Working in pairs, ask pupils to decide which calculations are easy to work out in their heads and why. Pick some pairs to present their methods. Encourage the rest of the class to provide feedback about the explanations. You could then discuss what makes a good method, and a good explanation.

Literacy activity
- Divide the class into groups and give each pupil a key word from this chapter. Ask pupils to explain why their key word is the most important one of those in their group.

Part 2
- The class should be familiar with short multiplication and division when working with whole numbers. This section will extend that idea to decimals.
- Ask: '*What is the answer to 2.3 + 2.3 + 2.3 + 2.3 + 2.3?*'
- Pupils should be able to reach the answer of 11.5 fairly easily.
- Ask: '*Can this be done in a different way?*' Repeated addition is the same as multiplication, in this case: 5×2.3.

Demonstrate how to do this using the column method:

$$
\begin{array}{r}
2.3 \\
\times \quad 5 \\
\hline
1\,1.5 \\
1
\end{array}
$$

- Repeat with 7×6.3 (= 44.1), 8×3.4 (= 27.2). Emphasise the need to keep the decimal points aligned (or to estimate the answer).
- Now demonstrate short division with decimals. For example:

  $46.5 \div 3$ is written as: $\dfrac{1\,5.5}{3\,\overline{)4^16.^15}}$

- Repeat with $27.48 \div 6$ (= 4.58), $17.78 \div 7$ (= 2.54). Once again, emphasise that the points stay aligned (or that the answer can be estimated).
- **Pupils can now do Exercise 4E from Pupil Book 1.1.**

Part 3

- Review the methods of long multiplication, for example: 14×36 (= 504)
- Ask for the answer to 1.4×3.6 (= 5.04). What about the answer to 0.14×3.6?
- Is there any connection to the answer to 14×36 and the decimal places in the second and third products?
- Establish the rule that there are: the same number of decimal places in the answer as in the original product.
- Then give the class the product 32×63. Ask for the answers to various connected products, for example: 3.2×63 or 3.2×6.3
- Repeat with other products if necessary.

Answers

Exercise 4E

	a	b	c	d	e	f	g	h
1	a 175	b 344	c 48	d 108	e 215	f 496	g 249	h 468
2	a 12	b 14	c 29	d 19	e 18	f 19	g 14	h 17
3	a 15.75	b 58.56	c 14.16	d 31.92	e 30.17	f 19.72	g 25.4	h 55.35
4	a 2.3	b 5.5	c 8.4	d 6.7	e 1.57	f 1.97	g 2.54	h 4.2
5	a 5.5	b 8.4	c 2.6	d 12.6	e 20.5	f 18.6	g 32.4	h 30.5
6	a 2	b 1.5	c 2.5	d 3.5	e 4.5	f 5.5	g 6.5	h 7.5

7   a $7 \times 13 = 91$ b $15 \times 5 = 75$ c $18 \times 4 = 72$

8	a 22.5	b 25.6	c 8.1	d 16.8	e 18.5	f 41.6	g 22.5	h 54.9
9	a 2.1	b 5.1	c 8.3	d 6.1	e 1.7	f 1.7	g 2.4	h 4.5

10 0.7 m   11 0.26 kg

12 £0.75   13 £3.40

14 11.2 kg   15 £1.02

16 £8

17 a 24 910   b 24 910   c 249.1   d 249.1

18 No, the pasta and sauce cost £7.75 so there is only £2.25 left over

Reasoning: The same digits

A   a 1564   b 156.4   c 15.64   d 0.1564

B   There should be the same total number of decimal places in the answer as in the calculation.

C   a 68.40   b 68.40   c 0.6840   d 684 000

Review questions (Pupil Book pages 80–81)

- The review questions will help to determine pupils' abilities with regard to the material within Chapter 4.
- These questions also draw on the maths covered in earlier chapters of the book to encourage pupils to make links between different topics.

Financial skills – Shopping for leisure (Pupil Book pages 82–83)

- This activity is designed to apply the skills learnt in this chapter to a multi-step problem. The context may be familiar to pupils but they are unlikely to have engaged with it themselves.
- As a warm-up to this activity, ask pupils to talk to their parents or caregivers about how they would make decisions about some familiar household purchasing activity, for example, buying a new computer.
- As is often the case with these types of functional problems the maths is not difficult, but pupils struggle to decode the mathematics from the words. You could work through an example in a different context, modelling the process and stressing the strategies they could use such as text marking important information. Discuss with them the clues they can find within the words that will help them to decide what maths to use. All the information required to answer the questions is given but pupils will need to read and think about it carefully. Remind them to highlight the key information they will need.
- Pupils can now work on the questions. Working individually would benefit **more able** pupils; **less able** pupils would benefit from working in groups. Encourage pupils to present or even role-play their solutions.
- You could ask pupils to develop this topic further by using the internet to research jobs that may use purchasing skills as part of their everyday work. For example, purchasing agents buy things for companies such as raw materials, products, and any other services. Encourage pupils to think about the contexts they encounter every day that require purchasing decisions, and how these might be made. Ask pupils to consider who does the purchasing in the school and how the people responsible for this make their decisions. If possible, ask a local employer to visit the class and discuss this with pupils.

Answers to Review questions

1 **a** 36   **b** 5   **c** 396
2 996, because $1000 - 996 = 4$, but $1006 - 1000 = 6$
3 16
4 **a** 27   **b** £12
5 5.38, 5.83, 8.35, 8.53, 53.8
6 £50.19
7 £45.85
8 **a** C, 25.2 cm   **b** C, 25.4 cm^2
9 **a** 9, 10.5, 12   **b** 9.1, 11.8, 14.5   **c** 7.0, 6.9 , 6.8

Answers to Financial skills – Shopping for leisure

The Bishop family
£207.50

A gift for Pat Visser
Rounding each value to the nearest pound and adding gives £30 + £21 + £5 = £56 so she doesn't have enough.

Abbas' outdoor area
He can purchase the following for exactly £200 – outdoor speakers, table, 2 chairs, 2 mats, 2 planters and 6 Fuchsia.

5 Working with numbers

Learning objectives

- How to round whole numbers
- The order of operations
- How to carry out long multiplication
- How to carry out long division
- How to calculate with measurements

Prior knowledge

- How to square a number
- Multiplication tables up to 12 × 12
- Place value of digits in a number such as 23.508
- How to use a calculator to do simple calculations
- How to convert units of measurement
- By the end of KS2, pupils should be comfortable with number facts up to 12 × 12. They will have spent some time securing their understanding of place value as a key concept in mathematics. This is reinforced in Chapter 4. Pupils will also have made some connections between mental methods and more formal methods of calculation.

Context

- The objectives in this chapter are probably some of the most widely used objectives in terms of real-life application. It is important for pupils to build on their mental methods when developing written methods, so that they understand why they are doing this, and are not just applying a set of rules that they do not understand.
- Remind pupils that these objectives will be very useful in building confidence and fluency in applying their financial skills in the questions and in real life.
- Search on the internet for 'Chinese multiplication' and 'alternatives to the usual approach to multiplication' for interesting links. This link might be useful: **http://youtu.be/pOYuEUkE06I**.

Discussion points

- What numbers, and how many, can you make with 2, 4 and 5 in five minutes?
- Can you give me an example of a calculation you would do in your head, and why? Can you change it so that it becomes a calculation that you will need to work out with a calculator? (To help them decide if they think they have done the written example correctly, pupils could discuss how they might use the example they have done in their heads.)
- Can you tell me two lengths that make 1 metre? What about 1 centimetre or 1 kilometre?

Associated Collins ICT resources

- Chapter 5 interactive activities on Collins Connect online platform
- *Using BIDMAS* video on Collins Connect online platform
- *Kinsale market* Wonder of Maths on Collins Connect online platform
- *Square numbers and square roots* and *Rounding* Worked solutions on Collins Connect online platform

Curriculum references

Number

- Use the four operations, including formal written methods
- Use conventional notation for the priority of operations, including brackets, powers, roots and reciprocals
- Use integer powers and associated real roots
- Round numbers and measures to an appropriate degree of accuracy
- Use a calculator and other technologies to calculate results accurately and then interpret them appropriately
- Use standard units of mass, length and other measures, including with decimal quantities

Develop fluency

- Consolidate their numerical and mathematical capability from KS2
- Select and use appropriate calculation strategies to solve increasingly complex problems

Solve problems

- Develop their use of formal mathematical knowledge to interpret and solve problems, including in financial mathematics

Fast-track for classes following a 2-year scheme of work

- Pupils will have considered written methods for working with numbers in KS2. After a brief recap of methods, pupils should concentrate on the **MR** and **PS** questions in Exercise 5D and Exercise 5E of lessons 5.4 and 5.5.

Lesson 5.1 Square numbers

Learning objective
- To recognise and use square numbers up to 225 (15 × 15)

Resources and homework
- Pupil Book 1.1, pages 85–87
- Intervention Workbook 2, pages 28–29
- Intervention Workbook 3, pages 31–32
- Homework Book 1, section 5.1
- Online homework 5.1, questions 1–10

Links to other subjects
- **Design and technology** – to find out areas when given lengths and lengths when given areas

Key words
- integer
- square number
- power
- squaring

Problem solving and reasoning help
- The **PS** questions 4 and 6 in Exercise 5A of this chapter require pupils to apply their understanding to examples of short rich tasks to check that they can transfer their understanding to more complex, less familiar situations.

Common misconceptions and remediation
- Be very clear about the notation of example 3^2, which is consistently misinterpreted by some pupils as 3×2. The use of visual images such as arrays will help **less able** pupils to understand square numbers. Pupils who learn about square numbers without any visual imagery often fail to remember that a square number means 'a number multiplied by itself'.
- You could do an internet search for 'picturing of squares' or 'arrays, general use'. Or, you could look at the following links to investigate square numbers, or to focus on the more general use of arrays: **http://nrich.maths.org/2275**; **http://nrich.maths.org/2469**.

Probing questions
- Explain why the answer to 3^2 is not the same as 3×2.
- Why is 2^2 special and why is it not a good example to use for someone who has not worked with square numbers before?
- Explain to a partner how you would use the square root to find the dimensions of a square when you know the area.
- When you use a square root to find the dimensions of a square you are using a … operation.

Part 1
- Ask the class for numbers with only two factors. Ask what the special name is for these numbers. Pupils should remember that they are *prime numbers*.
- Then ask the class for some numbers that have exactly three factors. What if one of the three factors is even, for example, $1 \times 2 \times 7$?
- Pupils' suggestions could lead to a class discussion. Write the numbers on the board. Let pupils find a few before leading into what is special about these numbers. (Hopefully the class will come up with the answer.)
- The numbers are all even. Pupils may discuss the fact that it does not matter how many factors you have; if just one number is even, then the number of the total must be even.

Literacy activity
- Ask pupils to write a sentence explaining why you cannot have a negative square number.

Part 2

- Introduce pupils to the notation used for squaring, for example, 3^2. Ask pupils to write down the first 15 square numbers: $1^2 = 1$, $2^2 = 4$, …. The first 15 are on page 85 of Pupil Book 1.1.
- These square numbers are important, and pupils will see many more in future.
- Introduce the idea of a square root as the root or starting point of a square number. Ask the class: '*What is the square root of …?*' Go through most of the square numbers up to 15×15.
- Remind the class about the square root symbol and how it is used.
- Include pupils' calculators. Note: There may be several different types of calculators among pupils, so ensure that everyone knows how to use the square root key on their calculator.
- **MR** question 1 in Exercise 5A encourages pupils to question the connections between terms. **More able** pupils will see the link immediately. Guide **less able** pupils to see the link.
- A variation of this lesson plan is to start with an investigation of **MR** question 1, and use it to talk about square numbers and the way the sequence is developed.
- **Pupils can now do Exercise 5A from Pupil Book 1.1.**

Part 3

- This is the point where consolidation of the learnt square numbers can take effect.
- Call out various numbers from 1 to 15 and ask for their squares, in rapid response mode.

Answers

Exercise 5A

1 **a** 4, 9, 16, 25   **b** square numbers   **c** 1 + 3 + 5 + 7 + 9 + 11 + 13
2 **b** they are all in a diagonal line
3 1, 4, 9, 16, 25, 36, 49, 64, 81, 100, 121, 144, 169, 196, 225
4 **a** 25   **b** 36   **c** 9, 49, 169, 196   **d** no number 7
5 **b** 25 + 144 = 169   **c** 49 + 576 = 625   **d** 81 + 1600 = 1681
6 **a** $(2^2 + 5^2)$ **b** $(7^2 + 6^2)$ **c** $(5^2 + 8^2)$
7 **a** $(13^2 - 5^2)$ **b** $(15^2 - 9^2)$ **c** $(11^2 - 7^2)$

Problem solving: Squares and products
A **e** just one apart
B **b** again, just one apart

Lesson 5.2 Rounding

Learning objective
- To round numbers to the nearest whole number, 10, 100 or 1000

Resources and homework
- Pupil Book 1.1, pages 88–90
- Intervention Workbook 1, pages 6–7
- Intervention Workbook 3, pages 9–10
- Homework Book 1, section 5.2
- Online homework 5.2, questions 1–10

Links to other subjects
- **Science** – to present results to an appropriate degree of accuracy
- **Design and technology** – to give measurements to the degree of accuracy appropriate to the situation

Key words
- round
- round down
- round up

Problem solving and reasoning help
- In this chapter, the **PS** questions, 6 and 9, require pupils to apply their learning to real life situations. Pupils need to understand that in many mathematics situations there will be more than one possible answer, so they must be able to explain and justify their solutions.

Common misconceptions and remediation
- Pupils sometimes have problems with numbers that end in 9 (see Probing questions) especially if there are several. Pupils may also struggle with numbers with trailing zeros. Provide plenty of opportunity to discuss examples.

Probing questions
- Explain whether the following are true or false:
    - 4.399 rounds to 4.310 to two decimal places (false)
    - 6.5999 rounds to 6.6 to one decimal place (true)
- How do you go about rounding a number to one decimal place?
- Why might it not be possible to identify the first three places in a long jump competition if measurements were taken in metres to one decimal place?
- Show me a length that rounds 5.6 m to one decimal place. Are there other lengths?

Part 1
- In pairs, encourage pupils to discuss their response to this question: What is the same, or different, about these numbers: 56.532 and 56.536?
- Take feedback, focusing on pupils' understanding of place value. Ask which number is closer to 56.53/4 and why? You could use a number line to support this discussion.

Literacy activity
- Ask pupils to explain how to write numbers to the nearest 10, 100, 1000.

Part 2

- Draw a number line on the board with 10 segments marked on the line. Mark one end with 0 and the other end with 100.
- Mark a point with an arrow, as shown on the number line. Ask pupils to estimate the value of the number (63). What is it to the nearest 10 (60)? Repeat with other examples. Make sure that at least one number ends in 5, so that you can emphasise the rule about rounding up.

- Change the scale from 0 to 1000. Repeat, rounding off the numbers to the nearest 100.
- Do some examples without the scale. For example:
  Round 546 to the nearest: 10, 100, 1000
  Round 3098 to the nearest: 10, 100, 1000
- **Pupils can now do Exercise 5B from Pupil Book 1.1.**
- Pupils may use their calculators.

Part 3

- Write a variety of numbers on the board and ask pupils to round them off to various accuracies: to the nearest 1000, 100, 10, or whole number.
- Examples of numbers: 3219, 34.65, 31.07, 103.9, 5244, 829, 0.632, 3.438
- Discuss the techniques.

Answers
Exercise 5B
1 a 1100   b 1090
2 a £300   b £270
3 a £7500   b £7500
4 a £300   b £330
5 a £1500   b £1460
6 a 62 300, 62 000; 85 600, 86 000; 86 300, 86 000
   b because one's much higher than the other.
7 a 4640, 4600, 5000   b 980, 1000, 1000   c 1230, 1200, 1000
   d 5680, 5700, 6000   e 1260, 1300, 1000   f 3950, 3900, 4000
   g 2010, 2000, 2000   h 6000, 6000, 6000   i 1050, 1100, 1000
   j 6130, 6100, 6000   k 4200, 4200, 4000   l 1200, 1200, 1000
8 a 13 000, 143 000, 7000, 5000, 50 000, 2000, 121 000, 51 000, 12000
   b Mercury c Jupiter   d Venus
9 a 20, 17   b 20, 25   c 50, 51   d 70, 72   e 50, 54   f 90, 94 g 110, 106
   h 800, 800 i 80, 85   j 70, 72   k 100, 102 l 140, 143
10 a 50   b 10   c 60   d 140   e 30   f 170
11 a 34, 44   b 25, 35
Problem solving: Think of a rounded number
There are five possibilities: 150, 151, 152, 153, 154.

Learning objective

- To use the conventions of BIDMAS to carry out calculations

Resources and homework

- Pupil Book 1.1, pages 91–93
- Intervention Workbook 3, page 15
- Homework Book 1, section 5.3
- Online homework 5.3, questions 1–10

Links to other subjects

- **Design and technology** – to calculate correctly when using multiplicative and additive relationships to calculate quantities

Key words

- BIDMAS
- order of operations
- operation

Problem solving and reasoning help

- Make pupils aware of the real-life implications of the incorrect use of the order of operations. Do this, for example, by using real-life situations involving money.

Common misconceptions and remediation

- It is important for pupils to understand that the order of operations is a convention that works to describe reality. In other words, it is a way to communicate, which ensures that we get a common answer. It can be helpful to link the order of operations to verbal descriptions of real-life situations. Pupils need to understand that this is a convention.
- Explain why this answer is incorrect: $3 + 5 \times 2 = 16$
- What should the answer be and why? (13, because $5 \times 2 = 10 + 3 = 13$)
- How could you use brackets to make sure that the answer is calculated correctly? (Put brackets around 5×2.)
- Which operation will you need to do first? Why? (Multiply; order of BIDMAS)

Probing questions

- Show pupils a calculation such as $8 + 5 \times 2$ and ask: '*What steps do you need to take in order to get the correct answer? What is the first step? How do you know this?*'

Part 1

- Give each small group the same five numbers, for example: 2, 4, 5, 7, 10 (four for **less able** pupils). In a timed five-minute session, ask pupils to write down as many sums as possible using these numbers. Make the rules flexible to suit the group, for example:
  - Answers such as $24 + 5 = 29$ are acceptable, or all the numbers must be used individually, for example: $2 \times 4 + 5 = 13$.
  - Not all the numbers need to be used, for example: $2 \times 5 - 7 = 3$, or, they must all be used, for example: $2 + 4 + 5 - 7 + 10 = 14$.
- Remind pupils that they must show all their working and answers.
- Give pupils a target number such as 80. Ask them to make a calculation using all the numbers with 80 as the answer. For example: $(2 \times 7 - 10) \times 4 \times 5$
- After five minutes, ask pupils to score 1 point for every sum, and 5 points for each sum that gives the target number. Record the scores, but do not check yet. (Collect pupils' sheets.)

Literacy activity

- In pairs, ask pupils to come up with three false and three true calculations using the lesson objectives. Swap these and ask pupils to explain orally why a statement is true or false.

Part 2

- Give pupils word problems and calculations, for example:

  Sarah has £22 in her piggy bank. She is given two 5 pound notes for her birthday. How much does she have? (Answer: 22 + 2 × 5)

  Sarah has a £10 note in her piggy bank. At the end of the week she adds £3 pocket money to it. Her grandfather says that he will double what she has in her piggy bank for her birthday. How much will she have? (Answer: 10 + 3 × 2)

- Ask pupils to identify which sum is correct or not, and why.
- Encourage **more able** pupils to explain how they might use brackets in the second example and to design some examples of their own. Support **less able** pupils by using real money to demonstrate the example.
- **Pupils can now do Exercise 5C from Pupil Book 1.1.**

Part 3

- Use a visualiser to display each group's answers to Part 1. Check the answers for accuracy and correct use of BIDMAS. Score each sheet. Check the score that each group recorded. Deduct 5 when a total is wrong; add 5 when a total is correct. Declare a winning group.

Answers
Exercise 5C

1 **a** 11 **b** 34 **c** 55 **d** 62 **e** 89 **f** 72 **g** 87 **h** 132

2 **a** 5 **b** 34 **c** 23 **d** 53 **e** 52 **f** 31 **g** 42 **h** 5

3 **a** ×, 7 **b** ÷, 8 **c** ×, 10 **d** ÷, 1 **e** +, 9 **f** −, 6 **g** +, 48 **h** −, 9

4 **a** 5 **b** 5 **c** 13 **d** 15 **e** 6 **f** 14 **g** 45 **h** 4 **i** 20
   j 16 **k** 5 **l** 6 **m** 49 **n** 29 **o** 13 **p** 3

5 **a** $1 \times (5 + 4)$ **b** $(2 + 5) \times 3$ **c** $(2 + 3) \times 2$ **d** $(5 + 2)^2$ **e** $(6 + 2)^2$
   f $2 \times (5 + 3)$ **g** $4 \times (7 + 1)$ **h** $(3 + 4) \times 7$ **i** $8 - (4 - 1)$ **j** $(7 - 5) \times 2$
   k $(3 \times 3) \div 2$ **l** $(1 + 4)^2$

6 **a** 4×2^2 **b** $(4 \times 2)^2$

7 **a** 2 **b** 5 **c** 6 **d** 4 **e** 0 **f** 5 **g** 20 **h** 30 **i** 125

8 **a** $2 \times 10 + 3 \times 20$ **b** \$80

9 **a** $6 \times 2.50 + 5$ **b** £20

Problem solving: All the fives

A **a** 11 **b** 30 **c** 50

Lesson 5.4 Long and short multiplication

Learning objective
- To choose a written method for multiplying two numbers together
- To use written methods to carry out multiplications accurately

Resources and homework
- Pupil Book 1.1, pages 94–95
- Intervention Workbook 1, pages 14–15
- Intervention Workbook 2, pages 14–19
- Intervention Workbook 3, pages 18–19
- Homework Book 1, section 5.4
- Online homework 5.4, questions 1–10

Links to other subjects
- **Science** – to use pencil and paper methods for calculating in a range of scenarios

Key words
- column method
- long multiplication
- grid or box method

Problem solving and reasoning help
- Easy access to technology in our modern society means that written methods of calculation are not used daily. However, pupils need to develop confidence and fluency with these methods in order to consolidate their understanding of concepts such as place value and magnitude. They also need to make links between mental methods and written calculations in order to support their assessment of the accuracy of calculations that they have not done manually. Real-life examples might be calculating bills or charges for services.

Common misconceptions and remediation
- Pupils need to make links to the informal mental calculation methods they use and progress towards formal written methods at a speed that is appropriate for them. If less able pupils are struggling, revisit the progression in calculation in the primary programme of study. The NCETM website has a set of videos that might also be useful in identifying gaps in understanding of calculation from primary level:
  https://www.ncetm.org.uk/resources/

Probing questions
- Provide an example for pupils. Say: '*Think about the example: How would you do this in your head? Now try using a pencil and paper method. What are the similarities and differences?*'
- Ask pupils to carry out multiplication using the grid method and a compact standard method.
- Ask them to describe the advantages and disadvantages of each method.

Part 1 including literacy activity
- Focus on spellings and definitions of mathematical terms.
- Ask a pupil to spell the word 'factor', and write it on the board. Ask another pupil to define a square. For difficult words such as 'multiply', ask pupils to give an example.
- Repeat with other pupils. Suitable words (based on number) are: multiple, prime (number), square (number), triangle (number), multiply, divide, multiplication, division, addition, subtraction, decimal, hundredth, tenth, thousandth, million.

Part 2

- Multiply 5 by 413. Pupils may have a variety of methods to discuss. The likely methods are:

Box method (partitioning)

×	400	10	3	
5	2000	50	15	2000 + 50 + 15 = 2065

Column method (expanded working)

```
      1 3
   ×    5
      1 5
      5 0
  2 0 0 0
  2 0 6 5
```

Column method (compacted working)
(136 × 5)

```
    1 3 6          136 × 5
  ×     5          136 × 5
    6 8 0
    1 3
```

Napier's bones or Chinese multiplication (possibly the best method)

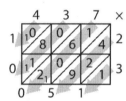

- **Pupils can now do Exercise 5D from Pupil Book 1.1.**

Part 3

- Recapitulate the methods with an example that extends pupils: 234 × 7 (= 1638)
- Which method is best?

Answers

Exercise 5D

1 **a** 75   **b** 84   **c** 57   **d** 204   **e** 144   **f** 56   **g** 405   **h** 1080
2 **a** 115   **b** 186   **c** 129   **d** 90   **e** 116   **f** 294   **g** 412   **h** 1170
3 **a** 100   **b** 132   **c** 172   **d** 108   **e** 85   **f** 132   **g** 625   **h** 1236
4 168
5 190
6 £312
7 **b** adds up to 75   **d** adds up to 240
8 **a** 4 × 10 × 18 = 720   **b** 4 × 18 + 5 × 18 = 162   **c** 40 × 18 + 9 × 18 = 882

Lesson 5.5 Long and short division

Learning objectives

- To choose a written method for dividing one number by another
- To use written methods to carry out divisions accurately

Resources and homework

- Pupil Book 1.1, pages 96–97
- Intervention Workbook 1, pages 14–15
- Intervention Workbook 2, pages 14–19
- Intervention Workbook 3, pages 18–19
- Homework Book 1, section 5.5
- Online homework 5.5, questions 1–10

Links to other subjects

- Science – to use pencil and paper methods for calculating in a range of scenarios

Key words

- long division
- short division
- repeated subtraction

Problem solving and reasoning help

- Easy access to technology in our modern society means that written methods of calculation are not used daily. However, pupils need to develop confidence and fluency with these methods in order to consolidate their understanding of concepts such as place value and magnitude. They also need to make links between mental methods and written calculations in order to support their assessment of the accuracy of calculations that they have not done manually. Real-life examples might be calculating bills or charges for services.

Common misconceptions and remediation

- Pupils need to link their informal mental calculation methods, and progress towards formal written methods at their own speed. With **less able** pupils, revisit useful strategies such as jottings, number lines and partitioning. If there are gaps in pupils' understanding, revisit the progression in calculation in the primary programme of study. The NCETM website has a set of video clips that might be useful for identifying gaps in understanding of calculation from primary level: **https://www.ncetm.org.uk/resources/**. Before pupils attempt formal division calculations, they need to understand the process of repeated subtraction.

Probing questions

- Provide an example. '*How would you work this out in your head or using long multiplication or division? Now use short multiplication or division. Name the similarities and differences.*'
- Provide examples of divisions with errors. Ask pupils to identify and discuss the errors.

Part 1

- Have a set of 'Follow me' cards, for example the Worksheet – Working with numbers on the Collins Connect platform, which use approximations. Hand these out to pairs or groups. There is no set method of rounding, so discussion is important.

Literacy activity

- In groups, ask pupils to write a set of guidelines that would help to solve division problems. Pupils should share their suggestions to generate a class set of guidelines.

Part 2

- A fleet of 53-seater coaches is taking 539 pupils and staff to a theme park. How many coaches are needed? Discuss the operation (division). Estimation gives $500 \div 50 = 10$.
- Solve using repeated subtraction ('chunking'). That is: $10 \times 53 = 530$, giving $539 - 530 = 9$
  So, 11 coaches are needed to carry all pupils and staff. The standard method of long division can be used if appropriate.
- **Pupils can now do Exercise 5E from Pupil Book 1.1.**

Part 3

- Give pupils examples of divisions with mistakes and ask them to identify the mistakes and talk through what is wrong and how to correct the mistakes.
- Recapitulate the methods with an example to extend them: $3132 \div 8$ (= 391 rem 4)
- Which method is best?

Answers

Exercise 5E
1	**a** 6	**b** 8	**c** 10	**d** 15	**e** 25		
2	**a** £5	**b** £12	**c** 7 kg	**d** 11 kg	**e** 30 m		
3	**a** 14	**b** 15	**c** 19	**d** 9	**e** 31	**f** 14	**g** 124	**h** 29
4	**a** 13	**b** 21	**c** 13	**d** 20	**e** 36	**f** 36	**g** 106	**h** 75
5	**a** 40	**b** 20	**c** 16	**d** 28	**e** 45	**f** 30	**g** 72	**h** 45
6	**a** 55	**b** 280	**c** 2	**d** 45	**e** 55	**f** 31	**g** 320	**h** 111

7 **a** $300 \div 5$ **b** $244 \div 4$ **c** $722 \div 6$

8 12

9 15 m

10 14

11 **a** 15 **b** 3

12 **a** 468 **b** £2808

Activity: Cross-number puzzle

1	7	0	■	2
■	1	■	8	1
2	■	9	■	6
7	■	1	6	■
0	■	1	2	0

Lesson 5.6 Calculations with measurements

Learning objectives

- To convert between common metric units
- To use measurements in calculations
- To recognise and use appropriate metric units

Links to other subjects

- **Design and technology** – to calculate the material needed
- **Science** – to use metric conventions in experiments

Resources and homework

- Pupil Book 1.1, pages 98–101
- Intervention Workbook 1, pages 46–47
- Intervention Workbook 2, pages 56–58
- Homework Book 1, section 5.6
- Online homework 5.6, questions 1–10

Key words

- cent-
- centi-
- conversion
- convert
- metric
- milli-

Problem solving and reasoning help

- The **MR** and **PS** questions in Exercise 5F require pupils to see how they can apply the number skills they have learnt in this chapter across different mathematics and in real-life contexts. Pupils need to realise that good number skills support sound financial skills, so while role-playing real-life situations they should include using number skills incorrectly.

Common misconceptions and remediation

- Pupils need a sound understanding of place value when working with metric measures. When working with time and money, pupils need to understand that they are working in a different base and need to adjust their calculations accordingly.

Probing questions

- How many 30 g blocks of chocolate will weigh 1.5 kg, using 1.5 kg ÷ 30 g?
- Which is longer: 300 cm or 30 000 mm? Explain how you worked it out.
- What clues do you look for when deciding which metric unit is bigger?
- Explain how you would convert metres to centimetres. How do you change: grams into kilograms; millilitres into litres; kilometres into metres, and so on?

Part 1

- Practise mental multiplication of multiples of 10. Ask for the answer to 50 × 40 (= 2000). Discuss the methods for doing this.
- Repeat with other examples: 30 × 70 (= 2100) 20 × 20 (= 400).
- Now ask for the answer to 300 ÷ 50 (= 6). Discuss the methods for doing this.
- Repeat with other examples: 300 ÷ 30 (= 10); 600 ÷ 40 (= 15)
- Write these on the board as fractions so that pupils can see the cancellation.

Literacy activity

- Explain how you would convert metres to centimetres. Ask pupils how they would change: grams to kilograms; millilitres to litres; kilometres to metres, and so on.

Part 2

- Brainstorm units and equivalences; establish the relationships between units, giving their abbreviations:

  length kilometre (km), metre (m), centimetre (cm), millimetre (mm)

  mass kilogram (kg), gram (g), milligram (mg)

  capacity litre (l), centilitre (cl), millilitre (ml)

- This table can be used to establish the equivalent units. For example:

8	0	0	0			
			4	0	0	
0	3	7	2			
0	0	4	5	0	0	0
			0	0	7	2

8 000 m = 8 km

4 l = 400 cl

0.372 kg = 372 g

0.045 km = 45 000 mm

72 ml = 0.072 l

- **Pupils can now do Exercise 5F from Pupil Book 1.1.**

Part 3

- Put a variety of scales on the board and mark points on them, for example:

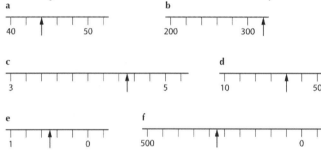

- Discuss the important things when reading scales: divisions (calibrations) and their direction.

Answers

Exercise 5F

1   **a** 40 m   **b** 50 m   **c** 50 m   **d** 20 m   **e** 40 m

2   **a** 50 kg   **b** 70 kg   **c** 40 kg   **d** 60 kg   **e** 40 kg

3   **a** 600 cm   **b** 200 cm   **c** 1200 cm   **d** 50 cm   **e** 1730 cm

4   **a** 7000 g   **b** 3000 g   **c** 11 000 g   **d** 500 g   **e** 21 400 g

5   **a** £7   **b** £5   **c** £1.50   **d** £2.75   **e** £3.14

6   **a** 4000 m   **b** 13 000 m   **c** 6300 m   **d** 21 500 m   **e** 5460 m

7   **a** 30 mm   **b** 110 mm   **c** 51 mm   **d** 356 mm   **e** 7 mm

8   **a** 3 kg   **b** 5.5 kg   **c** 0.5 kg   **d** 0.2 kg   **e** 0.035 kg

9   **a** 4000 g   **b** 8000 g   **c** 9500 g   **d** 700 g   **e** 450 g

10   **a** 1 h 30 min   **b** 2 h 10 min   **c** 1 h 25 min   **d** 3 h 20 min   **e** 10 h 30 min

11   yes, it's 3.05 kg

12   **a** 2.5 kg   **b** 150 g   **c** 50 g   **d** 40   **e** 120   **f** 10

Challenge Activity

A   (500 g, 100 g), (200 g, 200 g, 200 g)

B   (500 g, 100 g), (200 g, 200 g, 100 g, 100 g)

C   (1 kg, 250 g, 200 g), (1 kg, 300 g, 100 g, 50 g)

D   (1 kg, 200 g, 50 g), (750 g, 500 g)

Review questions
(Pupil Book pages 102–103)

- The review questions will help to determine pupils' abilities with regard to the material within Chapter 5.
- These questions also draw on the maths covered in earlier chapters of the book to encourage pupils to make links between different topics.

Problem solving – What is your carbon footprint?
(Pupil Book pages 104–105)

- This activity is designed to use the skills covered in this and earlier number chapters to give a real-life context to mathematics.
- All the information required to answer the questions is given within the spread. Advise pupils to read the information sections first.
- A discussion about the meaning of a 'carbon footprint' may be a good starter.
- Ask pupils further questions as a warm-up to start working on the questions in the Pupil Book. Here are some examples:
    o Which of your activities can leave a carbon footprint?
    o Which of these activities can you avoid doing?
    o Which of these activities can you keep to a minimum?
- Pupils can now work on the questions individually or in groups.
- You could ask pupils to develop this topic further by using the internet for further research or project work.

Answers to Review questions

1   **a** 2100   **b** 2090
2   **a** 25, 36   **b** 100
3   **a** 23   **b** 33   **c** 32
4   A, 150 cm^2
5   4°C
6   700, 900, 200
7   40 kg
8   **a** 17   **b** 2

Answers to Problem solving – What is your carbon footprint?

1   £8000
2   60 000 kg
3   18%
4   8400 million tonnes
5   1.5 tonnes
6   **a** true   **b** true

6 Statistics

Learning objectives

- How to calculate the mode, the median and the range for a set of data
- How to interpret statistical diagrams and charts
- How to collect and organise data
- How to create data-collection forms
- How to create questionnaires
- How to use frequency tables
- How to draw simple conclusions from data

Prior knowledge

- How to interpret data from tables, graphs and charts. In Year 6, pupils connect their work on angles, fractions and percentages to the interpretation of pie charts.
- How to draw frequency tables and bar charts
- How to create a tally chart
- How to draw bar charts and pictograms
- By the end of KS2, pupils will have encountered and drawn graphs relating two variables, arising from their own enquiry and in other subjects.

Context

- How many people are there in the world? Or even in our country? How do these people live? What do they eat and drink? How big are their families?
- Encourage pupils to consider the ways in which statistics are used to explore questions like these. For example, a census is a huge survey that is used to find out information about each man, woman and child in a country. Pupils need to consider how they could present this information.
- Pupils also need to think about how we use statistics to model populations where it is difficult, or in many cases impossible, to gather all the population information.

Discussion points

- For a given graph, table or chart, make up three questions that people can answer using the information represented.
- What makes the information easy or difficult to represent?

Associated Collins ICT resources

- Chapter 6 interactive activities on Collins Connect online platform
- *Finding the median, mode and range* video on Collins Connect online platform
- *Growth charts* Wonder of Maths on Collins Connect online platform
- *Mean from frequency tables* Worked solution on Collins Connect online platform

Curriculum references

Reason mathematically

- Explore what can and cannot be inferred in statistical settings, and begin to express their arguments formally

Solve problems

- Begin to model situations mathematically and express the results using a range of formal mathematical representations
- Select appropriate concepts, methods and techniques to apply to unfamiliar and non-routine problems

Statistics

- Describe, interpret and compare observed distributions of a single variable through: appropriate graphical representation involving discrete, continuous and grouped data; and appropriate measures of central tendency (mean, mode, median) and spread (range, consideration of outliers)
- Construct and interpret appropriate tables, charts, and diagrams, including frequency tables, bar charts, and pictograms for categorical data, and vertical line (or bar) charts for ungrouped and grouped numerical data

Fast-track for classes following a 2-year scheme of work

- If your pupils are confident with measures of central tendency and range (covered in KS2), you could leave out Lesson 6.1. Provide a brief recap and move on to the later lessons where you will need to encourage pupils to interrogate data and make choices and decisions about the statistical measures they use.

Lesson 6.1 Mode, median and range

Learning objective
- To understand the meaning of mode, median and range

Resources and homework
- Pupil Book 1.1, pages 107–110
- Intervention Workbook 2, pages 80–82
- Intervention Workbook 3, pages 67–68
- Homework Book 1, section 6.1
- Online homework 6.1, questions 1–10

Links to other subjects
- **Geography** – to compare climates
- **Science** – to work out average and range of results for experiments

Key words
- average
- median
- outlier
- data
- mode
- range

Problem solving and reasoning help
- Pupils apply their understanding to real-life problems, decoding the statistical meaning behind familiar and less familiar situations. The activity at the end of the lesson requires pupils to carry out their own research. Encourage them to think carefully about the statistical measures they use and why. Pupils can achieve differentiation by the amount of guidance and scaffolding they are given in terms of collecting the necessary data.

Common misconceptions and remediation
- Pupils often get confused because of the rather vague and often inaccurate use of the language for central tendency and range in real life. Encourage pupils to explore and critique the use of this language in real life. Help them to understand that all averages are a measure of central tendency and give them the opportunity to makes choices and decisions about which statistical measures to use for a given situation.

Probing questions
- Find five numbers that have mode as 7 and the range as 9. How did you do it?
- Two sets of data both have the same range but the first one has a median of 6 and the second has a mode of 6. Explain how these two distributions may differ.

Part 1
- Write a list of positive numbers on the board. For example: 7, 3, 9, 2, 10, 8, 5, 4, 14, 12
- Ask pupils to put the numbers in numerical order, with the smallest first.
- Ask pupils if they have any strategy for doing this.
- Repeat for another list of numbers. For example: 34, 67, 38, 19, 44, 57, 24, 31, 62, 20
- What about any strategies now? Identify the 10s column first.
- Write a list of positive and negative numbers on the board. For example:
- 2, –3, 1, 4, –4, 0, 5, –2
- Ask pupils to put the numbers in numerical order, with the smallest first.
- What about any strategies now? Remind pupils about the number line that they used in Chapter 1.

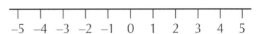

Literacy activity
- Write a sentence for a real-life situation using one or more of these words: total, range, mode, median.

Part 2

- Explain the term *average*, using everyday examples of when the word is used. For example: average rainfall, average examination mark, average height.
- Ask pupils for examples. (An average is a single value that represents a set of data.)
- Explain how to find the *mode* for a set of data.
- The mode is the value that occurs most often in a set of data. For example, in 5, 6, 8, 2, 4, 5, 3, 5; the mode is 5. Explain that for some sets of data there is no mode because all the values are different, or no single value occurs more often than other values.
- Explain how to find the *median* for a set of data.
- The median is the middle value for a set of data when the values are put in numerical order. For example: 6, 8, 3, 7, 5, 2, 4; in order: 2, 3, 4, 5, 6, 7, 8; so the median is 5.
- Show that for an odd number of values in a set, there is only one middle value.
- Show that for an even number of values in a set, there are two middle values and the median is the value in the middle of these two values.
  For example: 5, 7, 7, 8, 10, 12, 14, 15; the middle values are 8 and 10; the median is 9.
- Explain how to find the *range* for a set of data.
- The range is the largest value minus the smallest value.
- Explain that the range is not an average. It shows how data is spread out.
- A small range shows that the values in a set of data are similar in size.
- A large range shows that the values in a set of data differ considerably.
- **Pupils can now do Exercise 6A from Pupil Book 1.1.**

Part 3

- On the board, write two short lists of numbers. Ask the class to explain how to find the mode, the median and the range for each set of data.
- Ask pupils if they know of another average. Explain that the mean is the most common average used and will be discussed in the next lesson.

Answers

Exercise 6A

1   **a** yellow   **b** sun   **c** I   **d** ♥
2   **a** 6   **b** 23   **c** 24 and 25   **d** 102
3   **a** 19   **b** 6   **c** 27   **d** 14
4   **a** £0.80, £2.40   **b** 24 kg, 13 kg   **c** 33 cm, 19 cm   **d** 21 °, 6 °
5   **a** £2.30   **b** £1.70
6   **a** 5   **b** 18   **c** 14   **d** 104.5
7   **a** £1.80, £2.40, £3.25   **b** 19 kg, 14 kg, 14 kg
    c 111 cm, 19 cm, 119 cm   **d** 33 °, 6 °, 34 °
8   **a** for example 5, 5, 5   **b** for example 1, 2, 5, 6, 6
    c for example 2, 4, 4, 5, 6, 7, 8
9   **a** Helen   **b i** Helen   **ii** Tom
10   **a** for example 1 and 5, same birthday   **b** 0, born on the same day

Lesson 6.2 Reading data from tables and charts

Learning objective
- To read data from tables and charts

Resources and homework
- Pupil Book 1.1, pages 110–113
- Intervention Workbook 1, pages 60–63
- Online homework 6.2, questions 1–10

Links to other subjects
- **History** – to compare population data over time
- **Physical education** – to compare performance data to support athletic training programmes

Key words
- charts
- frequency

Problem solving and reasoning help
- The activity at the end of Exercise 6B in the Pupil Book requires pupils to find data using a suitable source, for example, the internet or a road map. Make sure pupils are confident in their understanding of two-way tables. Ask pupils to compare the data they have gathered from different sources. Write the data on the board and ask pupils to work out the mode, median and range of the data.

Common misconceptions and remediation
- Pupils are often unable to interpret the data given to them accurately. Provide plenty of opportunity for them to compare different representations. Encourage pupils to generate questions about the data and assess the advantages and disadvantages of different representations.

Probing questions
- You are told that the local bus service is not as good as it used to be. How could you find out if this is true?
- How do we define *good*? Frequency of service?

Part 1
- Write the following numbers on the board: 3 7 4 6 9 1 8 2.
- Ask the class to find the total of these numbers.
- What strategy did they use? Notice that the numbers are in four pairs that each sum to 10, giving a total of 40.
- Repeat for the following sets of numbers:
  - 16 13 4 18 2 14 7 6 (Total 80)
  - 14 12 16 9 13 15 11 10 (Total 100)

Literacy activity
- Ask pupils to explain the following statistics terms: mode, median and range.

Part 2

- Explain that data can be shown in various ways such as in lists, tables and charts.
- Ask the class to give examples of the different ways this can be done. For example:
  - shopping lists
  - menus
  - television programme times
  - calendars
  - bus and train timetables
  - mileage charts
  - football results
- Write all suggestions on the board.
- It is important to be able to read and interpret the data correctly from tables and charts. However, for example, many people find it difficult to read bus and train timetables.
- Show the class a selection of calendars, bus timetables, tables of sporting results, television listings of programmes from newspapers and magazines. Pupils may wish to cut out some of them and make a display of different ways to represent data.
- Discuss what each one shows and make sure that pupils can read them correctly.
- **Pupils can now do Exercise 6B from Pupil Book 1.1.**

Part 3

- Ask the class for examples of the types of tables and charts that are used to represent data.

Answers
Exercise 6B

1	**a** £40	**b** £35	**c** Year 9	**d** £165	
2	**a** Sophie	**b** 12	**c** 10	**d** 3	**e** 69
3	**a** Saturday	**b** 13th October	**c** 18	**d** Tuesday	
4	**a** 198	**b** 68	**c** London & York	**d** 139	
5	**a** 17	**b** Newcastle & Southampton			
	c i 34	**ii** Manchester United	**iii** Leicester		
6	**a** 1	**b** bus	**c** 32		
7	**a** 3	**b** 15	**c** 32	**d** 8	
8	**a** 10 °C	**b** 15 °C	**c** 9 degrees		

Learning objective
- To create and use a tally chart

Resources and homework
- Pupil Book 1.1, pages 114–116
- Intervention Workbook 1, pages 52–56
- Intervention Workbook 2, pages 66–68
- Homework Book 1, section 6.3
- Online homework 6.3–4, questions 1–10

Links to other subjects
- **Science** – to record population data
- **History** – to model survey data and how it is used for historical purposes

Key words
- tally
- modal

Problem solving and reasoning help
- Pupils develop fluency by applying their learning to a range of familiar contexts. Pupils will enjoy creating graphs using a spreadsheet.

Common misconceptions and remediation
- Pupils need to appreciate the need to be methodical when recording data. Give them opportunities to work with increasingly complex and unfamiliar situations.

Probing questions
- What was important in the way that you chose to collect data? How do you know that you will not need to collect any more data?

Part 1
- Ask pupils to move around the classroom asking pupils they know less well, how they travel to school. What do they think is the most common form of transport?

Literacy activity
- Ask pupils to feedback to the whole class about their discussions in Part 1.

Part 2
- Ask the class: '*What method of transport do pupils use to travel to school? Why?*'
- Write the questions on the board along with pupils' answers. Pupils can draw on the activity in Part 1 to help them answer the question.
- Keep the method of transport separate from the reasons why.
- Have another box on the board for '*Things that might affect their answers*'. Keep adding words as you discuss the question with the class. For example:
    - distance
    - why?
    - age
    - transport available
    - time
    - weather
- Tell pupils that you require some data from them. Ask for suggestions on how you might record the responses.
- Complete the tally chart by asking each pupil in turn, and logging their reasons, for example, as shown here.
- Pupils should now make their own record of the class data in their books.

Transport	Tally	Frequency	Reason 1	Reason 2	Reason 3
Bus	JHT JHT I	11	****** JHT II	******* III	****** I
Car	IIII	4	****** III	****** I	
Bike	I	1	****** I		
Walk	JHT JHT III	13	****** JHT I	******* JHT	****** II
Other	Other	1	****** I		

- **Pupils can now do Exercise 6C from Pupil Book 1.1.**

Part 3

- Revisit the example above. Discuss how to deal with the results. Do simple tables of results show clearly what is happening? Or, for example, do charts for each paper better illustrate the different distributions of sizes?
- How can we ensure that we can compare one group's results with those of another group?

Answers

Exercise 6C
1   **b** for example like paddling   **c** seaside
2   **b** for example Gran has a cat   **c** cat
3   **b** football
4   **b** maths
5   **b** Scott & Bailey

Lesson 6.4 Using data

Learning objective
- To understand how to use data

Resources and homework
- Pupil Book 1.1, pages 116–118
- Intervention Workbook 1, pages 52–53
- Online homework 6.3–4, questions 1–10

Links to other subjects
- **Science** – to record population data
- **History** – to model survey data and how it is used for historical purposes

Key words
- data-capture form
- sample

Problem solving and reasoning help
- Pupils develop fluency by applying their learning to a range of familiar contexts. Pupils will enjoy creating graphs using a spreadsheet.

Common misconceptions and remediation
- Pupils need to appreciate the need to be methodical when recording data. Give them opportunities to work with increasingly complex and unfamiliar situations.

Probing questions
- What information does a chart or table provide? How do charts, tables, and graphs help you to interpret data? How do you collect data?

Part 1
- Remind pupils that data can be shown in various ways, such as in lists, tables and charts. Recap the different ways in which this can be done, as discussed in Lesson 6.2.

Literacy activity
- As part of Part 2, ask pupils to read aloud sections from the newspapers you will distribute.

Part 2
- Ask the question, and write it on the board: 'Do certain newspapers use more long words than other newspapers?'
- Discuss this with the class to find possible theories. Ask how we can test these theories. What do we need to know?
- Lead the class to the idea that we need sample pages from different newspapers. Do we need to count all the words? If not, how many words should we use? Which pages do we use for counting purposes?
- Have ready, chosen pages (specially censored) from all the main newspapers. Avoid topics that you do not want to discuss in your classroom.
- Discuss with the class how to count and record the number of letters in each word. First, create a tally chart for words ranging from 1 to 10 letters. (Change this if necessary.)
- Arrange the class into groups. Each group should look at one newspaper.
- Discuss with the groups how they will organise their collection of data: one to keep the tally going; two to count the number of letters in words from different parts of the page; one to

keep a record of how many words they have counted. Ensure that groups work their way sequentially through a sentence and do not randomise around the page.

- Discuss special cases with the class. Ask: '*What shall we do with the numbers?*'
- It is probably best to ignore them, but let the groups decide. What about hyphenated words? Ignore the hyphen. Abbreviations? Just count as printed.
- Ensure that each group knows how they are going to count and how many words they are counting. Stop the survey when each group has reached the target number.
- Discuss the differences between each group's findings. Why do some newspapers use longer words than others? What is special about newspapers that use mostly short words?
- Discuss with the class if they would get similar results from any pages in the newspapers or would some pages give different figures. How could they test this?
- **Pupils can now do Exercise 6D from Pupil Book 1.1.**

Part 3

- Remind pupils of the importance of being able to read and interpret the data correctly from tables and charts, for example, bus, train and plane timetables.
- Show and discuss with the class a selection of calendars, bus timetables, tables of sporting results, television listings of programmes from newspapers and magazines.

Lesson 6.5 Grouped frequency

Learning objective
- To understand and use grouped frequency

Resources and homework
- Pupil Book 1.1, pages 118–120
- Intervention Workbook 2, pages 69–71
- Homework Book 1, section 6.5
- Online homework 6.5, questions 1–10

Links to other subjects
- **Geography** – to compare climate data
- **Science** – to compare population data

Key words
- class
- grouped frequency table
- grouped frequency
- modal class

Problem solving and reasoning help

- Pupils continue to develop fluency and make links to the different stages of the data-handling cycle by revisiting and applying their learning to a range of familiar contexts. In the challenge activity at the end of Exercise 6E in the Pupil Book, pupils are faced with a less familiar context and a slightly more complex data set. Encourage **less able** pupils to tackle this as a guided group work activity.

Common misconceptions and remediation

- A common source of confusion for pupils when using grouped data is deciding on the boundaries. Give pupils opportunities to explore what this means, using examples of discrete and continuous data. Discuss examples that involve measurements with which pupils are familiar, for example, age and height. This will encourage pupils to discuss what particular groupings actually mean. It will also allow them to make links to work they have done on degree of accuracy and how this affects the grouping.

Probing questions

- Can you give an example of when you might use grouped data in real life?
- Can you give one example using discrete data, and one using continuous data?

Part 1

- Write this statement on the board: *Girls walk to school more often than boys.*
- Ask pupils if they think this is true. How could they check? Take feedback.

Literacy activity

- Ask pupils to write a sentence explaining why we need to group data.

Part 2

- Ask the class: '*How many times have you walked to school this term?*'
- As the discussion develops about when and why pupils walk to school, write down the number of times (approximately) that each pupil has walked to school this term.
- Discuss the need to group some of these answers; otherwise you could have 30 different numbers to graph! This leads to class intervals and a grouped frequency table.
- Talk about how we could chart this. The obvious way is to use a bar chart, but show how you can put reasons onto the bars, to make the bar chart more interesting or informative.
- **Pupils can now do Exercise 6E from Pupil Book 1.1.**

Part 3

- Ask what class size we might use for a survey on pocket money. Bring into the discussion the aspect of no amount as a boundary of a class.
- Ask what class size we might use for car prices, again mentioning boundaries.
- Discuss with pupils if there is any type of data that does not have the problem of class boundaries. This could lead to a discussion on *discrete data*.
- Clearly illustrate the difference between discrete data and non-discrete data.
- You may wish to use the term *continuous*, though pupils need not know this term yet.

Answers

Exercise 6E

1   **b** Frequencies are 16, 17, 8, 16; Total = 57   **c** Bar chart showing values from b
    d 15–19
2   **b** Frequencies are 11, 17, 6, 5, 8, 9; Total = 56   **c** Bar chart showing values from b
    d 6–10
3   **a i** Frequencies are 31, 14, 7, 4, 5, 2; Total = 63
       ii Frequencies are 40, 13, 8, 2; Total = 63
    b Bar charts showing values from a   **c i** 0–2   **ii** 0–4   **d** class size of 5

Lesson 6.6 Data collection

Learning objective
- To gain a greater understanding of data collection

Links to other subjects
- **Design and technology** – to assess product needs among the population

Resources and homework
- Pupil Book 1.1, pages 121–123
- Homework Book 1, section 6.6

Key word
- No new key words for this topic

Problem solving and reasoning help

- In this lesson, pupils have an opportunity to apply what they have learnt in the chapter. In the investigation at the end of Exercise 6F in the Pupil Book, pupils apply a range of statistical ideas to a real-life example of the differences between the boys and girls as to the suggested length of time for the disco.

Common misconceptions and remediation

- Pupils are sometimes confused by the misleading use of data in everyday life. Provide plenty of opportunity to explore real-life examples of the use of data. As a class, or in groups, discuss how data is misleading, and reflect on whether this is due to lack of understanding or a deliberate desire to confuse.

Probing questions

- Is … a good example of the use of data? Why? What do you think the author is trying to achieve with the data?
- A friend says that a local service is not as good as it was. How will you find out if this is true?

Part 1

- Give pupils access to examples of real-life data. Ask them to pick one example and write a brief summary of whether they think it is good use of data or not and why.
- Ask **more able** pupils to find their own examples from a broader, less-defined range of sources. Give **less able** pupils specific examples with key questions to guide them.
- Try to provide current examples.
- Take feedback and agree on some general conclusions.

Literacy activity

- Discuss a problem that will involve all the Year 7 pupils or the whole school. For example: A school disco is to be planned at Christmas. What time should it start? What time should it finish? How much should we charge as the entrance fee?
- Discuss the possible range of answers and who might give these answers.
- What other questions might be asked?
  For example: What food should be available to buy? And drinks?

Part 2

- After brainstorming and writing down suggestions, discuss how to find out the information.
  - Who should they ask? (One year group or everyone?) How should they ask? (By using a questionnaire to be completed or asking at lunchtime, or some other method?)

- ○ How should they keep track of the data? (Type of data capture form)
- Pupils should work in pairs or groups of three to plan the survey: questions; how to word them; layout of data capture form.
- Pupils could run this as a competition, with a vote at the end to find the best data capture form. Then they could use that one. The class should do the survey during the week after you have replicated the data capture form. Part of the competition could involve groups explaining why they think their design is good.
- To end the lesson, choose the design and discuss how to capture the data. This could lead to another lesson wherein pupils capture the data, tabulate the results and draw the bar charts. Groups could split the work into years, as different years may show different results.
- Make sure you help the class to draw conclusions from the data recorded.
- **Pupils can now do Exercise 6F from Pupil Book 1.1.**

Part 3

- Why use a sample? How many people do we need to ask?
- Where else do people use a sample to show trends or results?
- Discuss the role of interviewers on the streets asking passers-by questions from their clipboards – general election or local elections if appropriate – polls give the current trends.

Answers

Exercise 6F
1   **b** the older groups want to charge more
2   **b** the older groups want to start later
3   **b** the younger group want to finish earlier
4   **b** Y7 like snacks, Y8 like hotdogs, Y9 like pizzas

Review questions (Pupil Book pages 124–125)

- The review questions will help to determine pupils' abilities with regard to the material within Chapter 6.
- These questions also draw on the maths covered in earlier chapters of the book to encourage pupils to make links between different topics.

Challenge – Trains in Europe (Pupil Book pages 126–127)

- This activity encourages pupils to think about statistics in train travel – a form of travel with which many pupils may be familiar
- Ask pupils to summarise what they have learnt in the chapter, explaining that they will use much of this material to complete the activity.
- Then ask pupils to look at the data provided in Table A, Table B and Table C.
- Brainstorm ideas such as: How was the information in the tables gathered? What are the possible reasons for the highest and lowest figures in each table? What information would they need to gather if they were planning a trip around Europe? How might they collect more data? How might they present their data?
- Pupils should then work small groups to answer questions 1–7. Once completed, individual group members could present their answers to the rest of the group.
- Support **less able** pupils by grouping them with **more able** pupils, who could act as tutors.

Answers to Review questions

1 **b** pizza
2 **a** 18   **b** 2   **c** bar chart to show 6 cars, 8 vans, 3 lorries and 1 taxi
3 £1
4 −2°C
5 4 cm²
6 **a** 0.9 kg   **b** 1.05 kg **c** 0.3 kg
7 **a** 30 × 1, 15 × 2, 10 × 3, 6 × 5   **b** 30 cm   **c** 40 cm
8 155–159

Answers to Challenge – Trains in Europe

1 France
2 Pictogram showing the following values: UK 60 billion, France 90 billion, Germany 80 billion, Italy 40 billion, Switzerland 20 billion
3 Germany
4 1100
5

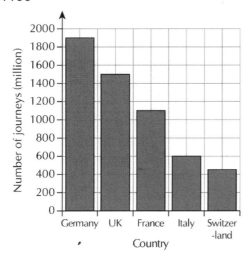

6 Switzerland
7

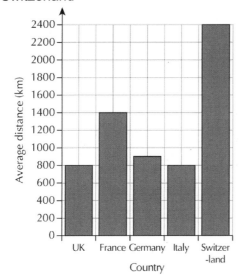

7 Algebra

Learning objectives

- How to use letters to represent numbers
- How to use the rules (conventions) of algebra
- How to simplify algebraic expressions
- How to use and write formulae

Prior knowledge

- How to apply the rules of arithmetic
- The meaning of the words 'term' and 'expression'

Context

- Introduce algebra as a universal language with rules that are used all over the world.
- Mathematicians have been developing the rules of algebra for over 3000 years. The Babylonians used a form of algebra by writing on clay tablets, some of which have survived until today.
- Show pictures of, or discuss, a range of examples in which algebra is used. For example, extend the classic handshakes problem or networks like the Königsberg bridge problem to a modern online community such as Facebook. Search on the internet for 'mathematics handshakes' or 'Königsberg bridge problem'. Or, look at these links: **http://nrich.maths.org/6708**; **http://nrich.maths.org/2484**.

Discussion points

- I think of a number and add 12. Do you know what my number is? Why or why not?
- I think of a number and add 12. The answer is 17. Do you know what my number is? Why?

Associated Collins ICT resources

- Chapter 7 interactive activities on Collins Connect online platform
- *Sagrada Familia* Wonder of Maths on Collins Connect online platform
- *Combining like terms*, *Formulae in words* and *Formulae* Worked solutions on Collins Connect online platform

Curriculum references

Develop fluency

- Use algebra to generalise the structure of arithmetic, including to formulate mathematical relationships

Solve problems

- Develop their mathematical knowledge, in part through solving problems and evaluating the outcomes, including multi-step problems
- Develop their use of formal mathematical knowledge to interpret and solve problems

Algebra

- Substitute values in expressions and simplify expressions
- Use and interpret algebraic notation, including:
    - ab in place of $a \times b$
    - $3y$ in place of $y + y + y$ and $3 \times y$
    - a^2 in place of $a \times a$, a^3 in place of $a \times a \times a$; a^2b in place of $a \times a \times b$
    - $\frac{a}{b}$ in place of $a \div b$
- Substitute numerical values into formulae and expressions, including scientific formulae
- Understand and use the concepts and vocabulary of expressions
- Simplify and manipulate algebraic expressions to maintain equivalence by:
    - collecting like terms
- Understand and use standard mathematical formulae

Fast-track for classes following a 2-year scheme of work

- **More able** pupils could skip every other question in the Pupil Book exercises of this chapter if they grasp the material quickly. However, it would be unwise to miss large chunks, as much of this material will be unfamiliar to the majority of pupils.

Lesson 7.1 Expressions and substitution

Learning objectives

- To use algebra to write simple expressions
- To substitute numbers into expressions to work out their value

Links to other subjects

- **Science** – to use and manipulate scientific formulae

Resources and homework

- Pupil Book 1.1, pages 129–133
- Intervention Workbook 3, pages 34–36
- Homework Book 1, section 7.1
- Online homework 7.1, questions 1–10

Key words

- expression
- term
- substitute
- variable

Problem solving and reasoning help

- The **PS** and **MR** problems require pupils to produce expressions from geometric shapes. Pupils need to be familiar with the meanings of perimeter and area from previous chapters.

Common misconceptions and remediation

- Pupils often struggle to recognise that letters represent variables and that the answer can vary depending on the situation. Provide lots of opportunities for pupils to see this in action in familiar contexts such *as 'Think of a number'* word problems.
- To avoid serious confusion when multiplying brackets, make sure pupils understand that letter symbols used in algebra stand for unknown numbers or variables and *not* labels. For example, $5b$ cannot mean '5 bananas'. If the b is interpreted as bananas when they meet $3b + b + 6$, pupils will ask: '6 *what?*' Or if a stands for apples, then what does ab mean?

Probing questions

- How do you know if a letter symbol represents an unknown or a variable?
- What are the important steps when substituting values into this expression?
- What would you do first? Why?
- How would you continue to find the answer?

Part 1

- Play the trial-and-improvement game of 'Guess my number'. Think of a number (less than 100 is best to start with) and ask pupils to say the right number in as few times as possible, by asking questions that can only be answered 'Yes' or 'No'. For example:
  - o Is it less than 50? Is it even? Is it larger than 25?
- Then include a number over 100, but do not make it too large.
- Allow the class to choose a number to see if you can guess it quicker than their best attempt.
- You could write the numbers on prepared cards, and stick them facing the wall. This would demonstrate that you have not changed your mind during the game.

Literacy activity

- Go through all the newly introduced algebra words with the class. Ask pupils to tell you what each word means. If you like, you could introduce this with a quick hangman-type game, using one of the more difficult words.
- The class should leave the lesson with a clear idea of the meanings of most of the words.

Part 2

- Go through the following ways of writing terms and expressions:
- $3n$ means 3 multiplied by the variable n (Explain the term 'variable' again.)
- $n + 7$ means 7 added to the variable n
- $8 - n$ means subtract n from 8
- $n - 1$ means subtract 1 from n (Explain the difference between these last two.)
- $\frac{n}{2}$ means n divided by 2.
- Each term and expression assumes a different value as the value of the variable changes. For example, when n is 6: $3n = 18$ $n + 7 = 13$ $8 - n = 2$ $n - 1 = 5$ $\frac{n}{2} = 3$
- Explain carefully to **less able** pupils, exactly what is being done. Use many examples to make sure that pupils grasp that the variable n can stand for millions of different numbers.
- **The class can now do Exercise 7A from Pupil Book 1.1.**

Part 3

- Write these mathematical equivalences on the board, and ask pupils to fill in the gaps.
    - o *number of days* = … times the number of weeks
    - o *cost* = price of … item × number of items
    - o *age in years* = age in months … 12
    - o *pence* = number of pounds × …
    - o *area of rectangle* = length × …
    - o *cost of petrol for a journey* = …
- You could ask **more able** pupils to design their own questions.
- Take feedback and discuss the meaning of the = sign in mathematics.

Answers

Exercise 7A

1   **a** 1   **b** 5   **c** 6   **d** 8
2   **a** 6   **b** 3   **c** 4   **d** 70
3   It is $t + t + t + t = 4t$
4   **a** $a + 21$ **b** $k + 27$ **c** $m + 17$
5   **a** $2y + 12$ **b** $2r + 60$ **c** $2f + 9$
6   $6h$
7   $5s$
8   **a** Add 4 cm to Alan's height.   **b** $h - 9$ **c** $6h$ cm
9   **a** Add 4.5 minutes to Lauren's time.   **b** $2m$ minutes
10   **a** $a + 12 + 10 = a + 22$ **b** 31   **c** 32.5   **d** 30.7
11   **a** 7   **b** 4.5   **c** 95   **d** 0
12   **a** 13   **b** 23   **c** 33   **d** 10.5
13   **a** 7   **b** 19   **c** 1   **d** 25
14   **a** $A + B$ **b** $2A$ **c** $2B$ **d** $A + 2B$
15   Own drawings made up of
     a 4 squares   **b** 2 squares and 1 triangle
     c 1 square and 4 triangles   **d** 2 squares and 4 triangles
16   **b** $c + d + 18$ **c** $e + f + 28$ **d** $2g + 4$ **e** $2h + 15$ **f** $2j + 2k$ **g** $2t + 2m + 12$

Investigation: Making shapes

Own shapes made up from
a   2 rectangles   **b** 2 semicircles   **c** 1 rectangle and 1 semicircle
d   1 rectangle and 2 semicircles   **e** 4 rectangles
f   4 rectangles and 4 semicircles

Lesson 7.2 Simplifying expressions

Learning objective

- To learn the rules for simplifying expressions

Links to other subjects

- **Science** – to simplify variables in experiments
- **Business and economics** – to develop simple algebraic formulae to express familiar everyday situations involving money

Resources and homework

- Pupil Book 1.1, pages 133–137
- Intervention Workbook 3, pages 34–36
- Homework Book 1, section 7.2
- Online homework 7.2, questions 1–10

Key words

- like terms
- simplify

Problem solving and reasoning help

- The **PS** questions and the investigation in Exercise 7B of the Pupil Book require pupils to write expressions in as many ways as possible. Giving pupils the opportunity to do this encourages them to be more fluent and confident in their use of algebra and to appreciate they are not always looking for 'the one correct' answer.

Common misconceptions and remediation

- The most common error when simplifying expressions is to write incorrectly:
  $3x + x + 5 = 9x$ instead of the correct: $4x + 5$
- This error stems from pupils' misunderstanding of variables as objects, as mentioned in the previous lesson. Provide examples of simplifying with errors similar to the one above and ask: '*What is wrong?*'

Probing questions

- Can you write an expression that simplifies to: $4x + 6$?
- What are the important points to remember when simplifying an expression?

Part 1

- Provide pupils with a set of cards with matching mathematical expression and/or word problems and mathematical sentences. For example:
  $a + a$ and $2a$, 6 more than w and $w + 6$.
- Include one spare example, in which pupils must identify the odd one out.

Literacy activity

- Write a short paragraph that explains how to simplify an expression.

Part 2

- Demonstrate simplifying using a few examples such as: $3c + 5b + 2c + 4b = 5c + 9b$
- *Remember: Do NOT turn the letters into objects such as cups and buns.*
- Talk about like terms. Like terms are terms that are multiples of the same letter, or the same combination of letters, for example, here the cs and the bs are like terms.
- Write another term on the board with a different variable (letter), for example: $5p$

- Ask for like terms for 5p. Write these on the board around the 5p. Then choose another term, for example, 2y, and ask for like terms.
- Now explain why we cannot simplify: 5c + 7 to 12c.
- When the question of 1a or 1p, for example, arises (hopefully this comes from pupils, but if not raise it yourself), explain that the 1 is unnecessary because the unit value of the coefficient is self-evident. So, by convention, the 1 is never written.
- Demonstrate how like terms can be added or subtracted to simplify an expression.
- Explain that the convention is to change an expression with a mixture of terms into alphabetical order. For example, an answer would not be left as: 3b + a; it would be put in order as: a + 3b
- **Pupils can now do Exercise 7B from Pupil Book 1.1.**

Part 3

- Ask pupils what like terms are. Can we add them? Can we subtract them?
- Ask why the answer to the sum 5a − a is not 5. (Some pupils may believe it is!) Ask some pupils to try to explain that the a is really 1a, so the sum is: 5a − 1a
- Remind pupils that they have been looking at the language of algebra, and that it is important to understand these basic ideas in order to be able to solve the more difficult questions that they will tackle later.
- Finally, ask pupils to write a text message that they can send to a friend, with hints and tips on how to simplify expressions.

Answers

Exercise 7B

1 a 2a   b 3b   c 7c   d 3d   e 4x   f 4z   g 10k h 9p   i 7q   j 15x   k 10y l 3z
2 a 5c   b 11d   c 10p d 12x   e 8t   f 6m   g 2q   h 4a   i 2p   j 10w k 5t   l 2g
3 a 5t + 16   b 3k + 9   c 4m + 32   d 9x + 28   e 3w + 1   f 4w + 1
4 a 2a + 8   b 3d + 40   c 5x + 30   d 4t + 8
5 a 9x   b 6y   c 4e   d 3w   e 4n   f 6k
6 a 8a + 7   b 3m + 3   c 9t + 9   d p − 6   e 8x + 8   f 5a + 13
7 a 4a + 6b   b 4x + y   c 4e + 6f   d x + y   e 8x + 8   f 5a + 13
8 a 16   b x + 13   c t + 15   d w + 9   e k + 10   f m + 16
9 a 2a + 9   b 2d + 10 c 2x + 14
10 a 3a + 6   b 3x + 10 c 3m + 4
11 a 4x   b 9x   c 7x + 15
12 a 3x   b 3x and 2 c 2a and 5b

Challenge: Making addition sentences

a   x − 2
b   x + 1 and x + 2
c   2x + 3
d   2x + 1
e   x + 1 and x − 2
f   x + 2 and x − 1 and x − 2 in any order

Lesson 7.3 Using formulae

Learning objective
- To use formulae

Resources and homework
- Pupil Book 1.1, pages 137–140
- Intervention Workbook 3, pages 34–36
- Homework Book 1, section 7.3
- Online homework 7.3–4, questions 1–10

Links to other subjects
- **Food technology** – to interpret recipes as formulae
- **Science** – to use formulae that pupils will encounter during their science lessons
- **Business and economics** – to use and interpret financial formula

Key words
- formula
- formulae

Problem solving and reasoning help
- The challenge activity at the end of Exercise 7C requires pupils to use their understanding in a real-life context that might be a little less familiar to them. Encourage pupils to ask questions about the context. They could role-play this in groups. They could build on this by designing their own word problems in familiar and unfamiliar contexts.

Common misconceptions and remediation
- Difficulties with substitution into formulae often come from a failure to grasp the basics of BIDMAS and negative numbers, along with an inability to recognise that letters represent variables. When this is the case, pupils tend to want to substitute specific values. Provide opportunities for pupils to see this in action in familiar contexts before moving on to more complex or abstract examples.

Probing questions
- How do you go about linking a formula that has been expressed in words, to a formula that has been expressed algebraically?
- Could you express this formula in a different way, so that it is still the same?

Part 1
- Ask if anyone knows approximately how many kilometres are in 5 miles. It would help if there were a specific place 5 miles from school on which you could focus.
- By trial and discussion, let the class arrive at approximately 8 km.
- Offer a variety of multiples of 5 miles and ask for their kilometre equivalents. For example: '*Approximately how many kilometres are in 10 miles, 15 miles, 25 miles, …?*'
- Then ask: '*Approximately how many kilometres are there in 18 miles?*'
- Lead the discussion along the lines of: '*15 miles are 24 km, 20 miles are 32 km, so 18 miles are in between, but closer to 32 than 24, say about 29 or 30 km.*'
- Ask a few more similar questions. Use the following table to help.

Miles	18	22	38	44	53	59	62	72	98
Kilometres	29	35	61	70	85	94	99	115	157

- Discuss different speeds. '*What is equivalent to 30 mph, 40 mph, …?*'

Literacy activity

- Give pupils a formula such as $C = 3h + 9$ and ask them to write it in words and explain a real-life scenario about how the formula was constructed.

Part 2

- Tell the class a story, for example: While talking to my window cleaner the other day, I asked how he worked out how much to charge for cleaning the windows in different-sized houses. 'Easy', he said, 'I use a rule of 50p plus 70p for every big window cleaned, plus 20p for every small window cleaned.' I thought that was rather clever and that I would write down the rule, but as a mathematician, I wrote it down as a *formula*. What do you think I wrote?
- Lead the class to something like: $C = 50 + 70B + 20w$. (Let the class choose the letters for the variables, but do give guidance on suitable letters.)
- Explain how useful it is to write down rules as formulae.
- Ask pupils to work out a few charges. For example:
  Mrs Smith: 4 big windows and 5 small windows give: $50 + (70 \times 4) + (20 \times 5) = 430$ pence
  Mr Jordan: 6 big windows and 7 small windows give: $50 + (70 \times 6) + (20 \times 7) = 610$ pence
- **Pupils can now do Exercise 7C from Pupil Book 1.1.**

Part 3

- Ask pupils to try to explain the meaning of a formula.
- Ask if they are able to explain the difference between a term, an expression and a formula.

Answers
Exercise 7C
1   a £16   b £40   c £80
2   a £70   b £140   c £280
3   a 48 km   b 16 km   c 32 km
4   a 2 feet   b 5 feet   c 10 feet
5   a 3   b 5   c 17
6   a 18   b 48   c $2 \times (5 + 4) = 2 \times 9 = 18$ and $2 \times (20 + 4) = 2 \times 24 = 48$
7   a $252   b $630   c $2998.80
8   a £10   b £50   c £250
9   a £65   b £90   c £115
10 a i 70   ii 100   b i 38   ii 46
Challenge: Lines and dots
A $L = 3 \times 6 + 1 = 19$ and $D = 2 \times 6 + 2 = 14$
B   31 lines, 22 dots
C   61 lines, 42 dots
D   301 lines, 202 dots

Lesson 7.4 Writing formulae

Learning objectives

- To write formulae

Resources and homework

- Pupil Book 1.1, pages 141–143
- Homework Book 1, section 7.4
- Online homework 7.3–4, questions 1–10

Links to other subjects

- **Food technology** – to design recipes as formulae
- **Science** – to use and manipulate scientific formulae
- **Business and economics** – to use and interpret financial formula

Key words

- No new key words for this topic

Problem solving and reasoning help

- In Exercise 7D of the Pupil Book, pupils are required to apply their understanding of other areas of mathematics to word problems, to write them algebraically. In the investigation at the end of the exercise, pupils need to apply their understanding of formulae and sequences to a problem.
- A discussion on using formulae in real-life situations would be beneficial.

Common misconceptions and remediation

- Pupils need to make links to their work in number and see algebra as a generalised form of number. In response to this, pupils need the opportunity to discover formulae for themselves. If they discover the power of algebra in terms of generalisation they are more likely to engage with it as a short method of finding an answer.

Probing questions

- How do you go about linking a formula that has been expressed in words to a formula that has been expressed algebraically?
- Could this formula be expressed in a different way, but still be the same?

Part 1

- Write the following question on the board, linking it to Lesson 7.1. In pairs, ask pupils to think of as many examples as they can in five minutes.
    - When you substitute $a = 3$ and $b = 8$ into the formula $t = 2a + b$, you get 14. Can you make up some more formulae that also give $t = 14$ when $a = 3$ and $b = 8$ are substituted?
- Encourage pupils to be methodical, for example: $2a + b = 14$, $3a - 3 + b = 14$. Ask **more able** pupils to explain this algebraically.
- Provide examples for **less able** pupils to explain and/or match.
- Take feedback.

Literacy activity

- In pairs, ask pupils to write a formula in words, then swap formulae and solve them.

Part 2

- Give pupils three sets of cards: the first with formulae in words, the second with the same formulae but expressed algebraically, the third with a range of calculations that match the formulae (more than one for each).
- Ask pupils to sort the cards. The formulae should involve up to two operations.
- Use different sets of cards for different abilities, with some that include brackets. Use grouping to support and challenge pupils. Encourage **more able** pupils to design their own sets of cards using templates.
- **Pupils can now do Exercise 7D from Pupil Book 1.1.**

Part 3

- How do you go about constructing a formula from information given in a problem?
- How might you check if the formula works?

Answers

Exercise 7D

1 $R = 102P$
2 $A = 1.7P$
3 $K = 8.3E$
4 **a** £27.20   **b** $c = 1.36l$
5 **a** $A = 12k$ **b** $P = 2k + 24$ or $P = 2(k + 12)$
6 **a** $8 + t$ **b** $A = 3(8 + t)$ **c** $P = 2t + 22$
7 **a** $c = t + 7$ **b** $a = 2(t + 7)$
8 **a** $20x$ **b** $30y$ **c** $20x + 30y$
9 **a** 25   **b** 19   **c** $p = 3w + d$
10 $t = x + 11$
11 **a** $t = y + 10$ **b** $t = 2k + 11$ **c** $t = 2w + 17$

Investigation: Dots and squares

B   shape B, $a = 10$ and $i = 3$; shape C, $a = 13$ and $i = 6$; shape D, $a = 7$ and $i = 0$
C $a = i + 7$

- The review questions will help to determine pupils' abilities with regard to the material within Chapter 7.
- These questions also draw on the maths covered in earlier chapters of the book to encourage pupils to make links between different topics.

Problem solving – Winter sports (Pupil Book pages 146–147)

- Discuss with pupils the data shown in the table in the Pupil Book. In particular, make sure that pupils note the following:
    - that the 'deals' have different names, for example, 'Adult Platinum'
    - the types of skis mentioned under each deal 'Salomon Crossmax W12 – or equivalent'
    - that the 8-day price is not four times the 2-day price.
- Encourage pupils to suggest questions that they can ask from the information. They could do this in small groups or individually, and then present their questions to the class. Discuss what else might happen in real-life situations, for example, discounts, rebates, paying deposits.
- Once pupils are familiar with the idea and the process of equipment hire, they can answer questions 1–8 in the activity.
- Discuss the reality of buying on the internet: why it is cheaper (no labour costs), possible fraud, and the fact that the company usually requires a deposit upfront and full payment by a certain date.
- The deposit required is 20%. Recall how to work out 20%. Pupils should suggest finding 10%, then doubling the answer.
- Round off the costs to the nearest €10 (€190, €170, €140, €100, €60 and €40) and ask pupils to work out the deposits mentally.
- Ask pupils further questions as suggested below. They will need the information in the key to work out the answers.
    - The exchange rate is £1 = 1.10 (or use today's rate). Work out, to the nearest penny, how much eight days' hire of the 'Platinum' deal would be in pounds and pence.
    - Work out the cost of 10 days' hire of the Children's 'Kid' deal.
    - The deals shown include boots. If boots are not required, 15% is deducted from the cost. How much would the 8-day 'Silver' deal cost without boots?

Answers to Review questions

1 **a** $x + 15$ **b** $3y + 5$ **c** $3t + 14$
2 **a** 12 **b** 7 **c** 13 **d** 18 **e** 17 **f** 5 **g** 16 **h** 2
3 both 69
4 **a** $2t + 4$ **b** $5x$ **c** $a + 7b$ **d** $5d + 2$ **e** $2A + 4$ **f** $10w - 25$
5 **a** $p = 8 + t + 8 + 2t = 16 + 3t$ **b i** 34 **ii** 49 **iii** 44.5
6 **a** £16 **b** £400 **c** £13.20
7 **a** $t = 3c + 5$ **b** $t = 2c + 24$ **c** $t = 5c + 9$
8 **a** $G + 20$ **b** $2G$ **c** $T = 4G + 20$ **d** 240
9 **a i** 2 **ii** 5 **iii** 8 **iv** 11 **v** 14
   b i 17 **ii** $3 \times 6 - 1 = 17$
   c i 29 **ii** 59

Answers to Problem solving – Winter sports

1 £88
2 £52
3 £16
4 £52
5 £472
6 **a** 104 120 136 152 168 **b** £16
7 **c** graph with straight line from (1, 24) to (10, 168)
   d graph with straight line from (1, 16) to (10, 124)

8 Fractions

Learning objectives

- How to find equivalent fractions
- How to write a fraction in its simplest form
- How to add and subtract fractions with the same and different denominators
- How to convert a simple improper fraction to a mixed number
- How to convert a mixed number into an improper fraction
- How to add and subtract simple mixed numbers

Prior knowledge

- How to recognise and use simple fractions
- How to compare and order fractions with the same denominator

Context

- Fractions as we know them did not exist in Europe until the 17th century. At first, fractions were not even thought of as numbers in their own right, simply as a means of comparing whole numbers with one another. Who first used fractions? Were they always written in the same way? How did fractions reach us here? To find out more, search on the internet for 'history of fractions' or see: http://nrich.maths.org/2515

Discussion points

- Ask pupils to explain why some fractions are easy to compare, for example: $\frac{1}{3}$ and $\frac{1}{7}$ or $\frac{2}{5}$ and $\frac{8}{7}$. Also ask for examples of fractions that are less easy to compare and why this is, for example: $\frac{3}{7}$ and $\frac{2}{5}$.

Associated Collins ICT resources

- Chapter 8 interactive activities on Collins Connect online platform
- *Addition and subtraction of fractions* video on Collins Connect online platform
- *Swimming* Wonder of Maths on Collins Connect online platform
- *Equivalent fractions and cancelling* and *Calculations involving mixed numbers* Worked solutions on Collins Connect

Curriculum references

Develop fluency

- Consolidate their numerical and mathematical capability from key stage 2 and extend their understanding of the number system to include fractions
- Move freely between different numerical representations [for example, equivalent fractions]

Solve problems

- Develop their mathematical knowledge, in part through solving problems and evaluating the outcomes, including multi-step problems

Number

- Order fractions
- Use the four operations, including formal written methods, applied to proper and improper fractions and mixed numbers

Fast-track for classes following a 2-year scheme of work

- By the end of KS2, pupils will have compared and ordered fractions and identified simple equivalent fractions. If they can demonstrate confidence and fluency with the KS2 content they could move straight to applying their understanding to the problem solving and mathematical reasoning questions in each exercise in the Pupil Book of this chapter. Check pupils' understanding by using one or two simple examples and/or the probing questions. **More able** pupils could leave out Exercise 8A and Exercise 8B and move on to Exercise 8C.

Learning objectives

- To find simple equivalent fractions
- To write fractions in their simplest form

Resources and homework

- Pupil Book 1.1, pages 149–152
- Intervention Workbook 1, pages 26–28
- Intervention Workbook 2, pages 40–42
- Intervention Workbook 3, pages 11–12
- Homework Book 1, section 8.1
- Online homework 8.1, questions 1–10

Links to other subjects

- **Design and technology** – to compare different portion sizes or packaging

Key words

- denominator
- equivalent
- equivalent fraction
- numerator
- simplify
- simplest form

Problem solving and reasoning help

- Question 1 of Exercise 8A in the Pupil Book uses multiplicative reasoning to explore the relationship between the numerator and denominator in equivalent fractions, horizontally and vertically. This will prepare pupils for later work on proportional reasoning. To help **less able** pupils with **PS** question 5, revise multiples before they start. **PS** question 10 is simply a variation on 'cake problems'; revise the words 'clockwise' and 'anticlockwise'.

Common misconceptions and remediation

- Pupils are often aware of the role of the denominator when finding equivalent fractions but may fail to understand the role of the numerator. Working with visual images may help.

Probing questions

- Give me two equivalent fractions. How do you know they are equivalent?
- Can you draw me a diagram to convince me that one-third is the same as four-twelfths? Can you use more than one diagram or image?

Part 1

- Use a target board such as this one to recall strategies for doubling and halving. Ask: '*How can we extend this to multiplying by 4 and dividing by 4?*' (Answer: Double and double again. Halve and halve again.)
- Randomly select pupils; ask them to '*times by 4*' the number pointed at. Discuss strategies again. For example:

28	38	7	22	60
8	16	14	26	48
30	52	36	9	13
32	15	12	24	34

  - $2 \times 38 = 2 \times 30 + 2 \times 8 = 60 + 16 = 76$
  - $2 \times 76 = 140 + 12 = 152$

- Randomly select pupils and ask them to '*divide by 4*' the number pointed at.
- Discuss the strategies for dividing by 4. For example:
  - Half of 26 = half of 20 + half of 6 = 13
  - Half of 13 = half of 10 + half of 3 = $6\frac{1}{2}$

- Ask pupils to pick out pairs on the target board that are four times, or a quarter of each other. Make them say the relationship in full. For example: '*Eight is a quarter of thirty-two.*' '*Twenty-eight is four times seven.*'

- Pairs on the target board are (7, 28), (13, 52), (8, 32), (12, 48), (15, 60).

Literacy activity

- Ask pupils to write down the new words they have learned this lesson and what they mean in mathematics. (Pupils could also give alternative meanings in other curriculum areas.)

Part 2

- Draw a number line on the board, or use a counting stick with eight divisions marked on it. Mark one end as 0 and the other end as 1 (each division will be one-eighth).
- Ask pupils to identify the first mark as a fraction. Then ask, in order, for other marks as fractions. Pupils may call the second mark a quarter. If so, ask for any other ways to identify the second mark.
- Do this with all the marks and end up with a diagram like this:
- Make sure that pupils are familiar with these terms: *numerator, denominator, equivalent fraction, proper fraction, fraction in its simplest form (lowest terms).* Now ask for the missing number in $\frac{3}{8} = \frac{}{24}$. How can pupils find this?

0	$\frac{1}{8}$	$\frac{2}{8}$	$\frac{3}{8}$	$\frac{4}{8}$	$\frac{5}{8}$	$\frac{6}{8}$	$\frac{7}{8}$	$\frac{8}{8}$
0		$\frac{1}{4}$		$\frac{2}{4}$		$\frac{3}{4}$		$\frac{4}{4}$
0				$\frac{1}{2}$				$\frac{2}{2}$

- What is the inverse operation of multiplication?
- What is the missing number? (9)
- How do we write the proper $\frac{12}{20}$ fraction in its lowest terms (simplest form)? $\frac{12}{20} \div 4 = \frac{3}{5}$
- Encourage pupils to show (at least at first) what they are doing.
- **Pupils can now do Exercise 8A from Pupil Book 1.1.**

Part 3

- Write some fractions on the board in random order, for example: $\frac{1}{2}, \frac{3}{4}, \frac{12}{18}, \frac{4}{5}, \frac{20}{25}, \frac{6}{8}, \frac{2}{3}, \frac{15}{30}, \frac{15}{20}, \frac{7}{14}, \frac{6}{9}, \frac{12}{15}$. Ask the class to identify the proper fractions and then group the fractions in sets of equivalent fractions. Discuss how they know that fractions are equivalent.
- Write these four fractions (or similar) on the board: $\frac{24}{30}, \frac{9}{12}, \frac{14}{20}, \frac{25}{15}$. Ask pupils to cancel them to their lowest form, explaining the process as they do so.
- Why is the last one different? Briefly introduce the idea of a top-heavy fraction.

Answers

Exercise 8A

1   b $\frac{2}{5} = \frac{6}{15}$ c $\frac{1}{3} = \frac{4}{12}$ d $\frac{5}{6} = \frac{10}{12}$

2   own diagram showing $\frac{2}{5} = \frac{4}{10}$

3   a $\frac{9}{12}$ b $\frac{4}{20}$ c $\frac{8}{12}$ d $\frac{15}{24}$

4   a yes   b no   c yes   d no

5   a $\frac{6}{8}, \frac{9}{12}, \frac{12}{16}$ and $\frac{15}{20}$

   b $\frac{6}{10}, \frac{9}{15}, \frac{12}{20}, \frac{15}{25}$

   c $\frac{8}{10}, \frac{12}{15}, \frac{16}{20}, \frac{20}{25}$

6   a $\frac{5}{15}$ and $\frac{8}{24}$ b $\frac{12}{48}$

7   a $\frac{3}{4}$ b $\frac{3}{5}$ c $\frac{1}{2}$ d $\frac{3}{8}$

8   a $\frac{2}{3}$ b $\frac{1}{2}$ c $\frac{4}{9}$ d $\frac{1}{5}$

9   a $\frac{3}{4}$ b $\frac{5}{8}$ c $\frac{2}{5}$ d $\frac{3}{4}$

10   a $\frac{1}{4}$ b $\frac{1}{4}$ c $\frac{1}{2}$ d $\frac{3}{4}$ e $\frac{3}{4}$ f $\frac{3}{8}$

11   a $\frac{3}{5}$ b no   c $\frac{7}{10}$ d $\frac{3}{4}$ e $\frac{4}{5}$ f no   g $\frac{9}{10}$

Problem solving: Fractions of shapes

A $\frac{5}{8}$ B $\frac{5}{8}$

Lesson 8.2 Comparing fractions

Learning objective
- To compare and order two fractions

Resources and homework
- Pupil Book 1.1, pages 152–154
- Intervention Workbook 2, pages 40–42
- Intervention Workbook 3, pages 11–14
- Homework Book 1, section 8.2
- Online homework 8.2, questions 1–10

Links to other subjects
- **Food technology** – to compare quantities in different packaging to evaluate different offers such as buy one get one free.
- **Art** – to use the rule of thirds as a means of composing images that are most pleasing to the eye

Key word
- fraction wall

Problem solving and reasoning help
- Pupils use the visual image of a fraction wall to reinforce the concept of equivalent fractions. This will help them combine and apply their understanding of ordering fractions and equivalent fractions. It also provides pupils with a mental image they can use when they start working with more complex and less familiar fractions.

Common misconceptions and remediation
- Pupils are often pushed into doing calculations with fractions too quickly, using rules they do not really understand. It is important that pupils spend time comparing and ordering fractions so they acquire a sound understanding of fractions as points on a number line as well as operators.

Probing questions
- Explain how you would fill in the missing numbers, to show these lists of fractions from smallest to largest. $*\dfrac{\square}{5}$, $*\dfrac{\square}{6}$, $*\dfrac{\square}{4}$ $\dfrac{3}{*}, \dfrac{2}{*}, \dfrac{5}{*}$
- Then fill in the numbers in a different way, to show the fractions from largest to smallest.

Part 1
- Draw a number line on the board, or use a counting stick. Mark 10 divisions, starting with 0 on the left. Mark the second division as 10. Ask the class to identify the remaining marks.
- As a class or with one pupil, count on in 15s. Point out the positions until you reach the end. Then let pupils continue without prompts. Repeat, to establish a class 'record'.
- Repeat the activity with the 0 mark on one end, and 1 on the second division, using fractions rather than decimals. (Take the opportunity to link the equivalent fractions and decimals.)
- Ask for the connection between this counting-on activity and the last activity.
- Repeat with the line or stick, with the 0 mark on one end and 25 on the first division, then again with the 0 on one end, and $\dfrac{1}{4}$ on the first division. Establish the connection between these two counting-on activities.

Literacy activity
- Write three top tips for comparing and ordering fractions.

Part 2

- Display an image of a fraction wall. Pupils should work in pairs.
- Write $\frac{1}{4}$ and $\frac{1}{2}$ on the board. Ask which is bigger or smaller, and to explain how they know this. Pupils might say: '*There are four quarters in a whole and only two halves, so one-quarter will be less than half*'. They can use the fraction wall to support their explanations.
- Ask pupils if this was difficult, and why. They should be familiar with these fractions.
- Now write $\frac{2}{5}$ and $\frac{4}{5}$. Again, ask which fraction is bigger or smaller and to explain why.
- Pupils should explain that though these fractions are less familiar, the denominator is the same, so they can decide which fraction is bigger or smaller by referring to the numerator.
- This time, write $\frac{3}{8}$ and $\frac{4}{6}$ on the board. Ask which is bigger or smaller. Give pupils time to discuss and share ideas and consider how they can explain their answer.
- Depending on the group, you may want to refer to the fraction wall and ask probing questions, for example: Is $\frac{3}{8}$ less than or more than $\frac{1}{2}$? Is $\frac{4}{6}$ less than or more than $\frac{1}{2}$?
- Ask pupils what strategies they used, such as comparing them to fractions with which they are more familiar, or changing them to equivalent fractions with the same denominator.
- **Pupils can now do Exercise 8B from Pupil Book 1.1.**

Part 3

- Write a set of fractions on cards, giving one to each pupil. Ask pupils to line up; then by discussing their card with a pupil in front or behind, to stand in order from smallest to largest.
- Ask pupils to show their cards. Challenge individuals to explain why they are in the right place. You could ask other pupils if they agree or disagree and what they have learned.
- If pupils want to challenge anyone they can, but they should justify their challenge. Other pupils can join in the challenge using the stems '*I agree/disagree with [name] because ...*'.
- Pair **less able** pupils with **more able** pupils and let them work together.

Answers

Exercise 8B

1 $\frac{2}{4}, \frac{3}{6}, \frac{4}{8}$

2 a $\frac{2}{6}$ b $\frac{4}{6}$ c $\frac{2}{8}$ d $\frac{6}{8}$

3 a $\frac{1}{3}$ b $\frac{2}{5}$ c $\frac{5}{6}$ d $\frac{2}{7}$
   e $\frac{4}{5}$ f $\frac{2}{7}$ g $\frac{3}{5}$ h $\frac{5}{8}$

4 a equal to b larger than c smaller than
   d equal to e larger than f smaller than

5 a i $\frac{2}{10}$ ii $\frac{4}{10}$ iii $\frac{6}{10}$ iv $\frac{8}{10}$
   b i $1\frac{1}{10}$ ii $\frac{3}{5}$ iii $\frac{3}{10}$ iv $\frac{7}{10}$

6 a i $\frac{6}{12}$ and $\frac{4}{12}$ ii $\frac{1}{2}$ b i $\frac{4}{12}$ and $\frac{3}{12}$ ii $\frac{1}{3}$
   c i $\frac{9}{12}$ and $\frac{10}{12}$ ii $\frac{5}{6}$ d i $\frac{10}{12}$ and $\frac{8}{12}$ ii $\frac{5}{6}$

7 a i $\frac{8}{16}$ ii $\frac{1}{2}$ b i $\frac{12}{16}$ ii $\frac{7}{16}$

c i $\frac{6}{16}$ ii $\frac{5}{16}$ d i $\frac{14}{16}$ ii $\frac{7}{8}$

8 a $\frac{1}{4}$ because $\frac{2}{12}$ is less than $\frac{3}{12}$
   b $\frac{3}{4}$ because $\frac{6}{8}$ is more than $\frac{5}{8}$
   c $\frac{2}{3}$ because $\frac{6}{9}$ is more than $\frac{5}{9}$
   d $\frac{5}{12}$ because $\frac{4}{12}$ is less than $\frac{5}{12}$

Problem solving: Fraction wall

A halves, quarters, eighths and sixteenths

B $\frac{1}{16}$ $\frac{1}{8}$ $\frac{3}{16}$ $\frac{1}{4}$ $\frac{5}{16}$ $\frac{3}{8}$ $\frac{7}{16}$ $\frac{1}{2}$ $\frac{5}{8}$ $\frac{3}{4}$ $\frac{7}{8}$ $\frac{9}{8}$

Lesson 8.3 Adding and subtracting fractions

Learning objectives

- To add and subtract fractions with the same denominators
- To add and subtract fractions with different denominators

Links to other subjects

- **Food technology** – to calculate total daily calorific requirements of food groups using fractions

Resources and homework

- Pupil Book 1.1, pages 155–159
- Homework Book 1, section 8.3
- Online homework 8.3, questions 1–10

Key words

- addition
- lowest common multiple
- subtraction

Problem solving and reasoning help

- The word problems at the end of Exercise 8C and 8D in the Pupil Book require pupils to apply what they have learned. Pupils need to be able to decode questions and identify the mathematics within them. Encourage **more able** pupils to write their own questions, and to assess what makes the questions easy or difficult. For example, they can use mathematical criteria such as: *'Are the fractions unitary or not?'* or *'How familiar are the contexts?'* or *'In terms of difficulty, are the questions single or multi-step problems?'*

Common misconceptions and remediation

- Pupils often get taught rules without actually understanding where the rules originate. As a result, pupils may struggle to apply the rules in different contexts. For example, they confuse the rules for adding and subtracting fractions with those for multiplying and dividing fractions.
- Another problem is that pupils may add or subtract the denominators as well as the numerators when adding and subtracting fractions.

Probing questions

- Why are equivalent fractions so important when adding or subtracting fractions?
- What strategies do you use to find a common denominator when you add or subtract fractions?
- Is there only one possible common denominator? What happens if you use a different common denominator?

Part 1

- Ask the class to count on using Figure 1.

Figure 1

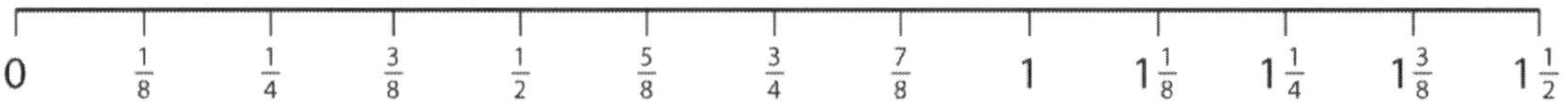

| 0 | $\frac{1}{8}$ | $\frac{1}{4}$ | $\frac{3}{8}$ | $\frac{1}{2}$ | $\frac{5}{8}$ | $\frac{3}{4}$ | $\frac{7}{8}$ | 1 | $1\frac{1}{8}$ | $1\frac{1}{4}$ | $1\frac{3}{8}$ | $1\frac{1}{2}$ |

- Ask pupils to study Figure 2 for a few moments. Cover the grid. Have prepared cards of diagrams, as in Figure 3. Ask pupils to add the missing numbers. They can copy them into their books or fill them in on the board. Finally, reveal the grid to check the answers.

Figure 2

$1\frac{1}{4}$	$1\frac{1}{2}$	$1\frac{3}{4}$	2
$2\frac{1}{4}$	$2\frac{1}{2}$	$2\frac{3}{4}$	3
$3\frac{1}{4}$	$3\frac{1}{2}$	$3\frac{3}{4}$	4
$4\frac{1}{4}$	$4\frac{1}{2}$	$4\frac{3}{4}$	5

Figure 3

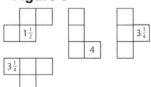

- Repeat with other grids, for example:

| $1\frac{1}{8}$ | $1\frac{1}{4}$ | $1\frac{3}{8}$ | $1\frac{1}{2}$ | $1\frac{5}{8}$ | $1\frac{3}{4}$ | $1\frac{7}{8}$ | 2 |
| $2\frac{3}{8} \cdot 1\frac{3}{4}$ | $7\frac{1}{4}$ | $7\frac{3}{8}$ | $7\frac{1}{2}$ | $7\frac{5}{8}$ | $7\frac{3}{4}$ | $7\frac{7}{8}$ | 8 |

Part 2

- For **more able** pupils, leave out Exercise 8C, and go straight to the explanation on how to add fractions with different denominators. The grids from Part 1 should be useful.

- What is $\frac{1}{8}+\frac{2}{8}$? Say it is like adding apples: 1 apple + 2 apples = 3 apples, so $\frac{1}{8}+\frac{2}{8}=\frac{3}{8}$

- What is $\frac{1}{8}+\frac{3}{8}$? How can we use the grids to do this?

- It is also possible to use a number line or a ruler marked in eighths.

- **Pupils can now do Exercise 8C from Pupil Book 1.1.**

- When pupils are ready, or in small guided groups, show the following example: $\frac{}{3}+\frac{}{4}$

- Ask pairs to discuss why this is more difficult (fractions are different types; different denominators). Ask how to add these fractions (think of equivalent fractions). Show pupils a fraction wall (page 157 of the Pupil Book) and ask if it helps them to visualise the equivalent fractions and how to use them to complete the sum.

- Remind pupils about LCM and ask them, in pairs, to find the LCM of, for example, 3 and 4. Encourage more able pupils to try difficult, or more than two numbers.

- Now draw the example on the right on the board and talk through it step by step.
  Pupils should repeat the process for $\frac{1}{4}$. Ask pupils how they can use the LCM to find the equivalent fractions and therefore to add $\frac{}{3}+\frac{}{4}$. Let pupils share ideas, then take feedback. Finally, demonstrate how to complete the original sum.

$\times 4$

$\frac{2}{3}+\frac{8}{12}$

$\times 4$

- **Pupils can now do Exercise 8D from Pupil Book 1.1.**

Part 3

- Using the fraction charts or the number line from the start of the lesson, ask pupils to explain how they would solve addition and subtraction problems such as:

  a $1\frac{3}{4}+2\frac{3}{8}$　　**b** $2\frac{3}{8}-1\frac{3}{4}$　　**c** $\frac{7}{10}+\frac{9}{10}$　　**d** $\frac{5}{9}-\frac{2}{9}$

- Discuss methods and rules. What about $\frac{1}{2}+\frac{1}{3}$? How could we do this? Discuss methods.

Answers

Exercise 8C

1　**a** $\frac{2}{5}$　**b** $\frac{2}{5}$　**c** $\frac{4}{5}$　**d** $\frac{4}{5}$

2　**a** $\frac{2}{8}=\frac{1}{4}$　**b** $\frac{6}{8}=\frac{3}{4}$　**c** $\frac{6}{8}=\frac{3}{4}$　**d** $\frac{8}{8}=1$

3　**a** $\frac{4}{10}=\frac{2}{5}$　**b** $\frac{8}{10}=\frac{4}{5}$　**c** $\frac{6}{10}=\frac{3}{5}$　**d** $\frac{10}{10}=1$

4　**a** $\frac{1}{5}$　**b** $\frac{2}{5}$　**c** $\frac{2}{5}$　**d** $\frac{1}{5}$

5　**a** $\frac{2}{8}=\frac{1}{4}$　**b** $\frac{2}{8}=\frac{1}{4}$　**c** $\frac{6}{8}=\frac{3}{4}$　**d** $\frac{4}{8}=\frac{1}{2}$

6　**a** $\frac{2}{10}=\frac{1}{5}$　**b** $\frac{4}{10}=\frac{2}{5}$　**c** $\frac{8}{10}=\frac{4}{5}$　**d** $\frac{2}{10}=\frac{1}{5}$

7　**a** 1　**b** $\frac{7}{9}$　**c** $\frac{5}{7}$　**d** $\frac{1}{2}$　**e** $\frac{2}{3}$　**f** $\frac{3}{8}$　**g** $\frac{5}{8}$　**h** 1

8　**a** $\frac{2}{3}$　**b** $\frac{3}{9}$　**c** $\frac{4}{7}$　**d** $\frac{1}{3}$　**e** $\frac{1}{2}$　**f** $\frac{1}{4}$　**g** $\frac{1}{4}$　**h** $\frac{3}{8}$

9　**a** $\frac{3}{8}$　**b** $\frac{1}{2}$　　10 $\frac{3}{4}$

6　**a** $\frac{1}{6}$　**b** $\frac{2}{9}$　**c** $\frac{1}{9}$　**d** $\frac{1}{4}$　**e** $\frac{1}{12}$　**f** $\frac{1}{4}$　**g** $\frac{1}{2}$　**h** $\frac{7}{12}$

7　**a** $\frac{3}{8}$　**b** $\frac{7}{8}$　**c** $\frac{7}{8}$　**d** $\frac{5}{8}$　**e** $\frac{3}{5}$　**f** $\frac{4}{5}$　**g** $\frac{1}{3}$　**h** $\frac{5}{6}$

8　**a** $\frac{1}{8}$　**b** $\frac{3}{8}$　**c** $\frac{2}{5}$　**d** $\frac{1}{5}$　**e** $\frac{5}{8}$　**f** $\frac{1}{6}$　**g** $\frac{1}{12}$　**h** $\frac{1}{6}$

9　**a** $\frac{3}{6}$ and $\frac{2}{6}$　**b** $\frac{1}{6}$

10　**a** $\frac{4}{12}$, $\frac{8}{12}$ and $\frac{3}{12}$　**b i** $\frac{7}{12}$　**ii** $\frac{1}{12}$　**iii** $\frac{5}{12}$　**iv** $\frac{11}{12}$

11　$\frac{5}{8}$ litre　　12 $\frac{1}{2}$

Investigation: Ancient Egyptian fractions

A　**a i** $\frac{3}{4}$　**ii** $\frac{5}{8}$　**iii** $\frac{7}{12}$　**iv** $\frac{9}{16}$　**v** $\frac{11}{20}$

b The numerator increases by 2 each time and the denominator increase by 4. (numerator – 1) × 2 = denominator

B　**a i** $\frac{2}{3}$　**ii** $\frac{3}{5}$　**iii** $\frac{4}{7}$　$\frac{5}{9}$

b The numerator increases by 1 each time and the denominator increases by 2. Numerator × 2 – 1 = denominator

Exercise 8D

1　$\frac{2}{4}=\frac{3}{6}=\frac{4}{8}$　　2 **a** $\frac{3}{4}$　**b** $\frac{2}{3}$　**c** $\frac{5}{8}$　**d** $\frac{7}{8}$

3　**a** $\frac{1}{4}$　**b** $\frac{3}{8}$　**c** $\frac{1}{8}$　**d** $\frac{1}{3}$　　4 $\frac{2}{6}=\frac{3}{9}=\frac{4}{12}$

5　**a** $\frac{1}{2}$　**b** $\frac{4}{9}$　**c** $\frac{5}{9}$　**d** $\frac{5}{12}$　**e** $\frac{3}{4}$　**f** $\frac{11}{12}$　**g** $\frac{5}{6}$　**h** $\frac{3}{4}$

Lesson 8.4 Mixed numbers and improper fractions

Learning objectives

- To convert mixed numbers to improper fractions
- To convert improper fractions to mixed numbers

Resources and homework

- Pupil Book 1.1, pages 160–162
- Homework Book 1, section 8.4
- Online homework 8.4, questions 1–10

Links to other subjects

- **Food technology** – to work out portion sizes

Key words

- convert
- improper fraction
- mixed number

Problem solving and reasoning help

- The questions in Exercise 8E of the Pupil Book require pupils to combine the specific mathematical skills they are learning with the generic skills of matching and sorting.
- As in the previous lesson, ask **more able** pupils to write and assess their own questions.

Common misconceptions and remediation

- Pupils sometimes assume that fractions are always less than 1. Using improper fractions and converting these to mixed number helps challenge this misconception.

Probing questions

- Use a visual image or diagram to show why $\frac{5}{2}$ is the same as $2\frac{1}{2}$.

Part 1

- True or false: '*Fractions are always less than 1*'. Justify your answer.
- Pupils should try to justify their answer with examples of visual images, if possible.
- Ask more able pupils to hold a discussion in pairs. One partner could be true and one false and they need to convince each other of the correct answer.

Literacy activity

- Ask pupils to write questions based on the lesson objectives, then swap in pairs and solve.

Part 2

- Write this sum on the board: $\frac{5}{6} + \frac{3}{6} + \frac{9}{6}$
- What can you say about the answer to this sum? (Brainstorm)
- If appropriate, use this image to support the discussion.
- How many sixths do we have in total? (17)
- Explain that $\frac{17}{6}$ is called an improper fraction. It is also equivalent to two whole 6s and five-sixths. This can be written as $2\frac{5}{6}$ and is called a mixed number.
- Write this definition on the board. **More able** pupils could write their own definition with examples. Support **less able** pupils by doing some more examples with them.
- **Pupils can now do Exercise 8E from Pupil Book 1.1.**

Part 3

- Choose two fractions that are less than 1. Add together the denominators and then the numerators to create two new fractions. Be careful how pupils write these, so that they are clear that they are creating a new fraction rather than adding the fractions. For example, write: $\frac{1}{3}$ and $\frac{2}{4}$ gives $\frac{3}{7}$

- Without doing any conversions, place all three in order. While doing so, explain why.
- Ask what pupils notice. (The new fraction is between the other two fractions.)
- Ask if they think this is always the case. Then try different examples with the class.
- Encourage pupils to use fractions greater than 1 (or more), and also mixed greater than and smaller than fractions.
- Ask **more able** pupils to suggest an extension, for example, using three fractions.

Answers

Exercise 8E

1 **b** $2\frac{1}{3} = \frac{7}{3}$ **c** $1\frac{1}{6} = \frac{7}{6}$ **d** $2\frac{3}{8} = \frac{19}{8}$ **e** $2\frac{4}{10} = \frac{24}{10}$ **f** $5\frac{1}{4} = \frac{21}{4}$

2 **a** $\frac{7}{2}$ **b** $\frac{11}{4}$ **c** $\frac{13}{8}$ **d** $\frac{22}{5}$

3 **a** 6   **b** 12   **c** 15   **d** 8   **e** 13

4 **a** 16   **b** 24   **c** 32   **d** 23   **e** 29

5 **a** $\frac{5}{2}$ **b** $\frac{9}{4}$ **c** $\frac{17}{8}$ **d** $\frac{21}{8}$

6 **a** $\frac{13}{4}$ **b** $\frac{24}{5}$ **c** $\frac{29}{20}$ **d** $\frac{29}{6}$ **e** $\frac{27}{4}$ **f** $\frac{17}{3}$ **g** $\frac{39}{8}$ **h** $\frac{46}{5}$

7 **a** $1\frac{1}{4}$ **b** $1\frac{4}{5}$ **c** $4\frac{1}{2}$ **d** $1\frac{5}{8}$ **e** $2\frac{1}{6}$ **f** $4\frac{1}{3}$ **g** $6\frac{1}{2}$ **h** $2\frac{1}{12}$

8 **a** $\frac{3}{2}$ **b** $\frac{7}{3}$ **c** $\frac{5}{2}$ **d** $\frac{5}{2}$

9 **a** $2\frac{1}{2}$ **b** $2\frac{1}{4}$ **c** $3\frac{1}{2}$ **d** $2\frac{1}{2}$ **e** $2\frac{1}{2}$ **f** 2   **g** $1\frac{1}{2}$ **h** $2\frac{1}{2}$

10 $1\frac{5}{8} = \frac{13}{8}$; $1\frac{1}{2} = \frac{12}{8}$; $2\frac{1}{4} = \frac{9}{4}$; $2\frac{3}{4}$; $2\frac{1}{2} = \frac{10}{4}$

Challenge: Fractions in sequence

A **a** $\frac{3}{4}$ $1\frac{1}{2}$ $2\frac{1}{4}$ 3 $3\frac{3}{4}$ $4\frac{1}{2}$ **b** $\frac{21}{4} = 5\frac{1}{4}$ and $\frac{24}{4} = 6$

B **a** $\frac{3}{8}$ $\frac{3}{4}$ $1\frac{1}{8}$ $1\frac{1}{2}$ $2\frac{1}{4}$ **b** $\frac{21}{8} = 2\frac{5}{8}$ and $\frac{24}{8} = 3$

Learning objectives

- To add and subtract simple mixed numbers with the same denominator
- To add and subtract simple mixed numbers with different denominators

Resources and homework

- Pupil Book 1.1, pages 163–165
- Homework Book 1, section 8.5
- Online homework 8.5, questions 1–10

Links to other subjects

- No links to other subjects

Key words

- No new key words for this topic

Problem solving and reasoning help

- The challenge question at the end of Exercise 8F makes links between fractions and the work pupils have done on multiples and number facts. The question has been designed to help to extend pupils' understanding of equivalent fractions beyond simply applying rules.

Common misconceptions and remediation

- Pupils often make mistakes when subtracting mixed numbers. For example: $2\frac{1}{3} - 1\frac{2}{3}$ to give, for example, $1\frac{1}{3}$. Pupils can avoid making this type of mistake if they always convert to mixed numbers before carrying out the calculation.

Probing questions

- Why is it okay to start with the whole numbers when adding mixed numbers, yet this can cause problems with subtraction? (Provide examples to show what you mean.)
- What strategy could you use that would work in every case for addition *and* subtraction?

Part 1

- What is the LCM of the numbers 3, 4, and 6?
- What is an easy way to identify a common multiple of two numbers, for example, 6 and 4? Is this the LCM: Sometimes, Always, Never?

Literacy activity

- Revisit the new key words in this chapter and explain their meanings and spell them.

Part 2

- Explain the method for adding and subtracting using improper fractions as described in example 10 in Pupil Book 1.1. Also show this alternative and more common method.
- Write this sum on the board: $3\frac{1}{4} + 2\frac{1}{2}$
- Have a class discussion about the answer. A number line might help. Using familiar fractions such as these, pupils should be able to see that that the answer is: $5\frac{3}{4}$
- Working in pairs, ask pupils to do an equivalent sum in written form. Work through the following sum. Meanwhile, pupils could compare and make notes on their own versions. First by partitioning – pupils should be used to this concept with whole numbers from KS2.

$$3\frac{1}{4} + 2\frac{1}{2} = 3 + \frac{1}{4} + 2 + \frac{1}{2}$$

Rearrange to give: $3 + 2 + \frac{1}{4} + \frac{1}{2} \longrightarrow 3 + 2 + \frac{1}{4} + \frac{2}{4}$ LCM of 2 and 4 is 4.

$= 5 + \frac{3}{4}$ Add the whole numbers and then the fractions.

$$= 5\frac{3}{4}$$ Simplified using equivalent fractions

- In pairs, ask pupils to write a set of steps or success criteria for adding fractions using this method. Take feedback and establish a class set of guidelines and/or success criteria.
- **More able** pupils could tackle this last part independently. **Less able** pupils could complete a set of guidelines that have already been partially completed, or complete a specific example based on a given set of success criteria.
- Then write the following example on the board: $3\frac{2}{3} - 1\frac{1}{4}$
- Ask pupils if they can apply the success criteria developed earlier to this example. Give them time to try it out; then work through it, as shown below. First by partitioning:

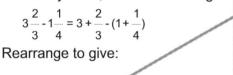

$$3\frac{2}{3} - 1\frac{1}{4} = 3 + \frac{2}{3} - (1 + \frac{1}{4})$$

Rearrange to give:

> Make sure you discuss why this is a plus, if pupils are confused and cannot see it from the previous step.

$$3 - 1 + \frac{2}{3} - \frac{1}{4} \longrightarrow 3 - 1 + \frac{8}{12} - \frac{3}{12}$$ LCM of 3 and 4 is 12.

$$= 2 + \frac{5}{12}$$ Subtract the whole numbers and subtracting the fractions.

$$= 2\frac{5}{12}$$ The answer cannot be simplified.

- **Pupils can now do Exercise 8F from Pupil Book 1.1.**

Part 3

- Using a fraction chart or number line, ask pupils to explain how they would solve addition and subtraction problems such as: $1\frac{3}{4} + 2\frac{3}{8}$ $2\frac{3}{8} - 1\frac{3}{4}$ $\frac{7}{10} + \frac{9}{10}$ $\frac{5}{9} - \frac{2}{9}$
- Discuss methods and rules. Then ask pupils to discuss the following: $3\frac{1}{4} - 2\frac{1}{2}$
- In pairs, ask pupils to identify the challenge within this subtraction: $\frac{1}{2}$ is larger than $\frac{1}{4}$. Then ask them to suggest a way of tackling this subtraction that would make sure they can deal effectively with this (change both fractions to mixed numbers).

Answers

Exercise 8F

1 a $1\frac{1}{2}$ b $1\frac{1}{4}$ c $1\frac{2}{5}$ d 2
   e 1 f $1\frac{1}{2}$ g $1\frac{2}{3}$ h $1\frac{3}{8}$

2 a $2\frac{1}{2}$ b 4 c $2\frac{1}{4}$ d $2\frac{1}{5}$
   e $2\frac{2}{3}$ f 2 g $3\frac{1}{3}$ h $4\frac{1}{5}$

3 a $1\frac{1}{2}$ b 4 c $1\frac{1}{4}$ d $1\frac{3}{5}$
   e $2\frac{1}{3}$ f $1\frac{3}{5}$ g $3\frac{2}{3}$ h $\frac{1}{2}$

4 a $1\frac{1}{2}$ b $2\frac{3}{5}$ c $1\frac{3}{4}$ d $1\frac{1}{2}$

5 a $2\frac{1}{4}$ b $3\frac{1}{4}$ c $2\frac{5}{8}$ d $2\frac{7}{10}$
   e $1\frac{3}{4}$ f $2\frac{3}{8}$ g $4\frac{5}{8}$ h $5\frac{5}{6}$

6 a $\frac{3}{4}$ b $2\frac{1}{4}$ c $1\frac{1}{8}$ d $2\frac{1}{10}$
   e $1\frac{1}{2}$ f $1\frac{1}{8}$ g $1\frac{7}{8}$ h $3\frac{1}{2}$

7 a $1\frac{5}{6}$ b $2\frac{2}{6}$ c $3\frac{1}{6}$ d $4\frac{5}{6}$
   e $1\frac{1}{6}$ f $1\frac{1}{6}$ g $1\frac{5}{6}$ h $1\frac{5}{6}$

8 a, d, f $2\frac{1}{4}$ b, c, e $1\frac{3}{4}$

Challenge

First row: $2\frac{3}{8}, 2\frac{5}{8}, 2\frac{3}{4}$

Second row: $2\frac{3}{4}, 3, 3\frac{1}{8}$

Third row: $3, 3\frac{1}{4}, 3\frac{3}{8}$

Review questions (Pupil Book pages 166–167)

- The review questions will help to determine pupils' abilities with regard to the material within Chapter 8.
- These questions also draw on the maths covered in earlier chapters of the book to encourage pupils to make links between different topics.

Challenge – Fractional dissections (Pupil Book pages 168–169)

- This activity explores partitioning, which is an important concept in understanding fractions. The tasks involve splitting a shape into unequal parts, which will help pupils' understanding of the part–whole relationship between the numerator and denominator in fractions.
- Tasks 1 and 2 involve pupils splitting shapes into three different fractions and cancelling down the fractions to their lowest terms. Explain that the shapes have grid lines and that only the divisions along the grid lines are allowed. Pupils could then show how they would add the three fractions together to make a whole by reversing the technique.
- You may want to ask pupils warm-up questions, depending on the group. For example:
    - Explain why these fractions are equivalent.
    - Draw a diagram to explain how you can add or subtract these fractions.
- Show pupils some shapes with gridlines on the interactive whiteboard or visualiser and ask:
    - Which shapes can be halved?
    - Which shapes can be split into thirds?
    - Which shapes can be split into quarters?
    - Can a shape that has been cut in half always be quartered?
- Pupils can now do tasks 1, 2 and 3, individually or in pairs.
- Pupils could present their solutions to the rest of the group. Encourage pupils to explain how they know they have all the solutions. Discuss the strategies they have used and what it means to be methodical.
- Task 4 is similar, except that pupils need to split the shape into unitary fractions. **More able** pupils could design their own questions, including shapes such as equilateral triangles or circles. Support **less able** pupils by encouraging guided group work. You may want to work through the first example together to make sure that pupils are happy with the way the colouring is used to illustrate the different unit fractions.
- You could extend this activity by exploring the two website links above, or by doing a search for 'Egyptian fractions'.

Answers to Review questions

1 **a** $\frac{5}{20}$ **b** $\frac{8}{12}$ **c** $\frac{9}{24}$ **d** $\frac{5}{25}$

2 **a** $\frac{1}{12}$ **b** $\frac{2}{3}$ **c** $\frac{1}{8}$

3 **a** $1\frac{1}{2}$ **b** $1\frac{1}{3}$ **c** $4\frac{1}{4}$ **d** $3\frac{3}{4}$

4 $2\frac{3}{4}, 3, 3\frac{1}{2}, 3\frac{3}{4}$

5 **a** $\frac{1}{2}$ **b** $\frac{3}{5}$ **c** $1\frac{2}{3}$ **d** $\frac{1}{2}$

6 **a** 4   **b** $\frac{3}{5}$ **c** $5\frac{1}{2}$ **d** $3\frac{2}{3}$

7 **a** $4\frac{5}{8}$ **b** $4\frac{3}{4}$ **c** $6\frac{1}{6}$ **d** $1\frac{5}{8}$

8 $8\frac{7}{8}$ cm

9 **a** $1\frac{1}{2}$ **b** $2\frac{2}{5}$ **c** $1\frac{3}{4}$

10 Put them in order and the middle one is $2\frac{1}{2}$ kg

11 Perry by $\frac{1}{8}$ m

Answers to Challenge – Fractional dissections

Task 1

a $\frac{3}{12} = \frac{1}{4}$ and $\frac{2}{12} = \frac{1}{6}$

b diagram divided into 9 squares, 2 squares and 1 square
c diagram divided into 3 squares, 4 squares and 5 squares

Task 2

a $\frac{1}{2} + \frac{1}{3} + \frac{1}{6}$

b $\frac{1}{2} + \frac{1}{5} + \frac{3}{10}$ or $\frac{1}{10} + \frac{2}{5} + \frac{1}{2}$

Task 3

Any one of the following: $\frac{1}{18} + \frac{1}{9} + \frac{5}{6}$ $\frac{1}{6} + \frac{2}{9} + \frac{11}{18}$ $\frac{1}{6} + \frac{5}{18} + \frac{5}{9}$

$\frac{1}{6} + \frac{1}{3} + \frac{1}{2}$ $\frac{1}{6} + \frac{7}{18} + \frac{4}{9}$ $\frac{1}{9} + \frac{7}{18} + \frac{1}{2}$ $\frac{2}{9} + \frac{5}{18} + \frac{1}{2}$

Task 4

A $\frac{1}{2} + \frac{1}{3} + \frac{1}{6}$ **B** $\frac{1}{2} + \frac{1}{3} + \frac{1}{8} + \frac{1}{24}$ **C** $\frac{1}{3} + \frac{1}{6} + \frac{1}{4} + \frac{1}{8} + \frac{1}{12} + \frac{1}{24}$

9 Angles

Learning objectives

- How to use a compass to give directions
- How to measure angles
- How to draw angles
- How to calculate angles at a point, angles on a straight line and opposite angles
- How to recognise parallel, intersecting and perpendicular lines
- How to explain the geometrical properties of triangles and quadrilaterals

Prior knowledge

- The names of the different types of angles
- The names of different triangles and quadrilaterals
- By the end of KS2, pupils can compare and classify geometric shapes based on their properties and find unknown angles in any triangles, quadrilaterals, and regular polygons. They can recognise angles where they meet at a point, are on a straight line, or are vertically opposite, and find missing angles.

Context

- In the real world, geometry is everywhere. Just a few examples include buildings, planes, cars and maps. Homes are made of basic geometric structures. Without an understanding of angles and their properties none of these structures would stay together. Show pupils examples of images of structures such as bridges and building where the angles are very clearly defined in terms of how they hold the structure together.
- Another use of angles in real life is how we find our way around the world. Without at least a basic understanding of angles in terms of a measure of rotation we would never be able to reach our destination.

Discussion points

- Can you describe a rectangle precisely in words so someone else can draw it?
- What mathematical words are important when describing a rectangle, triangle, …?
- What properties do you need to be sure a triangle is isosceles; equilateral; scalene?

Associated Collins ICT resources

- Chapter 9 interactive activities on Collins Connect online platform
- *Maths Man and the Undead* video on Collins Connect online platform
- *Trapeze artists* and *Snowboard angles* Wonders of Maths on Collins Connect online platform
- *Compass points* and *Exterior angle of a triangle* Worked solutions on Collins Connect online platform

Curriculum references

Reason mathematically
- Begin to reason deductively in geometry

Solve problems
- Develop their use of formal mathematical knowledge to interpret and solve problems
- Select appropriate concepts, methods and techniques to apply to unfamiliar and non-routine problems

Geometry and measures
- Draw and measure line segments and angles in geometric figures
- Describe, sketch and draw using conventional terms and notations: points, lines, parallel lines, perpendicular lines, right angles
- Use the standard conventions for labelling the sides and angles of triangle ABC, and know and use the criteria for congruence of triangles
- Derive and illustrate properties of triangles, quadrilaterals, circles, and other plane figures [for example, equal lengths and angles] using appropriate language and technologies
- Apply the properties of angles at a point, angles at a point on a straight line, vertically opposite angles

Fast-track for classes following a 2-year scheme of work

- Pupils following a two-year scheme of work will most likely be proficient at using a compass. If this is the case, then leave out Lesson 9.1 and start with Lesson 9.2.

Lesson 9.1 Using the compass to give directions

Learning objective

- To use a compass to give directions

Resources and homework

- Pupil Book 1.1, pages 171–175
- Online homework 9.1, questions 1–10

Links to other subjects

- **Geography** – to navigate using a map and a compass

Key words

- anticlockwise
- clockwise
- compass

Problem solving and reasoning help

- Make sure pupils understand the need to be accurate and give them time to practice if necessary. Using a visualiser is a great way of explaining this topic.

Common misconceptions and remediation

- Pupils need to learn the order of the compass points. Phrases such as 'never eat shredded wheat' or 'naughty elephants squirt water' will help pupils to remember the four compass points: north, east, south and west (clockwise).

Problem solving

- How do we use maps in everyday life?

Part 1

- Brainstorm why we should know the compass directions and how to use maps.
- Place 'North', 'South', 'East', and 'West', on the four walls of the classroom. Ask a pupil to follow directions such as two steps south, one step east, and so on, to find an object or treasure that you have hidden in the classroom before the lesson began.

Literacy activity

- Give pupils a map of the school. Using compass directions, ask them to write a story about, for example, moving around the school, visiting various classrooms and visiting the canteen.

Part 2

- Now introduce all eight cardinal points by placing the directions NE, NW, SE and SW in the corners of your classroom. Ask pupils the following questions.
- Which way are you facing if:
    - o you are facing north you make a half turn clockwise?
    - o you are facing south you make a quarter turn anticlockwise?
    - o you are facing northwest and you make half a turn anticlockwise?
    - o you are facing southeast and you make a full turn clockwise?
- Go around the class asking similar questions until pupils fully understand the topic. For more able pupils you could extend them by asking them questions in degrees such as:
    - o You are facing east and you turn $90°$ clockwise.
- **Pupils can now do Exercise 9A from Pupil Book 1.1**

Part 3

- In pairs, using square grid paper, encourage pupils to design their own map, showing different landmarks. Then pupils should take turns to explain, using directions, how to travel from landmark to landmark.
- You could place some of the good examples in the class under a visualiser and do this as a class activity.

Answers
Exercise 9A
1 **a** 3 squares North, then 4 squares East   **b** 4 squares South, then 5 squares West
   c 4 squares East, then 3 squares South   **d** 5 squares West, then 1 square North

2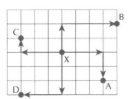

3 for example: 2 squares North, then 6 squares East and then 4 squares North
4 **a** $\frac{1}{4}$ turn anticlockwise   **b** $\frac{1}{4}$ turn clockwise   **c** $\frac{1}{2}$ turn clockwise

   d $\frac{1}{2}$ turn anticlockwise   **e** $\frac{3}{4}$ turn clockwise   **f** $\frac{3}{4}$ turn anticlockwise
5 **a** East   **b** South   **c** North   **d** West   **e** West   **f** North
6 **a** D   **b** E   **c** G   **d** F
7 **a** Leeds   **b** Lincoln   **c** Liverpool   **d** Leeds
Challenge: More directions
For example:
A   Oslo
B   Belgrade
C   Porto
D   Edinburgh
E   Venice
F   Berlin

Lesson 9.2 Measuring angles

Learning objectives

- To know the different types of angles
- To use a protractor to measure an angle

Resources and homework

- Pupil Book 1.1, pages 176–181
- Intervention Workbook 2, pages 59–61
- Intervention Workbook 3, pages 52–53
- Homework Book 1, section 9.1
- Online homework 9.2, questions 1–10

Links to other subjects

- **Design and technology** – to produce accurate design templates
- **Geography** – to navigate using a map and a compass

Key words

- acute angle
- degrees
- protractor
- angle
- obtuse angle
- right angle

Problem solving and reasoning help

- Make sure pupils understand the need to be accurate and give them time to practice if necessary. Using a visualiser is a good way to explain this topic.

Common misconceptions and remediation

- Pupils often do not grasp the need for accuracy when measuring angles. Pupils need plenty of practice in using a protractor accurately. They need to understand the concept of an angle as a measure of turn, as this may help them to understand why it is necessary always to measure from 0 when using a protractor. Alongside this they also need to understand that conventions such as 'always measuring a bearing from north ensures that we are able to communicate effectively with one another'. Demonstrate this actively for kinaesthetic learners. Show pupils examples of how being out by just a degree can make huge difference when working on a large scale.

Probing questions

- Why is it a good idea to estimate the size of an angle before measuring it?
- How would you explain to somebody how to use a protractor?

Part 1

- Draw 10 angles on the board to include right, acute and obtuse angles.
- Ask different pupils to name the acute angles, the obtuse angles and the right angles.

Literacy activity

- Ask pupils to write three tips in their books for measuring angles accurately. Take feedback and come up with a class list that can be displayed if appropriate.

Part 2

- Explain that this lesson is about how to measure angles.
- Draw an acute angle on the board.
- Show the class how to measure the size of the angle to the nearest degree using a board semi-circular protractor.

- You could use geometric software such as Geogebra to demonstrate this. **http://www.geogebratube.org/material/show/id/8409**. You can download Geogebra free of charge or use the HTML version if this is a problem.
- Explain how to use the two scales on the protractor and how important it is first to establish whether the angle is acute or obtuse.
- Ask the class to draw some acute angles in their books and to measure the size of each angle.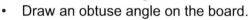
- Draw an obtuse angle on the board.
- Show the class how to measure the size of the angle to the nearest degree.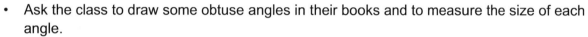
- Ask the class to draw some obtuse angles in their books and to measure the size of each angle.
- This activity can also be done using a full circular protractor, which many pupils find much easier to use, although semi-circular protractor provides an opportunity to reflect on a range of angle facts.
- **Pupils can now do Exercise 9B from Pupil Book 1.1.**

Part 3

- Draw a large triangle on the board or using a visualiser, ask pupils to come out and measure the size of each of the three angles using the board semi-circular protractor.

Answers
Exercise 9B
1 acute **a** and **c**; obtuse **b** and **d**
2 **a** 1   **b** 1   **c** 5
3 **a** and **d**
4 **b** and **d**
5 **d, b, c** and **a**
6 **d, a, c** and **b**
7 **a** 30°   **b** 50°   **c** 45°   **d** 40°   **e** 25°
   f 75°   **g** 120°   **h** 150°   **i** 95°   **j** 165°
8 **a** 50°, 60° and 70°   **b** 180°
9 **a** 30°, 50° and 100°   **b** 180°   **c** 180°
Challenge: Estimating triangles
C actual sizes are **1** 50°   **2** 80°   **3** 115°   **4** 110°

Lesson 9.3 Drawing angles

Learning objective

- To use a protractor to draw an angle

Links to other subjects

- **Geography** – to use bearings on a map
- **Design and technology** – to produce accurate design drawings

Resources and homework

- Pupil Book 1.1, pages 182–184
- Online homework 9.3, questions 1–10

Key words

- No new key words for this topic

Problem solving and reasoning help

- Make sure pupils understand the need to be accurate and give them time to practise if necessary. Using a visualiser is a good way to explain this topic.

Common misconceptions and remediation

- As pupils learned in the previous lesson, the need for accuracy when measuring angles is very important. Make sure pupils are given plenty of practice in using a protractor accurately. The concept of an angle as a measure of turn is also important for them to know, as this may help them to understand why they should always measure from 0 when using a protractor. Alongside this they also need to understand that conventions such as always measuring a bearing from north makes sure we are able to communicate effectively with one another. Demonstrate this actively for kinaesthetic learners. Showing examples of how being out by just a degree can make huge difference when working on a large scale. Encourage pupils to use a hard (HB or harder) sharp pencil when drawing angles.

Probing questions

- How would you explain to someone how to use a protractor?
- How would you draw an angle larger than $180°$?

Part 1

- Draw 10 angles on the board to include right, acute and obtuse angles.
- Invite pupils to put the angles in order of size, starting with the smallest.
- Finish by asking pupils to estimate the size of each angle.

Literacy activity

- Ask pupils to write three tips in their books for drawing angles accurately. Take feedback and come up with a class list that can be displayed if appropriate

Part 2

- Explain that the lesson is about how to draw angles.
- Show the class how to draw an acute angle to the nearest degree using a board semi-circular protractor.
- You could use geometric software such as Geogebra to demonstrate this. **http://www.geogebratube.org/material/show/id/8409**. You can download Geogebra free of charge or use the HTML version if this is a problem.

- Explain how to use the two scales on the protractor depending which way the angle is facing.
- Ask the class to draw some acute angles in their books 30°, 45°, 80°.
- Show the class how to draw an obtuse angle to the nearest degree.
- Ask the class to draw some obtuse angles in their books 95°, 120° 135°
- This activity can also be done using a full circular protractor, which many pupils find much easier to use, although semi-circular protractor provides an opportunity to reflect on a range of angle facts.
- **Pupils can now do Exercise 9C from Pupil Book 1.1.**

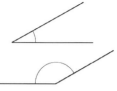

Part 3

- Ask pupils to come to the front of the class and draw angles under the visualiser, or using the board semi-circular protractor.

Answers

Exercise 8C

1	check angles: **a** 20°	**b** 40°	**c** 60°	**d** 80°
2	check angles: **a** 110°	**b** 130°	**c** 150°	**d** 170°
3	check angles: **a** 25°	**b** 45°	**c** 65°	**d** 85°
4	check angles: **a** 95°	**b** 125°	**c** 135°	**d** 185°
5	check angles: **a** 30°	**b** 75°	**c** 140°	

6 check pupils' diagrams
7 check clock face

Challenge: Drawing triangles

Check that the angles and pupils' drawings are accurate.

Lesson 9.4 Calculating angles

Learning objectives
- To calculate angles round a point
- To calculate angles on a line
- To calculate opposite angles

Links to other subjects
- **Geography** – to use bearings on a map
- **Design and technology** – to produce accurate design drawings

Resources and homework
- Pupil Book 1.1, pages 185–189
- Intervention Workbook 3, pages 54–56
- Homework Book 1, section 9.2
- Online homework 9.4, questions 1–10

Key words
- angles on a straight line
- angles round a point
- calculate
- opposite angles

Problem solving and reasoning help
- Encourage complete explanations that state clearly what facts are being used. Encourage accurate use of mathematical language.

Common misconceptions and remediation
- Pupils learn rules without really understanding where they come from. Use lots of visual images to support relational understanding.

Probing questions
- Can you show how to use the fact that the sum of the angles on a straight line is 180° to explain why the angles at a point are 360°?

Part 1 – including literacy activity
- Write down everything you are sure you know about angles, along with the things you think you know.
- Share with pupils what they have written. What is different about the things they know and the things they thought they know? Start a discussion about the idea of mathematical proof.

Part 2
- Explain that it is not always necessary to measure angles on diagrams.
- Angles can be calculated on diagrams by using given geometrical information. Angles whose values are not given are denoted by the letters a, b, c .... These are called *unknown angles*.
- Draw the following diagrams on the board and explain how to calculate the sizes of unknown angles by giving various examples.
  Sum of the angles around a point a + b + c = 360°
- Draw the following diagrams on the board and explain how to calculate the sizes of unknown angles by giving various examples.

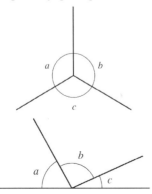

Sum of the angles around a point a + b + c = 360°

Sum of the angles on a straight line a + b + c = 180°

Practical work for pupils

You will need: coloured, gummed squares.

1   Draw a triangle on a gummed square and clearly mark each angle with a letter.
2   Cut out the triangle and tear off the three angles.
3   Stick each angle on a piece of paper so that the three angles are around a common point.
4   Ask the class to write down what this shows.

   Sum of the interior angles of a triangle   *a + b + c = 180°*

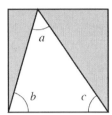 

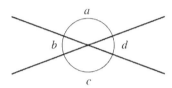   *Vertically-opposite angles*   *a = d and b = c*

- Vertically opposite angles are also called *opposite angles*.
  Notice that the adjacent angles add up to 180°: *a + b = 180°*
- **Pupils can now do Exercise 9D from Pupil Book 1.1.**

Part 3

- Ask some pupils to explain the meaning of: angles around a point, angles on a line, angles in a triangle and vertically opposite angles.
- Ask other pupils to make up an example to illustrate each of the above.

Answers

Exercise 9D

1   **a** 30°   **b** 50°   **c** 25°   **d** 45°
2   **a** 50°   **b** 125°   **c** 130°   **d** 65°   **e** 80°   **f** 40°
3   50°, 60° and 70° **(b, c and d)**
4   **a** 130°   **b** 160°   **c** 80°   **d** 225°   **e** 100°   **f** 150°
5   **a** 50°   **b** 140°   **c** 25°   **d** *d* = 65°, *e* = 115°
6   **a** 65°   **b** 68°   **c** 50°   **d** 72°   **e** 68°   **f** 54°
7   **a** 70°   **b** 162°   **c** 147°   **d** 53°   **e** 23°   **f** 73°
8   **a** *a* = 120°, *b* = 60°, *c* = 120°
    b *d* = 50°, *e* = 130°, *f* = 50°
    c *g* = 122°, *h* = 58°, *i* = 122°

Reasoning: Calculating angles

A   45°
B   90°
C   120°
D   20°
E   50°
F   130°

Lesson 9.5 Properties of triangles and quadrilaterals

Learning objectives

- To understand the properties of parallel, intersecting and perpendicular lines
- To understand and use the properties of triangles
- To understand and use the properties of quadrilaterals

Resources and homework

- Pupil Book 1.1, pages 190–195
- Homework Book 1, section 9.5
- Online homework 9.5, questions 1–10

Links to other subjects

- **Art** – to produce tessellated patterns that include triangles and quadrilaterals

Key words

- diagonal
- intersect
- perpendicular
- vertices
- geometrical properties
- parallel
- vertex

Problem solving and reasoning help

- Remember that pupils will often get confused between the names of different quadrilaterals. Use lots of visual images to support pupils' learning. This you tube video may also help: **http://www.youtube.com/watch?v=JP8kdf2Tn2A**.

Common misconceptions and remediation

- Pupils often learn rules without really understanding where they originate. Use lots of visual images to support relational understanding.

Probing questions

- Explain why a triangle cannot have two parallel sides.
- An isosceles triangle has one angle of 30°. Is this enough information to know the other two angles? Why?
- Sketch a shape to help convince me that a trapezium: might not be a parallelogram; or might not have a line of symmetry.

Part 1

- Is it possible to draw a triangle with:
    - one acute angle?
    - two acute angles?
    - one obtuse angle?
    - two obtuse angles?
- Give an example of the angles if it is possible.

Literacy activity

- Take feedback from Part 1, encouraging pupils to explain their answers.
- Use stems such as '*I agree or disagree with … because …*'.
- Did you know that *isosceles* comes from 'isos', 'equal' and 'skelos', a leg?

Part 2

- Ask the class to name all the different types of triangles that they know.

- Draw the following triangles on the board: scalene triangle, obtuse-angled triangle, right-angled triangle, isosceles triangle and equilateral triangle.
- Ask pupils to copy them and write the name underneath each triangle.
- Invite the class to describe the differences between the triangles.
- Next, ask the class to name all the different types of quadrilaterals they know.
- Draw the following quadrilaterals on the board or OHP: square, rectangle, parallelogram, rhombus, trapezium, kite. Ask pupils to copy them and write their names underneath them.
- Invite the class to describe the differences between these quadrilaterals.
- Ask the class to give examples of where they would see these shapes in real life. For example, triangles in structures such as bridges, rhombuses as diamonds in a pack of cards, arrowheads in company logos.
- **Pupils can now do Exercise 9E from Pupil Book 1.1.**

Part 3

- Draw examples of triangles and quadrilaterals on the board. Question pupils to explore their understanding of correct notation and angle facts of triangles and quadrilaterals. Examples:
  - o   What information is given in each diagram (angles, parallel or equal lines, etc.)?
  - o   Is there anything you do not know about the shape (such as is it an isosceles triangle)?
  - o   If so, what extra information or notation would answer any questions you might have?
- Do this as a class activity or ask pupils to do this in small groups or pairs.
- Take feedback, drawing out any remaining questions.

Answers

Exercise 9E

1 a

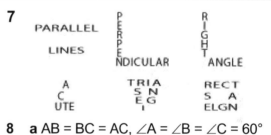

  b square, parallelogram, rectangle, kite, trapezium, rhombus

  c square, kite, rhombus

2 **b** and **d**

3 **b** and **c**

4 **a** and **c**

5 **b** and **d**

6 **a** rectangle   **b** isosceles triangle

  c right-angled triangle   **d** parallelogram

  e kite   **f** trapezium

7

PARALLEL LINES

PERPENDICULAR

RIGHT ANGLE

ACUTE

TRIANGLES

RECTANGLES

8 **a** AB = BC = AC, ∠A = ∠B = ∠C = 60°

  b AB = BC = CD = AD, ∠A = ∠B = ∠C = ∠D = 90°, AB is parallel to CD, AD is parallel to BC

  c AB = BC = CD = AD, AD is parallel to BC, AB is parallel to CD, ∠A = ∠C and ∠B = ∠D

9 **a** square, rectangle, parallelogram, isosceles triangle

  b 2 different trapeziums

  c square, parallelogram, isosceles triangle

Reasoning: Making triangles

A six different triangles

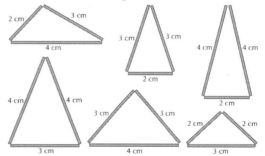

Review questions (Pupil Book pages 196–197)

- The review questions will help to determine pupils' abilities with regard to the material within Chapter 9.
- These questions also draw on the maths covered in earlier chapters of the book to encourage pupils to make links between different topics.

Investigation – Snooker tables (Pupil Book pages 198–199)

- This activity is designed to encourage pupils to think about how angles can affect a possibly familiar real-life situation – the way one plays the game of snooker.
- Before pupils start this activity, review the terminology used in this chapter such as the angle-naming rules. It is important that pupils understand and can use the mathematical language and symbolism used in the question.
- You could also reinforce the methods learned when drawing and measuring angles.
- Encourage pupils to read through the example on their own to remind them of the process and to check any outstanding questions they may have.
- You may want to ask pupils some warm-up questions, depending on the group. Here are some examples:
  1. What do they know about triangles?
  2. How any millimetres are there in a centimetre?
  3. How would you give 3.6 centimetres to the nearest centimetre?
- When you think that pupils feel confident in their understanding of Examples 1 and 2, they can work in pairs or groups to complete the table on page 199 of the Pupil Book.
- Go through the answers with pupils as a class. Use the opportunity to answer further questions and explain things that **less able** pupils may not have grasped.
- As a follow-up activity ask pupils to research 'snooker moves'. They may find it interesting to see how much mathematical calculation snooker players need to do to play a good game.

Answers to Review questions

1 **a** 3 squares north, then 2 squares east **b** 3 squares east, then 1 square south

2 **a** acute **b** acute **c** is acute **d** obtuse

3 For example:

a 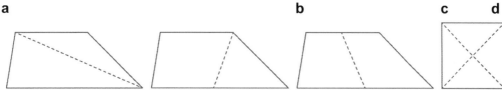 **b** **c** **d**

4 **a** 20° **b** 45° **c** 150° **d** 105°

5 check angles: **a** 50° **b** 65° **c** 100° **d** 145°

6 **a** 40° (angles add up to 90°)
  b 115° (angles on a line add up to 180°)
  c 145° (angles round a point add up to 360°)
  d 60° (opposite angles are equal)

7 The two short sticks would not meet.

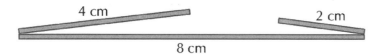

8 A = B = C = D = 80°, AB is parallel to AC, BC is perpendicular to BD

Answers to Investigation – Snooker tables

Example	Size of table	Final corner	No. of bounces
3	2 by 2	C	0
4	2 by 3	D	3
5	2 by 4	B	1
6	2 by 5	D	5
7	2 by 6	C	2
8	3 by 2	B	3
9	3 by 3	C	0
10	4 by 2	D	1

For example:
For square tables, the ball ends up in corner C after 0 bounces.
Balls never end up in corner

10 Coordinates and graphs

Learning objectives

- How to use coordinates
- How to draw graphs from functions and input/output diagrams
- How to recognise lines of the form $x = a$, $y = b$
- How to recognise the line $y = x$
- How to interpret and draw graphs that show real-life problems

Prior knowledge

- How to read a simple map

Context

- The use of graphs to represent data is probably one of the most common uses of mathematics in the modern world. Pupils may be surrounded to such an extent by visual representations of data in the media, and become so used to it, that they no longer notice it. The following website provides some interesting insights into the use of data in a modern society: **http://www.gapminder.org/**.

Discussion points

- What are the important conventions when describing a point using coordinates?
- I am thinking of a point that I want you to plot. I can only answer 'yes and 'no'. Ask me some questions so that you can plot the point.

Associated Collins ICT resources

- Chapter 10 interactive activities on Collins Connect online platform
- *Lines of the form $x + y = a$* Worked solution on Collins Connect online platform

Curriculum references

Algebra

- Recognise, sketch and produce graphs of linear functions of one variable with appropriate scaling, using equations in x and y
- Interpret mathematical relationships both algebraically and graphically

Develop fluency

- Consolidate their numerical and mathematical capability from Key Stage 2
- Develop algebraic and graphical fluency

Reason mathematically

- Identify variables and express relations between variables algebraically and graphically

Solve problems

- Begin to model situations mathematically and express the results using a range of formal mathematical representations

Fast-track for classes following a 2-year scheme of work

- If your class is confident at working with coordinates, they could move straight on to questions 7 and 8 and the investigation at the end of Exercise 10A in the Pupil Book, which is intended to be used as consolidating work from KS2.

Lesson 10.1 Coordinates

Learning objective
- To understand and use coordinates to locate points

Resources and homework
- Pupil Book 1.1, pages 201–203
- Intervention Workbook 2, pages 31–35
- Intervention Workbook 3, pages 37–39
- Homework Book 1, section 10.1
- Online homework 10.1, questions 1–10

Links to other subjects
- **Geography** – to read maps
- **Science** – to be able to plot graphs to display outcomes of experiments

Key words
- axes
- origin
- *x*-axis
- *y*-axis
- coordinate
- *quadrant*
- *x*-coordinate
- *y*-coordinate

Problem solving and reasoning help
- Pupils will need to apply their knowledge to answer **MR** questions 7 and 8 in Exercise 10A of the Pupil Book. The investigation checks their understanding of all four quadrants.

Common misconceptions and remediation
- Pupils tend to forget the conventions for reading coordinates. Help pupils to reinforce these by explaining the need to have a shared language to ensure effective communication. Real-life examples such as maps may be useful to reinforce this.

Probing questions
- How do you use the scale on the axes to help you to read the coordinates of a point that has been plotted?
- If these three points are vertices of a rectangle, how will you find the coordinates of the fourth vertex?

Part 1
- This starter reinforces pupils understanding of negative numbers, which they will need when working in all four quadrants.
- Draw the number line as shown on the board, and ask some pupils to come up and fill in the missing numbers.

  $-5 \qquad 0 \qquad 5$

- Now draw this number line on the board and ask some pupils to complete it.

  $-10 \qquad 0 \qquad 10$

- Repeat the activity using different scales on the number line.

Literacy activity
- To help pupils remember the rules for coordinates, give them the opportunity to physically enact these rules (outside if possible) by using coordinates to move around a real-life grid.

Part 2

- Explain that *coordinates* are used to locate a point on a grid. On the board, or on an OHT, draw the grid shown on the right.
- Explain the meaning of axes, the *x*-axis, the *y*-axis and the origin.
- A coordinate is written in the form (*x, y*).
- The first number is the *x*-coordinate, which is the number of units across the grid.
- The second number is the *y*-coordinate, which is the number of units up the grid. Point A has coordinates (4, 3) and can be written as A(4, 3).
- Plot other points on the grid and ask the class to write down their coordinates.
- Explain that the grid can be extended to use negative numbers. On the board or on an OHT, draw the grid shown below.
- Explain that the grid is divided into four quadrants. Ask the class to copy the grid and plot the points A, B, C and D.
- Explain how to write down the coordinates of the four points:
- A(4, 2), B(–4, 2), C (–4, –2) and D(4, –2).
- Plot other points on the grid and ask the class to write down their coordinates.
- **Pupils can now do Exercise 10A from Pupil Book 1.1.**

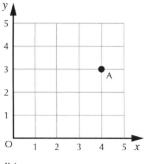

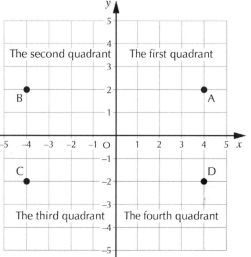

Part 3

- Have a prepared, large grid with axes from –10 to 10 and several points plotted on it.
- Ask the class to write down the coordinates of the points as you point to them.
- Link to the next lesson by explaining that the next stage is to find, using algebra, relationships for coordinates that follow a pattern.

Answers

Exercise 10A

1 A(1, 4), B(3, 2), C(4, 4), D(5, 2), E(0, 2), F(3, 0)
2 **c** (5, 1)
3 **a** A(2, 1), B(2, 5), C(6, 5), D(6, 1)   **b** (2, 3)   **c** (4, 1)   **d** (4, 3)
4 **a i** (5, 7), (3, 2), (7, 6), (2, 1)   **ii** (3, 6), (3, 2), (1, 5), (3, 4), (2, 7)
   iii (3, 6), (5, 5), (1, 3), (8, 1), (8, 4), (2, 1)
   iv (3, 4), (5, 5), (8, 4), (8, 1), (3, 8), (3, 2), (7, 3)
   b SEE YOU AT BREAK
5 A(2, 3), B(4, 4), C(6, 2), D(3, 0), E(1, 2), F(2, 5), G(5, 6), H(0, 0), I(0, 5), J(4, $1\frac{1}{2}$)
6 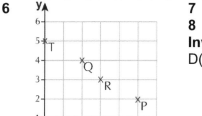   7 **a** A(1, 4) B(4, 5), C(5, 2)   **b** (2, 1)
   8 **a** L(1, 3), M(2, 1), N(5, 3)   **b** (4, 5) or (6, 1)
   Investigation: More space
   D(1, –5), E(3, 4), F(5, 2), G(–3, 2), H(–2, –4), I(–4, 0), J(0, –2)

Learning objective

- To work out coordinates from a rule
- To draw a graph for a simple rule

Resources and homework

- Pupil Book 1.1, pages 203–206
- Homework Book 1, section 10.2
- Online homework 10.2–3, questions 1–10

Links to other subjects

- **Science** – to identify relationships in experimental data

Key words

- graph
- rule

Problem solving and reasoning help

- The **MR** question 7 and the challenge after Exercise 10B in the Pupil Book begin to move pupils towards the work in the next chapter. Pupils can do the work independently or as part of a whole class discussion; or supported by guided group work.

Common misconceptions and remediation

- Pupils often struggle to decide on an appropriate scale for a graph, for example, labelled divisions representing 2, 5, 10 and 100. Give pupils lots of practice with different scales and encourage them to identify the criteria they need to use. Provide opportunities for pupils to see graphs that are used in a range of real-life situations.

Probing questions

- For a given graph, make up three questions that can be answered using the information represented.
- What makes the information easy or difficult to represent?
- Can you describe the rule used to produce this graph?

Part 1

- Ask the class: '*What is a complement? Start with 10 as an example.*'
- When 10 is the focus number, the complement of 3 is 7, of 8 is 2, ….
- Ask for a few more. Repeat with 20.
- Then focus on 50. Tell the pupils that this is useful for change from 50p.
- Go through some complements around 50 – say, 17, 28, …. Invite the class to discuss the strategy they used to get the complements. Then the class can blitz more complements around the number 50. Finish with complements around 100.

Literacy activity

- Give pupils plenty of opportunity to talk about the rules they are finding and how they know that these rules are correct.

Part 2

- Remind pupils about functions. Ask someone to give an example of a function. Go through input and output by means of one of the given examples, say: +3

- Input   Output
  - 3
  - 4
  - 5
  - 6
  - 7
- Put each input and output together to give ordered pairs: (0, 3), (1, 4), (2, 5), (3, 6), (4, 7)
- Reminding the class of coordinates, ask: '*Have you seen anything like this before? Let us treat these ordered pairs as coordinates and plot them on a graph. What else do we need?*'
- Ask pupils to discuss what they need to draw the graph. (A pair of axes)
- Label the horizontal axis *input* and the vertical axis *output*, but if a pupil suggests using *x* and *y* then add these axis labels, asking: '*Which is which?*'
- Say: '*What numbers do we need on the axes? The input must go from 0 to 4; the output must go from 1 to 7.*'
- Then say: '*Let us draw x from 0 to 5 (explain why) and draw the output from 0 to 8 (again, explain why).*'
- Remind the class about equal spacing between the numbers on the axes.
- Also remind pupils to label the calibration marks and not the spaces in between. These are both crucially important.
- Then plot the points. Remind the class that each point should be marked by a cross
- Ask: '*What do you notice?*' … '*A straight line of points.*' Draw in the straight line.
- **Pupils can now do Exercise 10B from Pupil Book 1.1.**

Part 3

- Ask the class what they have noticed about every graph they have drawn.
- Draw from pupils that the graphs were all (or should have been) straight lines.
- Discuss whether the graphs would continue as straight lines forever.
- Tell the class that in the next lesson they will learn how to name these graphs.

Answers

Exercise 10B

1

(1, 1), (2, 2), (3, 3), (4, 4), (5, 5), (6, 6)

3 One less than the number on the red dice

4 a

	Coordinates
0 → 2	(0, 2)
1 → 3	(1, 3)
2 → 4	(2, 4)
3 → 5	(3, 5)
4 → 6	(4, 6)
5 → 7	(5, 7)

b (2, 4), (3, 6), (4, 8), (5, 10)
c (4, 2), (6, 3), (8, 4), (10, 5) **d** (3, 7), (4, 8), (5, 9), (6, 10)

5 a (2, 2), (3, 3), (4, 4), (5, 5)
6 a iii subtract 4   **b iii** add 5
7 a (2, 5), (3, 6), (4, 7), (5, 8)
  b (2, 6), (3, 9), (4, 12), (5, 15)
  c (6, 2), (9, 3), (2, 4), (15, 5)
  d (5, 2), (6, 3), (7, 4), (8, 5)

Challenge: It all adds up

A **a** Any 5 from (0, 6), (1, 5), (2, 4), (3, 3), (4, 2), (5, 1), (6, 0)
   b Any 5 from (0, 8), (1, 7), (2, 6), (3, 5), (4, 4), (5, 3), (6, 2), (7, 1), (8, 0)
   c Any 5 from (0, 5), (1, 4), (2, 3), (3, 2), (4, 1), (5, 0)

C

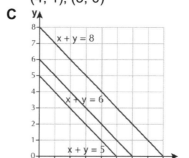

The lines are parallel.

Learning objective
- To recognise and draw line graphs of fixed values

Resources and homework
- Pupil Book 1.1, pages 206–209
- Homework Book 1, section 10.3
- Online homework 10.2–3, questions 1–10

Links to other subjects
- **Science** – to identify relationships in experimental data
- **History** – to identify trends in historical data

Key words
- No new key words for this topic

Problem solving and reasoning help
- The **MR** question 6 of Exercise 10C in the Pupil Book encourages pupils to apply what they have learned. The challenge links it to other areas of mathematics – area of a rectangle.

Common misconceptions and remediation
- Pupils often struggle with graphs of the form $x = c$ or $y = c$. Provide lots of opportunity for practice and link to other areas of mathematics such as symmetry, and to real-life situations.

Probing questions
- For a given graph, write three stories that could describe the information represented.

Part 1
- Put on the board 'cm, mm, km, m'. Ask the class what these abbreviations stand for. Discuss the relationship of one unit with another. Then ask for estimates of measurements, using the appropriate units. For example:
    - distance from school to London (km)
    - teacher's height (cm)
    - thickness of a pound coin (mm)
    - length of the room (m).
- Draw a line on the board (about 80 cm) and ask pupils its length. Write down suggestions. Discuss which ones look the most sensible, and why. Ask a pupil to measure it.
- Repeat for a shorter line of about 30 cm. Then repeat for a longer line of about 120 cm.
- Round this off with heights. '*What is the height of the shortest of us? What is the height of the tallest of us?*' Then measure these pupils.

Literacy activity
- Give pupils plenty of opportunity to talk about the rules they are finding and how they know that these rules are correct.

Part 2
- Remind the class that in the last lesson they learned about naming graphs from mappings. Ask what was special about each graph. (They were all straight lines.)
- Write the mapping below on the board:

    $1 \rightarrow 4$
    $2 \rightarrow 4$
    $3 \rightarrow 4$
    $4 \rightarrow 4$

- Introduce the idea of (x, y) as a general coordinate.
- The input number is called the x-coordinate.
- The output number is called the y-coordinate. What does y equal?
  - y is always 4, so we call the relationship $y = 4$. Let us draw the graph.
- Show the class how to go from the coordinates to the graph.
- Label the graph.

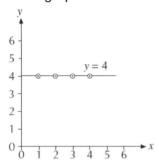

- Ask where the graph of $y = 3$ would be, drawn on the same axes.
- Discuss with the class the graph of $x = 2$. Let them see how this gives a vertical line from 2 on the x-axis.
- **Pupils can now do Exercise 10C from Pupil Book 1.1.**

Part 3

- On the board, write or put the labelled graph of the relationship: $y = 3$
- Choose any integer coordinate and ask what it is, and what it represents.
- Discuss with the class the fact that any point shows the y-value to be 3.
- Select a point, say (2.5, 3), and ask the same question.
- Discuss with the class the fact that *each* and *every* point on that line represents a point where the y-value is 3.

Answers

Exercise 10C
1 Any 6 from (0,4), (1,4), (2,4), (3,4), (4,4), (5,4), (6,4)
2 **a** Any 5 from (0,1), (1,1), (2,1), (3,1), (4,1), (5,1), (6,1)
   b Any 5 from (3,0), (3,1), (3,2), (3,3), (3,4), (3,5), (3,6)
   c (3,1)
3 **a** $y = 6$ **b** $x = 6$ **c** $y = 3$ **d** $y = 5$ **e** $y = 4$ **f** $x = 5$ **g** $x = 1$ **h** $y = 0$

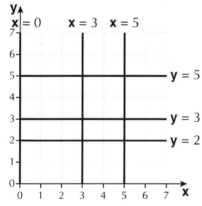

Challenge: Rectangles on grids
a 12 square units
b 15 square units
c 21 square units
d 20 square units
e 2 square units

Lesson 10.4 Graphs from the real world

Learning objectives
- To learn how graphs can be used to represent real-life situations
- To draw and use real-life graphs

Resources and homework
- Pupil Book 1.1, pages 209–211
- Intervention Workbook 2, pages 76–79
- Intervention Workbook 3, pages 73–77
- Homework Book 1, section 10.6
- Online homework 10.4, questions 1–10

Links to other subjects
- **Science** – to record experimental results
- **Geography** – to record environmental data

Key word
- conversion graph

Problem solving and reasoning help
- There are a number of **FS** questions in this chapter. These will help pupils to understand the meanings of graphs in familiar but slightly more complex real-life situations.

Common misconceptions and remediation
- Pupils are often confused by the complexity of the data in real life. Give them the opportunity to explore data in real-life situations, for example, in the media. Explain how it is often necessary to make assumptions and simplify data in order to be able to explore questions behind the data.

Probing questions
- For a given graph, ask pupils to write three stories that could describe the information represented.

Part 1
- Draw a couple of straight line graphs on the board.
- Read out a suitable story for one graph, and ask pupils which graph the story fits and why.
- Ask **more able** pupils to write their own story.

Literacy activity
- Graphs are used widely in real life. Give pupils the opportunity to discuss graphs used in forms of media they are used to.

Part 2
- Use the graph on page 209 of the Pupil Book, together with the table of values.
- Show how the ordered pairs can be used as coordinates to plot points, giving a straight line.
- This is a *conversion graph*, used to convert from litres of petrol to cost. Illustrate how to use the graph to find the cost of a specific amount of petrol.
- Explain that a straight-line graph represents a linear relationship.
- **Pupils can now do Exercise 10D from Pupil Book 1.1.**

Part 3

- Ask the class if they remember the name of the type of relationship that gives straight-line graphs. (This is called a linear relationship.)
- Ask pupils if they can think of other examples of situations in real life that might lead to straight-line graphs.
- Encourage discussion about why this is, making links to proportional reasoning.
- Ask **more able** pupils to sketch graphs of their examples. This could lead to discussions about intercepts and gradients.

Answers

Exercise 10D

1 2, 50, 12
2 **a** 79 million   **b** 2008   **c** 80 million
3 **a i** 11 pounds **ii** 17.5 pounds   **iii** 44 pounds   **b i** 6.8 kg   **ii** 9 kg   **iii** 36 kg
4 **a** 36 miles   **b** 12 miles **c** 2 h 30 min
5 **a** graph from (0, 0) to (34, 60)   **b i** 18 pints   **ii** 44 pints   **iii** 53 pints
       c i 6 litres   **ii** 14 litres **iii** 23 litres   **d** 2.3 litres   **e** 3.5 pints

Challenge: Taxi!

A **a** Does not start at the origin
       b £6.50
B **a**   **b** 3 kilometres

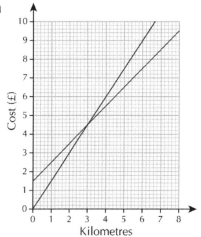

Review questions
(Pupil Book pages 212–213)

- The review questions will help to determine pupils' abilities with regard to the material within Chapter 10.
- These questions also draw on the maths covered in earlier chapters of the book to encourage pupils to make links between different topics.

Challenge – Global warming
(Pupil Book pages 214–215)

- This activity is designed to apply pupils learning in a real life topical situation.
- All the information required to answer the questions is given but pupils will need to think carefully about how they apply what they have learnt.
- Ask pupils further questions as a warm-up to start working on the questions in the Pupil Book. Here are some examples:
    - What do they know about global warming? You could have some web links ready to share with pupils.
    - What does it mean to estimate an answer? How do they decide how to round the numbers in their estimation?
- Pupils can now work on the questions individually or in groups. Use grouping to support or challenge pupils.
- Towards the end of the activity pupils are asked to extrapolate from the information given them. Pupils may find this challenging. You could approach this part of the activity as part as a class discussion or as part of guided group work.
- You could ask pupils to develop this topic further by using the internet to research other topics connected to global warming.

Answers to Review questions

1 **a** (1, 4), (5, 4), (5, 2), (1, 2)   **b** (3, 4)   **c** (1, 3)   **d** (3, 3)
2 **a** 0°C   **b** 9°C   **c** 11:45
3 **a** (1, 3), (2, 2), (3, 1)
   b

4 **a** (4½, 5) **b** (2, 3)
5 **a** Any 5 from (0, 5), (1, 5), (2, 5), (3, 5), (4, 5), (5, 5), (6, 5)
   b Any 5 from (4, 0), (4, 1), (4, 2), (4, 3), (4, 4), (4, 5), (4, 6)   **c** (4, 5)
6 **a** $x = 1$→Line through A and B; $x = 4$→Line through C and D;
   $y = 2$→Line through A and E; $y = x$→Line through E and D;
   $y = 5$→Line through B and C
   b 7 square units
7 **a** $x = 3$ **b** $y = 3$ **c** $x = 5$ **d** $y = 4$ **e** $x = 4$ **f** $x = 0$ **g** $x = 1$ **h** $y = 2$ **i** $y = x$

Answers to Challenge – Global warming

1 **a** 288 ppm   **b** 294 ppm   **c** 302 ppm   **d** 322 ppm
2 **a** 6 ppm   **b** 8 ppm
3 **a** 20 ppm   **b** 33 ppm
4 **a** For example, the level is increasing more quickly
   b For example, more cars on the roads, more flights being taken
5 Accept answers in the range 390-410 ppm
6 Around 2053

11 Percentages

Learning objectives

- How to interpret percentages as fractions
- How to work out a fraction or a percentage of a quantity
- How to write percentages as decimals
- How to work out a percentage of a quantity with or without a calculator
- How to work out the result of a simple percentage increase or decrease

Prior knowledge

- What the % sign means
- How to write fractions
- How to write decimals with up to two decimal places
- About units such as centimetres, metres, grams, kilometres and litres
- By the end of KS2, pupils will have solved problems involving the calculation of percentages such as 15% of 360 and the use of percentages for comparison.

Context

- Percentages are everywhere in real life – from bargains in the shops to taxes on payslips. In order to function in a modern society, it is important for pupils to be comfortable with calculating percentages. Encourage learners to role-play scenarios that involve percentages. They could write their own or perform scenarios from films, television or the internet

Discussion points

- What fractions/percentages can you work out easily in your head? Talk me through a couple of examples.

Associated Collins ICT resources

- Chapter 11 interactive activities on Collins Connect online platform
- *Finding fractions and percentages of quantities* video on Collins Connect online platform
- *Measures* Wonder of Maths on Collins Connect online platform
- *Very simple examples of percentages* Worked solution on Collins Connect online platform

Curriculum references

Number

- Define percentage as 'number of parts per hundred', interpret percentages and percentage changes as a fraction or a decimal, interpret these multiplicatively, express one quantity as a percentage of another, compare two quantities using percentages, and work with percentages greater than 100%
- Interpret fractions and percentages as operators
- Use a calculator and other technologies to calculate results accurately and then interpret them appropriately

Develop fluency

- Select and use appropriate calculation strategies to solve increasingly complex problems

Reason mathematically

- Extend and formalise their knowledge of ratio and proportion in working with measures and geometry, and in formulating proportional relations algebraically

Solve problems

- Develop their mathematical knowledge, in part through solving problems and evaluating the outcomes, including multi-step problems
- Develop their use of formal mathematical knowledge to interpret and solve problems, including in financial mathematics

Fast-track for classes following a 2-year scheme of work

- Work through some of the examples in the first three lessons as a class. Then work on the investigations or challenge questions at the end of each exercise, either as a class or pupils could work independently.
- Then move straight on to Lesson 11.4.

Lesson 11.1 Fractions and percentages

Learning objectives

- To understand what a percentage is
- To know the equivalence between some simple fractions and percentages

Resources and homework

- Pupil Book 1.1, pages 217–220
- Intervention Workbook 2, pages 40–42
- Intervention Workbook 3, pages 13–14
- Homework Book 1, section 11.1
- Online homework 11.1, questions 1–10

Links to other subjects

- **Business and economics** – to acquire fluency in this area

Key words

- decimal
- per cent (%)
- sector
- fraction
- percentage

Problem solving and reasoning help

- The investigation at the end of Exercise 11A of the Pupil Book reinforces the links between fractions and percentages.

Common misconceptions and remediation

- Lack of understanding as to what a fraction actually is:
  - Pupils view a percentage as a number rather than part of an amount.
  - Pupils have not made the link with fractions and so struggle to find 50% ($\frac{1}{2}$), 25% ($\frac{1}{4}$), 75% ($\frac{3}{4}$), 40% ($\frac{4}{10}$), and so on.

Probing questions

- Which sets of equivalent fractions, percentages do you know?
- From one set that you know (for example, $\frac{1}{2}$ = 50%) which others can you work out?
- How would you go about finding the decimal and percentage equivalents of any fraction?

Part 1

- Place a set of matching diagrams, % and percentages on the board, like the one below.

$\frac{1}{2}$ 50%   25%

- Include an odd one out. Pupils should identify the odd one out.

Part 2

- Introduce the 100-square grid.
- Colour in different amounts of the grid and discuss what fraction is coloured in? Here: $\frac{1}{4}$

- Remind or introduce pupils to the idea of percentages as number of parts per 100. Ask them how many small squares are coloured in (25). So $\frac{1}{4}$ is the same as 25%.
- Work through some other examples as appropriate.
- **The class can now do Exercise 11a from Pupil Book 3.** This exercise is non-calculator.

Part 3

- Have a set of 'Follow me' cards (for example see Worksheet – *Percentages* on Collins Connect online platform) that use equivalent fractions and percentages. Record the time that is taken to complete the activity. Pupils who finish quickly could challenge themselves to complete it faster and/ or to complete it faster.
- Pupils could use a 100-square grid to help them if necessary.
- Later, revisit the activity as an oral and mental starter to see if the time can be beaten.

Answers

Exercise 11A

1 **a** 30%　**b** 16%　**c** 55%

2 **a** 28%　**b** 28%　**c** 8%　　**d** 36%

3 **a** 50%　**b** $\frac{1}{2}$

4 **a** 25%　**b** 75%　**c** $\frac{1}{4}$　**d** $\frac{3}{4}$

5 $\frac{1}{4}, \frac{1}{2}, \frac{3}{4}$

6 **a** 10　**b** 10%　**c** $\frac{1}{10}$　**d** 20　**e** 20%　**f** $\frac{1}{5}$

7 The missing fractions are $\frac{3}{10}, \frac{2}{5}, \frac{1}{2}, \frac{3}{5}, \frac{7}{10}$

8 **a** $\frac{2}{5}$　**b** 40%　**c** $\frac{3}{5}$　**d** 60%

9 **a** 10%　**b** 20%　**c** 30%　**d** 40%　**e** 90%　**f** 70%　**g** 50%

10 **a** 4 red squares and 10 blue squares　　**b** 30%

11 yellow 60%, green 40%

12 **a** 30%　　**b** 2 out of 20 = $\frac{1}{10}$ = 10%

Challenge: Eighths as percentages

A　12.5%

B　37.5%

C　62.5% and 87.5%

D　own diagram

Lesson 11.2 Fractions of a quantity

Learning objectives
- To find a fraction of a quantity

Resources and homework
- Pupil Book 1.1, pages 220–222
- Intervention Workbook 1, pages 26–28
- Intervention Workbook 2, pages 40–42
- Intervention Workbook 3, pages 16–17
- Homework Book 1, section 11.2
- Online homework 11.2, questions 1–10

Links to other subjects
- **Food technology** – to use fractions of a quantity in recipes
- **Geography** – to compare heights and distances

Key word
- quantity

Problem solving and reasoning help
- The challenge at the end of Exercise 11B gives pupils an opportunity to apply their understanding to a familiar real-life situation. The situation is one that pupils fail to understand effectively, yet it is a common application in exam questions in KS4.

Common misconceptions and remediation
- Rather than simply learning a rule to calculate fractions of a quantity, pupils need to understand what they are doing and why. Make links to the visual images pupils have met at primary school to clarify this and provide real-life examples so that they realise why it is important to be able to calculate fractions of a quantity. It is essential that pupils have this knowledge of fractions before they can use fractions in a range of different contexts.

Probing questions
- What fractions of given quantities can you work out easily in your head? Talk me through a couple of examples.

Part 1
- Copy the fractions below on the board, leaving gaps for pupils to complete. Differentiate the task based on what and how much is removed.
- Encourage pupils to spot any patterns and explain them.

$$1 \times \frac{1}{4} = \frac{1}{4} \qquad \frac{1}{4} \text{ of } 1 = \frac{1}{4} \qquad 2 \times \frac{1}{4} = \frac{2}{4} = \frac{1}{2} \qquad \frac{1}{4} \text{ of } 2 = \frac{2}{4} = \frac{1}{2}$$

$$3 \times \frac{1}{4} = \frac{3}{4} \qquad \frac{1}{4} \text{ of } 3 = \frac{3}{4} \qquad 4 \times \frac{1}{4} = \frac{4}{4} = 1 \qquad \frac{1}{4} \text{ of } 4 = 1$$

$$5 \times \frac{1}{4} = \frac{5}{4} = 1\frac{1}{4} \qquad \frac{1}{4} \text{ of } 5 = \frac{5}{4} \qquad 6 \times \frac{1}{4} = \frac{6}{4} = 1\frac{2}{4} = 1\frac{1}{2} \qquad \frac{1}{4} \text{ of } 6 = \frac{6}{4} = 1\frac{2}{4} = 1\frac{1}{2}$$

$$7 \times \frac{1}{4} = \frac{7}{4} = 1\frac{3}{4} \qquad \frac{1}{4} \text{ of } 7 = \frac{7}{4} = 1\frac{3}{4} \qquad 8 \times \frac{1}{4} = \frac{8}{4} = 2 \qquad \frac{1}{4} \text{ of } 8 = \frac{8}{4} = 2$$

Literacy activity
- Provide opportunities for pupils to compare written forms of fractions with visual images.

Part 2

- Pupils will have met calculating fractions of a quantity at KS2, so use this opportunity to draw on this prior knowledge.

- Ask pupils for the answer to $\frac{1}{4}$ of £80. They should come up with £20.

- Ask pupils to outline the method clearly. That is, divide 80 by 4.

- What about $\frac{3}{4}$ of £80? Find $\frac{1}{4}$, then multiply by 3 to give £60.

- Try other examples if necessary.
- **Pupils can now do Exercise 11B from Pupil Book 1.1.**

Part 3

- Review the methods of calculating fractions of quantities and of multiplying fractions by an integer.

- Do examples such as $\frac{3}{7}$ of 63 (= 27), $\frac{3}{5}$ of 75 (= 45), $\frac{7}{10}$ of 120 (= 84). Ensure that pupils explain their methods clearly.

Answers

Exercise 11B
1 a 5 people b 10 people   c £6   d £12
2 a 5 kg   b 15 kg   c 20 m   d 60 m
3 a £2   b £8   c 12 people   d 40 cm   e 25 litres
4 a 4 people b £9   c 10 hours   d 27 km   e 20p
5 a £6   b £12 c £18   d £24
6 a 7 km   b 21 km   c 49 km d 63 km
7 a 9p   b 25 g   c 50 seconds   d 8 months
8 8 cm
9 80

10 a 26   b $\frac{3}{5}$ c 39

11 a 13 miles b 6 $\frac{1}{2}$ miles

12 a 1800   b 1600   c 900   d 2160
13 a 150 mm b 144 mm   c 120 mm   d It is 135 mm, between 120 and 144.
Challenge: fractions of a minute
Own answers. Some possible answers are:

$\frac{1}{2}$ = 30 seconds, $\frac{1}{3}$ = 20 seconds, $\frac{1}{4}$ = 15 seconds , $\frac{1}{5}$ = 12 seconds , $\frac{1}{6}$ = 10 seconds and

$\frac{1}{12}$ = 5 seconds

Lesson 11.3 Percentages of a quantity

Learning objectives

- To find a percentage of a quantity

Resources and homework

- Pupil Book 1.1, pages 222–225
- Intervention Workbook 3, pages 16–17
- Homework Book 1, section 11.3
- Online homework 11.3, questions 1–10

Links to other subjects

- **Food technology** – to use percentages of a quantity in recipes
- **Geography** – to work out the percentages of populations, urban geography

Key words

- No new key words for this topic

Problem solving and reasoning help

- The investigation after Exercise 11C encourages pupils to explain what they understand about the relationship between fractions and percentages, and apply this to justify the solutions to problems.

Common misconceptions and remediation

- Pupils realise a link with fractions but use the value of the percentage as the denominator and subsequently divide by that value. For example, they think 30% is equal to 1/30 and so to find 30% of 300 they would simply divide by 30.

Probing questions

- What percentages of given quantities can you easily work out in your head? Talk me through a couple of examples.
- When calculating percentages of quantities, what percentages do you usually start from? How do you use this percentage to work out others?

Part 1

- Use a target board such as the one shown on the right: two cards marked with × and ÷ and three cards marked with 10, 100 and 1000.

- Select a pupil, an operation, a power of 10 and a number. Ask the pupil for the result of the number multiplied (or divided) by 10, 100 or 1000. Repeat with other numbers.
- Recall the rules for multiplying and dividing by powers of 10.

28	38	7	22	60
8	16	14	26	48
30	52	36	9	13
32	15	12	24	34

Literacy activity

- Provide opportunities for pupils to compare the written form of percentages with visual images.

Part 2

- This lesson is primarily about the calculation of simple percentages of a quantity.
- Ask the class how to calculate 10 % of a quantity, for example: 10% of £40.
- Then ask the class how to calculate 15%, explaining how they have used their answer to the last example to help them.
- Find 10% (£4), then 5% (£2) and add (£6).
- Repeat with some slightly more complex examples.
- Ask the class to give any equivalent fractions, decimals or percentages that they know. Write these on the board.
- If only a couple are suggested, ask how to get others from these. For example: 5% is half of 10%. If sufficient have been collected, ask for the connections between them. For example: 20% and 10%, 75% and 25%.Then ask how to get others from these.
- **Pupils can now do Exercise 11C in Pupil Book 1.1.**

Part 3

- Write different quantities on the board (or have prepared cards available) such as: £45, 68 sweets, 560 penguins, 340 kg; and different percentages such as: 10%, 15%, 25%, 45%.
- Ask pupils to match a quantity to a percentage, and then to calculate the percentage of the quantity. If the opportunity arises, discuss why the percentages of some examples are easier to calculate than others.

Answers

Exercise 11C

1   a $\frac{1}{10}$ b i 2 cm   ii 5 people   iii 13 km   iv 30 ml

2   a $\frac{4}{5}$ b i 8 g   ii 44 m   iii £16   iv 100 ml

3   a 40 cm   b 60 cm   c 24 cm   d 64 cm   e 48 cm

4   a 8 people   b 1500 people c 1000 people

5   a 48   b 360   c 288   d 432

6   In order they are 260, 240, 225, 256 and 270

7   a i 45 people   ii 18 people   b i 63 people   ii 27 people

8   a i 330 animals   ii 88 animalsb i 418 animals   ii 242 animals

9   48 lime, 40 oak, 8 beech

10   a 6p   b 42p   c £1.26   d £3.24   e £5.94

11   a 23p   b 69p   c £2.30   d £9.20

12   a £24.60   b £36.90   c £6.15

13   a £428.40   b £642.60   c £107.10

14   a 320 kg   b 160 kg   c 224 kg   d 576 kg   e 633.6 kg

15   £30.38 (£49.00 − £18.62)

Investigation: Fractions for percentages

Own answers

Lesson 11.4 Percentages with a calculator

Learning objectives
- To write a percentage as a decimal
- To use a calculator to find a percentage of a quantity

Links to other subjects
- **Food technology** – to use percentages of a quantity in recipes
- **Geography** – to use percentages of populations, urban geography

Resources and homework
- Pupil Book 1.1, pages 225–227
- Homework Book 1, section 11.4
- Online homework 11.4, questions 1–10

Key word
- decimal

Problem solving and reasoning help

- The financial skills activity after Exercise 11D gives pupils the opportunity to see how percentages are used to support sound financial decision-making in a familiar real-life situation. Encourage pupils to discuss with family and friends when they might use percentages in real life and how they make decisions about when to use a calculator.

Common misconceptions and remediation

- Pupils often resort to using a calculator without considering if it is the best approach. Encourage pupils to ask the question: '*Can I do this easily in my head?*' Also, because pupils might not have strong mental strategies, they may be unable to say if their solution makes sense. Encourage pupils to have a mental estimate in their heads before using a calculator.

Probing questions

- Explain how you use a calculator to find a percentage of a quantity or a fraction of a quantity.

Part 1

- In pairs, ask pupils to work on this example. Encourage them to explain how they arrived at their answer: I divide a number by 10, and then again by 10. The answer is 0.3. What number did I start with? How do you know?
- Give **less able** pupils some simple examples to work on. Encourage **more able** pupils to give a range of their own examples using multiplication, division and different powers of 10.

Part 2

- Explain that sometimes it is easier to work out a percentage without using a calculator.
- Give an example such as: 30% of 120. Ask pupils to explain how they would do this.
- Divide 120 by 10 to give 10%; then multiply the answer to this by 3.
- Write this as a calculation: $\frac{120}{10} \times 3$.
- Is there another way to do this? 120 ÷ 100 to give 1%; multiply by 30. Write this as: $\frac{120}{100} \times 30$
- Show that both of these are equivalent to: 30 ÷ 100 × 120 OR: 0.3 × 100
- Pupils can use this calculation to find any percentage of a quantity using a calculator.
- Make sure pupils are confident with moving between percentages, fraction and decimals, and that they understand why this is useful when calculating more complex percentages using a calculator. Do a few more examples to reinforce this, starting with percentages that pupils are more comfortable with and then moving on to more complex examples.

- Now ask pupils to do 8% of £420 using a calculator. 8% of 420 = (8 ÷ 100) × 420 (or by converting directly to an equivalent decimal 0.08 × 420). Pupils may not see that the second way is more efficient, and may be happier with the calculation that uses a denominator of 100, as this enables them to recognise the percentage.
- If necessary, pupils may refer to Example 7 in the Pupil Book while doing the exercise.
- **Pupils can now do Exercise 11D from Pupil Book 1.1.**

Part 3

- Ask pairs to summarise for each other how they decide when to use a calculator rather than a mental or written method when finding percentages of quantities, giving some examples
- Write some percentages on the board such as: 25%, 14%, 32%, 60%, 7%, 92%, and various quantities such as £340, 45 books, 3.72 kg, 900 miles, 2500 bacteria, 1254 pupils.
- Link each of these as a percentage of a quantity, for example: 14% of 1254 pupils. First, ask for an estimate, then, if they could do the problem more easily using a calculator. Then ask the class to work out the answer using the appropriate method. Answers should be given to an appropriate accuracy, for example: 14% of 1254 pupils = 175.56 ≈ 176 pupils.
- For the percentages and quantities above, the answers and whether calculator (C) or non-calculator (N) are:
  - £340, £85 (N), £47.60 (C), £108.80 (C), £204 (N), £23.80 (C), £312.80 (C)
  - 45 books, 11 books (N), 6 books (C), 14 books (C), 27 books (N), 3 books (C), 41 books (C)
  - 3.72 kg, 0.93 kg (C), 0.5208 kg (C), 1.1904 kg (C), 2.232 kg (C), 0.2604 kg (C), 3.4224 kg (C)
  - 900 miles, 225 miles (N), 126 miles (N), 288 miles (N), 540 miles (N),63 miles (N), 828 miles (N)
  - 2500 bacteria, 625 bacteria (N), 350 bacteria (N), 800 bacteria (N), 1500 bacteria (N), 175 bacteria (N), 2300 bacteria (N)
  - 1254 pupils, 314 pupils (C), 176 pupils (C), 401 pupils (C), 752 pupils (C), 88 pupils (C), 1154 pupils (C).

Answers

Exercise 11D

1   a 0.45   b 0.13   c 0.09   d 0.03   e 0.3   f 0.7
2   a 63%   b 24%   c 7%   d 20%   e 60%   f 99%
3   a 0.42   b i 13.44 kg   ii 5.04 m   iii 3108 people   iv £12.18
4   a i 3/10   ii 0.3   b 63 children   c check
5   a £4.76   b 2898 km   c 4814 people   d 6552 years
    e 2.99 m   f £59.29
6   a £2.40   b 24p   c £31.68
7   a 26.6   b 292.6   c 2660
8   a i £10.54 ii £51.46   b because 17% + 83% = 100%
9   a i 2.1 kg ii 5.1 kg iii 8.1 kg iv 11.1 kg   b 47% of 30 kg = 14.1 kg
10 Reds 2272, Blues 2911, Yellows 1136
11 405
12 £4.20
13 Greater London 7.95 million and North East 2.65 million

Financial skills: Booking a holiday

A   £350
B   £101.50
C   £2128.50
D   £311.40

Lesson 11.5 Percentage increases and decreases

Learning objectives
- To work out the result of a simple percentage change

Resources and homework
- Pupil Book 1.1, pages 227–229
- Homework Book 1, section 11.5
- Online homework 11.5, questions 1–10

Links to other subjects
- **Business and economics** – to calculate interest and sale costs
- **Food technology** – to calculate dietary requirements

Key words
- decrease
- reduction
- increase

Problem solving and reasoning help
- The financial skills activity after Exercise 11E in the Pupil Book gives pupils the opportunity to see how percentages are used to support sound financial decision-making in a familiar real-life situation. Encourage pupils to ask family and friends: '*How often do you calculate VAT? What method do you use to calculate VAT?*'

Common misconceptions and remediation
- Pupils often fail to transfer what they have learned to real-life situations. Pupils could role-play situations where it would be useful to be able to calculate percentage change efficiently, for example, at sales. Pupils need a good understanding of 100% as a whole before tackling percentage increases and decreases successfully.

Probing questions
- Talk me through how you would increase or decrease £20 by, for example: 15%. Can you do it in a different way?
- The answer to a percentage increase question is £10. Make up an easy and a difficult question.

Part 1
- Recall fraction, percentage and decimal equivalences by asking pupils to complete a diagram similar to this one used in the starter of lesson 1
- Either give pupils a partially completed diagram, or they should produce it themselves.

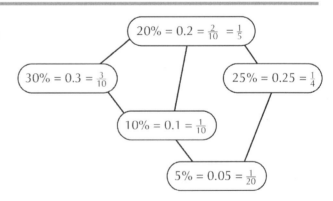

$$20\% = 0.2 = \tfrac{2}{10} = \tfrac{1}{5}$$

$$30\% = 0.3 = \tfrac{3}{10}$$

$$25\% = 0.25 = \tfrac{1}{4}$$

$$10\% = 0.1 = \tfrac{1}{10}$$

$$5\% = 0.05 = \tfrac{1}{20}$$

Literacy activity
- Encourage pupils to be careful when writing mathematical sentences. They need to use the correct mathematical notation. Sentences should not be mathematically inaccurate. A good example is stringing an argument together in a long line without realising that certain elements are mathematically incorrect. For example: 10% of £80 = £8 = £80 − £8 = £72

Part 2

- Recall how to calculate a percentage of a quantity. For example:
  - 20% of 420, which is 10% + 10% = 42 + 42 = 84
- Ask pupils how they would do this calculation on a calculator: 420×0.20
- Now ask what they think a percentage increase means? Give examples such as VAT.
- In pairs ask pupils to calculate: £400 +VAT
- Go through the correct answer: £400 + £80 = £480
- Now discuss percentage decrease. Make links to real-life examples, particularly sales.
- Do a few examples such as £80 reduced by 10%. Encourage pupils to do the calculation with and without a calculator.
- 10 % of £80 is £8. Subtract £8 from £80, which is equal to £72.
- Or, use a calculator: $£80 \times 0.10 = £8$. So the sale price will be: £80 – £8 = £72
- **Pupils can now do Exercise 11E from Pupil Book 1.1.**

Part 3

- The answer to a percentage increase question is £10. Make up an easy and a difficult question.
- Have a class discussion about what makes the questions easy or hard.

Answers

Exercise 11E

1   a £12   b £60
2   a 9   b 27
3   a 54 cm   b 594 cm
4   a 4 kg   b 44 kg
5   a 48   b 128
6   a 18   b 42
7   a £120   b £480
8   a 0.03   b £444   c £14 356
9   a 324   b 1044
10 a £26   b £546   c £494
11 a £56   b £2856   c £2744

Financial skills: VAT

A   a £9   b £54
B   a £78   b £468
C

VAT	2	4	10	20	40	100	200
cost	12	24	60	120	240	600	1200

Review questions (Pupil Book pages 230–231)

- The review questions will help to determine pupils' abilities with regard to the material within Chapter 11.
- These questions also draw on the maths covered in earlier chapters of the book to encourage pupils to make links between different topics.
- The answers are on the next page.

Financial skills – Income tax (Pupil Book pages 232–233)

- This activity is designed to use both the mathematical and transferable process skills covered in this chapter in a very important real-life context, which may be completely unfamiliar to pupils.
- All the information required to answer the questions is given but pupils will need to read it carefully. Remind them to highlight the key information they will need.
- A discussion about what they have already learnt about taxes may be beneficial.
- Ask pupils further questions as a warm-up to start working on the questions in the Pupil Book. Here are some examples:
    - What is tax?
    - Who pays tax?
- Pupils can now work on the questions individually or in groups.
- You could ask pupils to develop this topic further by using the internet to research other tax bands.
- **More able** pupils could look at national insurance. They could also research tax in other countries and devise what they believe is a fair tax system. Ask groups to present an argument for their tax system to the class.

Answers to Review questions

1 **a i** 10%   **ii** 24%   **iii** 48%   **iv** 14%   **b** 4% are white
2 **a** colour five parts   **b** colour two parts
3 58%
4 **a** $\frac{1}{2}$ **b** 50%   **c** 25%
5 **a** $\frac{3}{4}$ **b** $\frac{7}{10}$ **c** $\frac{3}{5}$ **d** $\frac{3}{10}$
6 **a** 5   **b** 15   **c** 4   **d** 16   **e** 6
7 **a** 28 cm   **b** 105 people   **c** 147 kg
8 **a** $\frac{2}{5}$ **b** 12 cm   **c** 96 kg
9 **a** 90 m   **b** 12 m   **c** 108 m   **d** 96 m
10 **a** 30p   **b** 94p   **c** 93p
11 **a** 20 cm   **b** 16 cm   **c** 25 cm^2 **d** 15 cm^2
12 **a** 0.06   **b i** 2.1 g   **ii** 28.2 km   **iii** 348 people
13 **a** £52.25   **b** £61.92   **c** £3.08
14 **a** 72°   **b** The third angle is 180 − 90 − 72 = 18° and 20% of 90° = 18°
15 **a** 12 cm   **b** 52 cm
16 **a** £54   **b** £36

Answers to Financial skills – Income tax

1 **a** £5000   **b** £5000, £1000
2 **a** £10 000   **b** £10 000, £2000
3 **a** £20 000   **b** £20 000, £4000
4 £1000 £2000 £3000 £4000 £5000
5 £6000
6 The second statement is true. He pays £4000 tax if he earns £30 000 which is more than double the £1000 he pays if he earns £15 000.
7 Straight line joining (10 000, 0) and (35 000, 5000)
8 £500
9 £3500
10 £32 500
11 **a** 25% 0f £5000 = £1250 **b** £2500   **c** £3750   **d** £5000
    e values above shown in table
    f Straight line joining the points (10 000, 0) and (30 000, 5000)

12 Probability

Learning objectives

- How to use words about probability
- How to work with a probability scale
- How to work out theoretical probabilities in different situations
- How to use experimental probability to make predictions

Prior knowledge

- Some basic ideas about chance and probability. This will be from outside the classroom or from extension work, as there is no formal requirement for probability in KS2.
- How to collect data from a simple experiment
- How to record data in a table or chart

Context

- Probability is an area of mathematics that pupils often find interesting but is contrary to what seems right. To engage pupils with this topic, you could use a website such as this link to National Lottery Statistics: **http://www.lottery.co.uk/statistics.**

Discussion points

- How likely do you think it is that it will rain tomorrow?
- Would your answer be different if it was January or August?
- Do you know for certain that it will rain more in January than August?

Associated Collins ICT resources

- Chapter 12 interactive activities on Collins Connect online platform
- *Probability words* and *Experimental probability* Worked solutions on Collins Connect online platform

Curriculum references

Probability

- Record, describe and analyse the frequency of outcomes of simple probability experiments involving randomness, fairness, equally and unequally likely outcomes, using appropriate language and the 0–1 probability scale
- Understand that the probabilities of all possible outcomes sum to 1

Reason mathematically

- Explore what can and cannot be inferred in statistical and probabilistic settings, and begin to express their arguments formally

Solve problems

- Begin to model situations mathematically and express the results using a range of formal mathematical representations

Fast-track for classes following a 2-year scheme of work

- You could briefly recap probability scales and equally likely outcomes using some of the examples in the Pupil Book if necessary. Check pupils' understanding using some of the probing questions. Provided pupils seem confident they could then move straight on to Lesson 12.3 on experimental probability.
- Support **less able** pupils using guided group work.

Lesson 12.1 Probability words

Learning objective
- To learn and use the words about probability

Resources and homework
- Pupil Book 1.2, pages 235–240
- Intervention Workbook 3, pages 61–66
- Homework Book 1, section 12.1
- Online homework 12.1, questions 1–10

Links to other subjects
- **Science** – to determine the likelihood of specific experimental or biological outcomes

Key words
- at random
- event
- likely
- probability
- random
- chance
- fair
- outcome
- probability scale

Problem solving and reasoning help
- The challenge activity at the end of Exercise 12A in the Pupil Book introduces the idea of a hypothesis and collecting evidence. As a class, before pupils work on the activity, discuss hypotheses and how to collect data to support them.

Common misconceptions and remediation
- The language of probability is often used in everyday terms, and pupils are not always aware of the difference between this more informal use of the language and the more precise use in mathematics. Give pupils opportunities to discuss the use of the language around probability in, for example, the media. Discuss how accurately, or not, it is being used.

Probing questions
- Give examples of probabilities (as whole number or fractions) for events that could be described using the following words:
  - impossible
  - almost (but not quite) certain
  - fairly likely
  - very likely
  - an even chance.

Part 1
- You will need a bag containing 50 counters in three different colours, in different amounts. For example, 10 red, 15 blue and 25 green.
- Ask a pupil to take a counter from the bag without looking, and replace it in the bag.
- Ask the class to name the colours of the counters in the bag.
- Shake the bag and repeat the activity about ten times.
- Tell the class that there are 50 counters in the bag.
- Ask pupils to write down how many counters of each colour they think are in the bag.
- Show the class the counters.

Literacy activity
- Give pupils plenty of opportunity to talk about the language of probability: how it is used in the real world; how its meaning can change depending on the context, who is using it, and for what purpose.

Part 2

- For this lesson, it would be helpful to have: dice, a pack of playing cards, cards numbered from 1 to 10, and various spinners. Make sure pupils are familiar with playing cards before using them as examples.
- Ask pupils to explain the term *chance* by giving everyday examples. Write pupils' explanations on the board. For example: the chance of getting a six when throwing a dice, the chance of rain tomorrow, the chance of winning the football pools.
- Draw the probability scale on the board as shown.

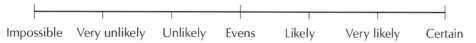

Impossible   Very unlikely   Unlikely   Evens   Likely   Very likely   Certain

- Ask for examples of *events* that describe any of the terms in the probability scale. Explain that *probability* is the mathematical way to describe the chance that an event will happen.
- Ask pupils: What other terms do you know that describe probability? For example: fair chance, 50–50 chance, uncertain.
- **Pupils can now do Exercise 12A from Pupil Book 1.1.**

Part 3

- What is the same or different for probability scales marked with: fractions
    - decimals
    - percentages
    - words?

Answers

Exercise 12A

1. **a i** 6   **ii** 0   **b i** 1   **ii** 2   **c i** 1   **ii** 4   **d i** 2   **ii** 1   **e i** 3   **ii** 7   **f i** 2   **ii** 1
   g circle   **h** certain   **i** impossible
2. **a i** 12   **ii** 6   **b** evens   **c i** 4   **ii** unlikely   **d i** 3   **ii** very unlikely
   e i equal to   **ii** more than   **iii** less than
   f i black   **ii** black   **iii** red   **g** triangle and rectangle
3. **a** impossible   **b** unlikely   **c** evens   **d** likely   **e** certain
4. **a** 11   **b i** I   **ii** I or B   **iii** P or R or O or L or T or Y
   c i 1   **ii** 3 or 4   **d i** unlikely   **ii** certain   **iii** very unlikely   **iv** impossible
5. A: certain B: fifty-fifty C: impossible D: very likely E: very unlikely F: very likely
   G: very likely or certain H: unlikely I: fifty-fifty chance J: likely K: very unlikely
6. F, D, C, B, A, E
7. **a** A   **b** B   **c** A

Challenge: Lucky for some

If the claim is true then you should get the most people choosing 7. If it isn't true then another number will have the most choices. If there is no preference all the numbers from 1 to 9 should be chosen about 3 or 4 times.

Lesson 12.2 Probability scales

Learning objectives

- To learn about and use probability scales from 0 to 1
- To work out probabilities based on equally likely outcomes

Links to other subjects

- Science – to record the likelihood of specific experimental or biological outcomes

Resources and homework

- Pupil Book 1.1, pages 241–244
- Intervention Workbook 3, pages 61–66
- Homework Book 1, section 12.2
- Online homework 12.2, questions 1–10

Key word

- probability fraction

Problem solving and reasoning help

- The activity at the end of Exercise 12B in the Pupil Book encourages pupils to start to apply their understanding and prepares them for the next lesson.

Common misconceptions and remediation

- Some pupils may misunderstand the concept of 0 or 1 on the probability scale. Allow time to discuss what this does and does not mean.

Probing questions

- Give examples of probabilities (whole numbers or fractions) for events that could be described using the following words:
    o   impossible
    o   almost (but not quite) certain
    o   fairly likely
    o   an even chance.

Part 1

- Refer to and remind pupils of the probability scale that you used in the previous lesson.
- Ask pupils to place to place these fractions on the number line. $\frac{1}{4}, \frac{1}{2}, \frac{3}{4}$
- Ask then what numbers are at either end of the number line and what they mean in terms of probability.
- Ask pupils if they can give an example of an event which has the probability of: $\frac{1}{2}$
- Ask **more able** pupils to design a context where there is a probability of: $\frac{1}{4}$ or $\frac{3}{4}$
- An example could be drawing a red ball from a bag with three white balls and one red ball.

Literacy activity

- Give pupils plenty of opportunity to talk about the language of probability and how it is used in the real world and how the use of this language can change depending on the context and often who is using it and for what purpose.

Part 2

- To describe probability more accurately, we use a scale from 0 to 1:

- Using a bag with 0 $\frac{1}{2}$ 1ₔ 4 in the Pupil Book.
- Explain that each time you draw a counter this called an *outcome for the event*. For this example, the possible outcomes are: Red (R) or Blue (B).
- Define the probability of an event:

$$P(\text{event}) = \frac{\text{Number of outcomes in the event}}{\text{Total number of all possible outcomes}}$$

- So, for the example in this case $P(R) = \frac{2}{5}$ and $P(B) = \frac{3}{5}$

- **Pupils can now do Exercise 12B from Pupil Book 1.1.**

Part 3

- Ask pupils to discuss the following statement: *In a lottery the six numbers 3, 11, 23, 36, 38, 45 are more likely to come up than the six numbers 1, 2, 3, 4, 5, 6.*
- In pairs, ask pupils to decide if the statement is true or false and why. This will give you the opportunity to discuss equally likely events and tackle misconceptions around this concept.

Answers

Exercise 12B

1 **a i** 12 **ii** 6 **iii** $\frac{6}{12} = \frac{1}{2}$ **b i** 1 **ii** $\frac{1}{12}$ **c i** 3 **ii** $\frac{3}{12} = \frac{1}{4}$ **d i** 2 **ii** $\frac{2}{12} = \frac{1}{6}$ **e** 1

2 **a** 16 **b i** $\frac{8}{16} = \frac{1}{2}$ **ii** $\frac{6}{16} = \frac{3}{8}$ **iii** $\frac{2}{16} = \frac{1}{8}$

3 **a** $\frac{1}{10}$ **b** $\frac{5}{10} = \frac{1}{2}$ **c** $\frac{2}{10} = \frac{1}{5}$ **d** $\frac{5}{10} = \frac{1}{2}$ **e** $\frac{2}{10} = \frac{1}{5}$

   f 1 **g** 0 **h** $\frac{3}{10}$ **i** $\frac{5}{10} = \frac{1}{2}$ **j** $\frac{3}{10}$

4 **a** $\frac{1}{8}$ **b** $\frac{2}{8} = \frac{1}{4}$ **c** $\frac{3}{8}$ **d** $\frac{2}{8} = \frac{1}{4}$ **e** 0

5 **a** $\frac{26}{52} = \frac{1}{2}$ **b** $\frac{13}{52} = \frac{1}{4}$ **c** $\frac{12}{52} = \frac{3}{13}$ **d** $\frac{1}{52}$ **e** $\frac{8}{52} = \frac{2}{13}$ **f** $\frac{4}{52} = \frac{1}{13}$

6 **a** $\frac{1}{6}$ **b** $\frac{3}{6} = \frac{1}{2}$ **c** $\frac{2}{6} = \frac{1}{3}$ **d** $\frac{5}{6}$ **e** $\frac{3}{6} = \frac{1}{2}$

   f $\frac{1}{6}$ **g** $\frac{2}{6} = \frac{1}{3}$ **h** 0 **i** $\frac{1}{2}$

7 $\frac{5}{20} = \frac{1}{4}$

8 $\frac{50}{400} = \frac{1}{8}$

Activity: Good guess!
1 higher as 1 is the lowest possible value
2 There are 3 cards left that are higher than 4 (5, 6 and 9) and only 1 lower than 4 (2).
3 **a** depends on your games
   b 1 and 9
   c 4, 5 and 6
   d If 1 has been seen then 2 will be the lowest card. Similarly if 9 is seen then 8 will be the highest card.

Lesson 12.3 Experimental probability

Learning objectives

- To learn about and understand experimental probability
- To understand the difference between theoretical probability and experimental probability

Resources and homework

- Pupil Book 1.1, pages 245–247
- Intervention Workbook 3, pages 61–66
- Homework Book 1, section 12.3

Links to other subjects

- **Science** – to conduct biological experiments
- **Geography** – to carry out social research

Key words

- experimental probability
- trial
- theoretical probability

Problem solving and reasoning help

- The activity after Exercise 12C gives pupils the opportunity to carry out their own experiment. Follow this activity with a discussion about *'how the more experiments that are conducted, the more accurate the predictions are likely to be'*.

Common misconceptions and remediation

- The concept of probability is in general use and is often used carelessly in the media. Give pupils the opportunity to discuss the use of probability in, for example, the media. Ask them to share some of their prior understanding of probability. This will help you to identify any misconceptions. Share real-life examples to explore the differences between theoretical and experimental probability. Discuss why theoretical probability is often difficult or impossible to calculate in complex real-life situations.

Probing questions

- Can you give me an example of an event for which the probability can only be calculated through an experiment?
- Can you give me an example of what is meant by 'equally likely outcomes'?

Part 1

- Ask one pupil to come up and write on the board one of the terms given below, and then to explain its meaning briefly. Repeat the activity with other pupils.
  - Average
  - Mean
  - Median
  - Mode
  - Modal class
  - Range
  - Frequency
  - Probability
  - Outcome
  - Event

Literacy activity

- The activity in Part 1 will give pupils an opportunity to revisit the language of statistics and probability. This may present an opportunity to discuss the links between these topics.

Part 2

- This lesson is mainly practical work. Pupils will need: coins, dice, packs of playing cards, card and cocktail sticks for making spinners, modelling clay or Plasticine.
- Explain that in the previous lesson, the probability of an event could be worked out because we knew that the outcomes were equally likely to happen: for example, the outcomes for throwing a fair dice.
- A probability calculated using equally likely outcomes is known as a *theoretical probability*.
- In other cases, it may not be possible to use equally likely outcomes. For example, the outcomes for throwing an unfair dice or a biased dice will have different probabilities for each outcome. In cases like these, we need to carry out an experiment to estimate the probability of an event happening. Here, we need to repeat the experiment a number of times in order to find the *experimental probability*. Each separate experiment is known as a *trial*. The results of all the trials can be recorded in a frequency table.

$$\text{Experimental probability of an event} = \frac{\text{Number of times the event occurs}}{\text{Total number of trials}}$$

- Notice that the experimental probability is a fraction, but as before, this can be written as a decimal or sometimes as a percentage.
- Explain that an experimental probability is an estimate for the theoretical probability. As the number of trials increases, the value of the experimental probability gets closer to the theoretical probability.
- If necessary, work through one of the examples in the pupil book as a class or with small groups as part of guided group work.
- **Pupils can now do Exercise 12C from Pupil Book 1.1.**

Part 3

- Ask pupils to explain the difference between theoretical probability and experimental probability.
- Make sure pupils understand 'equally likely outcomes' and 'trials'.

Answers

Exercise 12C

1-4 Check that the probabilities match the pupils' results.

5   a $\frac{2}{16} = \frac{1}{8}$

      b   Lucy knows that the other square must be one of A4, C4 and B2 so she has a 1 in 3 chance of getting the right square

6   a   The dice could be biased as all frequencies should be about 6 or 7 but 2 is 16 and 1 is only 3.

      b   She should do a lot more trials.

      c   The experimental probability of a 5 is $\frac{7}{40}$.

      d   The experimental probability of a 2 or 3 is $\frac{19}{40}$.

Activity: Spinners

The weighted face should appear more often. When the card is removed the spinner may still be biased as it is homemade and may not be accurately constructed. The theoretical probability is $\frac{1}{6}$ for each number. The spinner with card should not have experimental probabilities near $\frac{1}{6}$ but when the card is removed they should be fairly close to $\frac{1}{6}$.

Review questions (Pupil Book pages 248–249)

- The review questions will help to determine pupils' abilities with regard to the material within Chapter 12.
- These questions also draw on the maths covered in earlier chapters of the book to encourage pupils to make links between different topics.
- The answers are on the next page.

Financial skills – School Christmas Fayre
(Pupil Book pages 250–251)

- This activity combines pupils' understanding of experimental and theoretical probability and applies it in a real-life context.
- All the information required to answer the questions is provided in the text, which pupils will need to read and think about carefully. Remind them to highlight the key information.
- Support **less able** pupils with guided group work. This could include a discussion about what they have learnt about theoretical and experimental probability. Work through simpler examples with these pupils or let them work in pairs, before they work independently on the main activity.
- Pupils should work in small groups to encourage discussion. These groups could split into two groups, taking turns to work on a question and give feedback.
- Encourage **more able** pupils to develop this topic by designing a range of fair and unfair games. For ideas, pupils could do an internet search for: 'probability games, fair and unfair'.
- It might be a good idea to go through the answers as a class, answering and discussing any questions that pupils may still have.

Answers to Review questions

1 **a** very unlikely **b** very unlikely **c** certain **d** evens
   e impossible **f** very likely **g** certain
2 **a** evens **b** very unlikely **c** unlikely **d** likely
3 **a** $\frac{2}{6} = \frac{1}{3}$ **b** 2

4 **a**

   b i Blue **ii** It should have been about 15 but it is over three times that.

Answers to Financial skills – School Christmas Fayre

1 £850
2 $\frac{1}{10}$
3 Mr Buxton's daughter
4 less chance as $\frac{4}{50}$ is less than $\frac{20}{200}$
5 180 people have played so 20 ducks remain. 0.1 × 20 = 2 so 2 prizes are left.
6 £50 − £11.25 = £38.75
7 **a** $\frac{1}{25}$ **b** $\frac{3}{100}$ **c** $\frac{1}{50}$ **d** $\frac{1}{100}$
8 **a** $\frac{1}{25}$ **b** $\frac{1}{50}$ **c** $\frac{1}{50}$ **d** $\frac{1}{50}$
9 8, as there is a 1 in 8 chance of picking the egg
10 No, there were 10 prizes to start with and only 1 was £5 so the probability is $\frac{1}{10}$.
11 **a** $\frac{7}{100}$ **b** $\frac{1}{50}$ **c** $\frac{1}{100}$
12 more likely as 4 of the losing squares are blocked by his first 4 coins
13 £50 − 5 × £2 = £40
14 no, as the probabilities are experimental and the actual results may vary
15 To make a profit of 70p with 5 coins she has to win £1.20. Possible combinations are:
   50p, 50p, 10p, 10p, 0
   50p, 40p, 10p, 10p, 10p
   40p, 40p, 40p, 0, 0

13 Symmetry

Learning objectives

- How to recognise shapes that have reflective symmetry
- How to use line symmetry
- How to recognise and use rotational symmetry
- How to reflect shapes in a mirror line
- How to tessellate a shape

Prior knowledge

- How to recognise symmetrical shapes
- How to plot coordinates
- The mathematical names of triangles and quadrilaterals
- By the end of KS2 pupils should be able to describe positions in all four quadrants and draw and translate simple shapes and reflect them in the axes.

Context

- Symmetry is everywhere around us, both natural and human-made. Symmetry is probably one of the easier topics for pupils to see links to the real world, although some links may not be as obvious as others. This chapter provides many real-life examples, and each lesson has links to a number of these. An example that might spark pupils' interest in the concept of symmetry is the idea that their favourite celebrities are so attractive because their faces are more symmetrical than those of many other people. Search on the internet for 'facial symmetry' or look at this link, which shows research to support this idea: **http://www.faceresearch.org/students/symmetry**.
- One theory is that facial symmetry has an evolutionary advantage by indicating healthy members of the population for breeding purposes. Discuss this with pupils and ask for their views. The theory also links well with biology and scientific research.

Discussion points

- Explain how to reflect this shape into this mirror line. What would you do first?
- Make up a reflection that is easy to do. Make up a reflection that is difficult to do. What makes it difficult?
- How can you tell if a shape has been reflected or translated?

Associated Collins ICT resources

- Chapter 13 interactive activities on Collins Connect online platform
- *Symmetry* Wonder of Maths on Collins Connect online platform

Curriculum references

Develop fluency

- Use language and properties precisely to analyse 2D shapes

Geometry and measures

- Identify properties of, and describe the results of translations, rotations and reflections applied to given figures

Fast-track for classes following a 2-year scheme of work

- Many concepts in this chapter will be familiar to pupils from KS2. If pupils can demonstrate confidence with these basic concepts they can focus on working through the exercises and doing the activities after each exercise. Encourage pupils to explore the suggested links to real-life contexts.

Lesson 13.1 Line symmetry

Learning objectives

- To recognise shapes that have reflective symmetry
- To draw lines of symmetry on a shape

Resources and homework

- Pupil Book 1.1, pages 253–255
- Intervention Book 2, pages 53–55
- Intervention Book 3, pages 46–49
- Homework Book 1, section 13.1
- Online homework 13.1, questions 1–10

Links to other subjects

- **Art** – to think about the history of art
- **Physical Education** – to explore lines of symmetry in the layout of a range of pitches for example tennis and team sports

Key words

- diagonal
- line of symmetry
- reflect
- horizontal
- mirror line
- reflective symmetry
- vertical

Problem solving and reasoning help

- Pupils have several opportunities to apply their understanding to a range of problems in Exercise 13A in the Pupil Book. Support **less able** pupils by using templates and tracing paper. Encourage **more able** pupils to use visualisation or give them more abstract descriptions with which to work. Do an internet search for 'line symmetry images' or see this link: **http://patterninislamicart.com/drawingsdiagramsanalyses/**

Common misconceptions and remediation

- A common misconception is to think that all polygons have the same order of line symmetry as they do number of sides and/or angles. Avoid finding lines of symmetry only on regular polygons. Instead, provide a range of shapes. Encourage pupils to draw their own shapes on squared paper, with 'x' lines of symmetry.

Probing questions

- Can you think of a polygon with one line of symmetry? How could you check?
- Can you think of a polygon with more than one line of symmetry?

Part 1

- Ask pupils to imagine a square. In their minds, they should fold it in half. Then they should open out the square and describe the crease formed by folding the square once.
- Pupils should imagine another square. Ask them to fold it in half and in half again. Open it out and describe the creases formed by folding the square twice.
- Pupils should imagine a third square. They should fold it in half, again in half, and yet again in half. Open it out and describe the creases formed by folding the square three times.
- Discuss the possibilities, depending on the way pupils fold the square.

Part 2

- Each pupil will require a paper square, a mirror and tracing paper. Ask pupils to repeat the mental activity in Part 1 using the imaginary paper square.
- Show pupils the creases that can be formed with a paper square. The creases in the diagram are the *lines of symmetry* of the square. Each crease breaks the square into two equal parts, which fit exactly over each other. Use the mirror to

check that the image seen completes the square. A square has four lines of symmetry. Explain that there are two types of symmetry for 2D shapes: *line symmetry* and *rotational symmetry*. A shape has rotational symmetry if it can be rotated about a point to look the same in a new position.
- Repeat for a rectangle. A rectangle has two lines of symmetry and rotational symmetry of order 2. Repeat for a kite. A kite has one line of symmetry.
- Extension: visit **http://nrich.maths.org/5502** for ideas linked to symmetry in dance.
- **Pupils can now do Exercise 13A from Pupil Book 1.1.**

Part 3

- Have ready a set of cut-out shapes, or show shapes on a visualiser or IWB (Interactive whiteboard visualiser). Use triangles, quadrilaterals or other shapes cut from old magazines.
- For each shape, ask pupils to give the line symmetry.
- Explain that a circle has an infinite number of lines of symmetry (Some pupils may think that it has 360.) Ask them to explain 'infinity'. (You could mention the ∞ symbol for infinity here.)

Answers

Exercise 13A

1
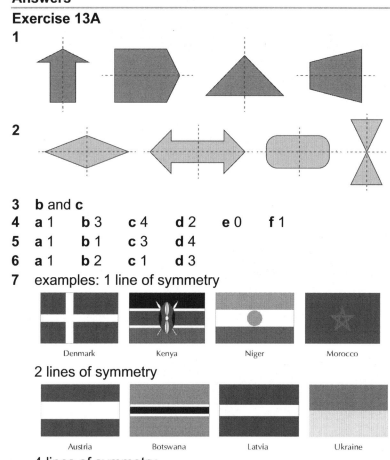

2

3 **b** and **c**
4 **a** 1   **b** 3   **c** 4   **d** 2   **e** 0   **f** 1
5 **a** 1   **b** 1   **c** 3   **d** 4
6 **a** 1   **b** 2   **c** 1   **d** 3
7 examples: 1 line of symmetry

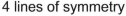

Denmark   Kenya   Niger   Morocco

2 lines of symmetry

Austria   Botswana   Latvia   Ukraine

4 lines of symmetry

Switzerland

8
The lines of symmetry produce the numbers 1   2   3   4   5   6   7

Lesson 13.2 Rotational symmetry

Learning objectives

- To recognise shapes that have rotational symmetry
- To find the order of rotational symmetry for a shape

Resources and homework

- Pupil Book 1.1, pages 256–259
- Intervention Book 2, pages 53–55
- Intervention Book 3, pages 46–49
- Homework Book 1, section 13.2
- Online homework 13.2, questions 1–10

Links to other subjects

- **Art** – to think about the history of art
- **Physical Education** – to explore rotational symmetry in gymnastics and dance.

Key words

- order of rotational symmetry
- rotational symmetry

Problem solving and reasoning help

- Pupils have several opportunities to apply their understanding to a range of problems in Exercise 13B in the Pupil Book. Support **less able** pupils by using templates and tracing paper. Encourage **more able** pupils to use visualisation or give them more abstract descriptions with which to work, for example, bell ringing. See this link: **http://plus.maths.org/content/ringing-changes**.

Common misconceptions and remediation

- A common misconception is to think that all polygons have the same order of rotational symmetry as they do number of sides and/or angles. Avoid finding lines of symmetry only on regular polygons. Instead, provide a range of shapes. Encourage pupils to draw their own shapes on squared paper, with 'x' order of rotational symmetry.

Probing questions

- Can you think of a polygon with rotational symmetry of order 1? How could you check?
- Can you think of a polygon with rotational symmetry of greater than order 1?

Part 1

- Ask pupils to imagine a square. In their minds, they should imagine a small red dot in the top right-hand corner of the square. Ask them to imagine turning the shape in their minds so the dot is now on the bottom right-hand corner.
- How many times could they rotate the square until the dot is back where it started?
- Now ask them to imagine doing the same thing with a rectangle.

Part 2

- Each pupil will require a paper square, a mirror and tracing paper. Ask the class to repeat the mental activity in Part 1 using the square and folding it.
- Remind pupils that there are two types of symmetry for 2D shapes: *line symmetry* and *rotational symmetry*. A plane shape has rotational symmetry if it can be rotated about a point to look the same in a new position.
- Ask pupils to trace the square. Ask them how many times the traced square will fit exactly on top of the original square as they rotate the tracing paper around the centre of the square – its point of symmetry. Pupils should say 'four' but a common response is 'lots of times'.

- If necessary, show pupils how to trace the square and turn the tracing paper until it fits exactly on top of the original square. The red dot will make it is easy to see when it has been rotated through 360°. So, the square has rotational symmetry of order 4. Repeat for a rectangle. A rectangle has rotational symmetry of order 2. Repeat for a kite. A kite has one line of symmetry but no rotational symmetry. It is said to have rotational symmetry of order 1.
- Extension: for ideas linked to symmetry in dance, visit **http://nrich.maths.org/5502**.
- **Pupils can now do Exercise 13A from Pupil Book 1.1.**

Part 3

- Have ready a set of cut-out shapes or shapes to show on a visualiser or IWB (Interactive whiteboard visualiser). Use triangles, quadrilaterals or shapes cut from old magazines.
- For each shape, ask pupils to give the order of rotational symmetry.
- Remind pupils that a circle has an infinite number of lines of symmetry. What do they think is the order of rotational symmetry? Order infinity for rotational symmetry. (Some pupils may think it has 360.) Ask pupils to explain 'infinity'. (Mention the ∞ symbol for infinity here.)

Answers
Exercise 12B
1	a 2	b 1	c 2	d 2	e 1	f 2
2	a 2	b 2	c 1	d 2	e 2	f 4
3	a 4	b 3	c 4	d 2		
4	a 3	b 4	c 2	d 2		

5 **a** For example 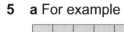 **b** For example   **c** For example

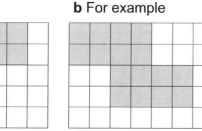
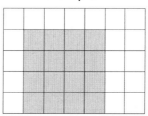

6

	Name of shape	Number of lines of symmetry	Order of rotational symmetry
a	Isosceles triangle	1	1
b	Equilateral triangle	3	3
c	Square	4	4
d	Rectangle	2	2
e	Parallelogram	0	2
f	Rhombus	2	2
g	Trapezium	1	1
h	Kite	1	1

7 **a** 3, 3, 3   **b** 4, 4, 4   **c** 5, 5, 5   **d** 6, 6, 6   **e** 8, 8, 8

For regular shapes, the number of lines of symmetry is the same as the order of rotational symmetry.

Learning objectives

- To understand how to reflect a shape
- To use a coordinate grid to reflect shapes

Resources and homework

- Pupil Book 1.1, pages 259–263
- Intervention Book 2, pages 53–55
- Intervention Book 3, pages 46–49
- Homework Book 1, section 13.3
- Online homework 13.3–4, questions 1–10

Links to other subjects

- **ICT** – to use software such as LOGO
- **Design and technology** – to use symmetry in design and technology

Key words

- image
- reflect
- object
- reflection

Problem solving and reasoning help

- Pupils have several opportunities to apply their understanding to a range of problems in this lesson. Support less able pupils by using templates and tracing paper and focus on simple mirror lines. Encourage more able pupils to work with more complex, less familiar shapes and more complex mirror lines. Do an internet search for 'symmetry in design' or look at this link: **http://sixrevisions.com/web_design/symmetry-design/**.

Common misconceptions and remediation

- Pupils often have trouble visualising the effect of a reflection on a shape. Provide plenty of opportunity for pupils to use real objects or tracing paper to help them develop the ability to visualise the effect of any transformation, including reflections. Use a range of mirror lines. The 'Imagine' activity in Part 1 of Lesson 13.1 is useful for developing visualisation skills.

Probing questions

- Draw me a shape that is easy to reflect.
- Now draw me one that is more difficult. Why is it more difficult?

Part 1

- For this activity, you will need a pinboard (or a large square of card). Each pupil will need paper or a small whiteboard. Make a square in one quadrant of the pinboard, as in the diagram.
- Show the class the pinboard. Flip over the pinboard along the axis DE so that the square is now facing you.
- Ask the class to draw a sketch of what *you* can see on the pinboard.
- Repeat the activity using other axes, such as BG, AH or CF.
- Make this more difficult by using other shapes such as a rectangle or a right-angled triangle.

Part 2

- The class will require mirrors, tracing paper and squared paper.
- Ask pupils to copy the triangle on squared paper, put a mirror along the dotted line and draw, on the squared paper, the triangle that they can see in the mirror.
- Explain the terms 'object', 'image', 'mirror line' and 'reflection.'
- Ask the class to describe the position of the image in relation to the object. They should notice that the corresponding points on the object and the image are at the same distance

from, and the lines joining them perpendicular to, the mirror line. This is a condition for all reflections.

- Explain that the position of the shape has been changed by the reflection, and that a reflection is an example of a *transformation*.
- Explain the notation used for reflecting shapes in a mirror line. ΔABC is mapped onto ΔA´B´C´ by a reflection in the mirror line.
- When reflecting shapes in a diagonal line, take care to make sure that corresponding points in the object and the image are at the same distance from, and the lines joining them perpendicular to, the mirror line. Explain how to do this by using the example.
- Use tracing paper to check this.
- **Pupils can now do Exercise 13B from Pupil Book 1.1.**

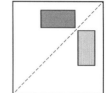

Part 3

- Show the class the square on the pinboard, as in Part 1.
- Ask pupils to explain if any properties of the square are changed after any reflection, or do they remain the same? For example: left becomes right if the square has been flipped over; the image is the same shape and size; the angles stay the same; the area stays the same.
- Emphasise the importance of these properties of reflections.

Answers
Exercise 13C

1
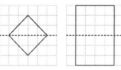

3 a 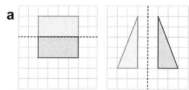 **b**

2
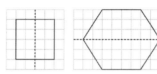

c 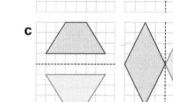 **d**

4 c A´(1, 1), B´(2, 2), C´(3, 5) and D´(5, 6)

5 a
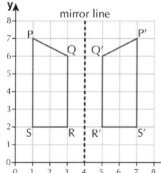

b

	Object		Image	
Point	Coordinates		Point	Coordinates
P	(1, 7)		P´	(7, 7)
Q	(3, 6)		Q´	(5, 6)
R	(3, 2)		R´	(5, 2)
S	(1, 2)		S´	(7, 2)

6
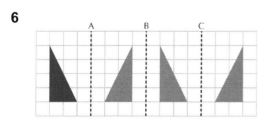

Lesson 13.4 Tessellations

Learning objective
- To understand how to tessellate shapes

Resources and homework
- Pupil Book 1.1, pages 264–265
- Homework Book 1, section 13.4
- Online homework 13.3–4, questions 1–10

Links to other subjects
- **Art** – to the use of tessellation
- **Religious education** – to think about other religions

Key word
- tessellation

Problem solving and reasoning help

- Pupils have several opportunities to apply their understanding to a range of problems in this lesson. Support **less able** pupils by using templates and tracing paper. Encourage **more able** pupils to use visualisation or give them more abstract descriptions with which to work. You could do some internet searches for: 'tessellations, fun with mathematics', 'mathematical art, Escher' or 'Islamic art'. Or, look at these links:
  http://xploreandxpress.blogspot.co.uk/2010/12/fun-with-mathematics-tessellations.html
  http://www.youtube.com/watch?v=yGp29Flirl8.

Common misconceptions and remediation

- This is probably the easiest of the transformations, but pupils often make careless mistakes. In particular they confuse whether to move horizontally or vertically first. Make clear links to the work on coordinate geometry that pupils have done.

Probing questions

- Name two regular pentagons that will not form a tessellation on their own. Explain why.

Part 1

- Ask the class to imagine a tiling pattern made from squares. Ask individual pupils to describe their patterns to the class. How many different patterns can they make?
- Repeat for a tiling pattern made from rectangles.
- Ask the class to name other shapes that will form a tiling pattern.

Part 2

- This work will involve a good deal of drawing, and so should cover at least two lessons. It is an ideal end-of-year activity.
- Pupils will require square grid paper and triangular grid paper. Crayons or felt-tipped pens will be useful for making display work. It will be helpful to have examples of tessellations already prepared on card or on a PowerPoint/whiteboard presentation.
- Explain to pupils that the patterns discussed in Part 1 are examples of *tessellations*. Identical shapes are said to tessellate if they fit together exactly, leaving no gaps. To show a tessellation, it is usual to draw about 10 copies of the shape to make sure there are no gaps.

- Show the class examples of squares and rectangles tessellating. Point out that a tessellating shape does not have to be in a regular grid layout. For example, a rectangle can tessellate to form a herring-bone pattern, as shown.
- Stress the importance of using colour to show a tessellation. Sometimes three or four colours may have to be used.
- The shape used can be rotated, reflected or translated to complete a tessellation. For example, look at the isosceles triangle pattern.
- A triangular grid is useful to draw more complex tessellations: For example, a rhombus (see diagram).
- Encourage pupils to work in pairs or groups to design wall posters on which to display their own tessellations.
- **Less able** pupils can be supported with more examples or partly completed patterns. Also use grouping to support or challenge.
- **Pupils can now do Exercise 13D from Pupil Book 1.1.**

Part 3

- Working in pairs, ask pupils to explain why one can make a tessellation where each vertex is made up of two hexagons and two equilateral triangles. Is there any other combination of hexagons and equilateral triangles that will tessellate? If so, explain why.
- To help **less able** pupils, do the explanation as a class. Then, working in pairs, ask pupils to repeat the explanation to their partner.
- The partner should then provide formative feedback on the quality of the explanations.

Answers
Exercise 13D
Check that pupils' tessellations are correct.
Activity: Tessellation poster
Check that pupils' tessellations are correct.

Review questions (Pupil Book pages 266–267)

- The review questions will help to determine pupils' abilities with regard to the material within Chapter 13.
- These questions also draw on the maths covered in earlier chapters of the book to encourage pupils to make links between different topics.
- The answers follow.

Activity – Landmark spotting (Pupil Book pages 268–269)

- This activity is designed to reinforce the use of the techniques from this chapter in a practical and creative context.
- The basic design on square dotty paper can be attempted by all pupils.
- Discuss the number of lines and order of rotational symmetry in each pattern.
- Pupils can then try designs on an 8 × 8 grid or 10 × 10 grid.
- Once pupils have completed the basic design ask questions such as:
    - How would you increase the lines of symmetry?
    - If you increase the lines of symmetry would the order of symmetry also increase?
- Pupils can now draw Rangoli patterns on triangular dotty paper in order to make more complex designs.
- **More able** pupils could make their own designs on plain paper.
- Pupils could investigate symmetry in art as a homework activity.

Answers to Review questions

1 **a** b, e and f

2 **a** 2   **b** 4   **c** 5   **d** 6

3 **a** For example   **b** For example   **c** For example

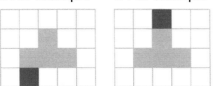

4 **a** 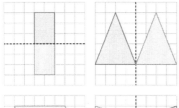 **b**

   c 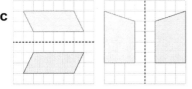 **d**

5 **a** A(1, 7), B(7, 6) and C(3, 5)

   b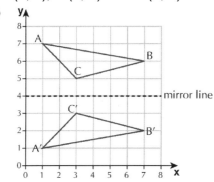

   c A(1, 1), B(7, 2) and C(3, 3)

6 **a** 2   **b** 3   **c** 1   **d** 4

7 **a** 4 different shapes   **b** 3, 4, 6 and 12

Answers to Activity – Landmark spotting

Pupils' own answers

14 Equations

Learning objectives
- How to solve simple equations
- How to set up equations to solve simple problems

Prior knowledge
- How to write and use simple expressions, using letters for numbers
- How to substitute numbers into expressions to work out their value
- How to write and use simple formulae using words or symbols
- By the end of KS2, pupils should have been introduced to the use of symbols and letters to represent variables and unknowns in familiar mathematical situations.

Context
- The history of algebra goes back to ancient Egypt and Babylon. However, it is not just an ancient topic. Most of our modern society is dependent on the use of algebra. For more information search the internet for: 'mathematician Andrew Wiles' or 'Fermat's last theorem'.

Discussion points
- Why do we sometimes use letters in mathematics?

Associated Collins ICT resources
- Chapter 14 interactive activities on Collins Connect online platform
- *Simple equations* video on Collins Connect online platform
- *Traffic jam* Wonder of Maths on Collins Connect online platform
- Equation balancer tool on Collins Connect platform

Curriculum references

Develop fluency
- Use algebra to generalise the structure of arithmetic, including to formulate mathematical relationships
- Substitute values in expressions, rearrange and simplify expressions, and solve equations

Solve problems
- Develop their mathematical knowledge, in part through solving problems and evaluating the outcomes, including multi-step problems

Algebra
- Use and interpret algebraic notation, including
  - ab in place of $a \times b$
  - $3y$ in place of $y + y + y$ and $3 \times y$
  - a^2 in place of $a \times a$, a^3 in place of $a \times a \times a$; a^2b in place of $a \times a \times b$

- $\circ$ $\dfrac{a}{b}$ in place of $a \div b$
  - $\circ$ coefficients written as fractions rather than as decimals
  - $\circ$ brackets.
- Use algebraic methods to solve linear equations in one variable (including all forms that require rearrangement)

Fast-track for classes following a 2-year scheme of work

- Recap 'Finding unknown numbers' in Lesson 14.1 and run through 'Solving equations' in Lesson 14.2, before moving on to Lesson 14.3 and Lesson 14.4.

Lesson 14.1 Finding unknown numbers

Learning objective
- To find missing numbers in simple calculations

Resources and homework
- Pupil Book 1.1, pages 271–274
- Homework Book 1, section 14.1
- Online homework 14.1, questions 1–10

Links to other subjects
- **Business and economics** – to use simple equations to generalise cost calculations

Key words
- Algebra
- unknown number

Problem solving and reasoning help
- **PS** questions 8, 9 and 10 of Exercise 14A of the Pupil Book require pupils to work backwards. They may relate this to earlier work on number machines. The challenge activity at the end of the exercise encourages pupils to apply their skills to an increasingly difficult multi-step problem.

Common misconceptions and remediation
- Pupils may not understand the role of the letters as unknowns. Spend time making links between number and algebra so that pupils understand that algebra is generalised number.

Probing questions
- How do you know if a letter symbol represents an unknown or a variable?

Part 1
- On the board, write 25. Around it write 3, 4 and 7.
- Ask: *'How can I make 25 using these three small numbers?'* (Answer: $3 \times 7 + 4$)
- Then ask: *'Is there another way?'* We're now looking for: $7 \times 4 - 3$.
- Then give pupils three different small numbers: 2, 3 and 5, but keep the 25.
- Ask: *'How many different ways can we now see of making 25?'* Only one way: $(2 + 3) \times 5$.
- Change the numbers to 4, 7 and 8, and the target number to 24.
- Ask: *'How many now?'* Again there is only one: $(7 - 4) \times 8$.
- Now add another small number, 6, and ask: *'How many different ways can we now find of making 24?'* $[4 \times 6 \times (8 - 7)]$, $[(4 \times 6) \div (8 - 7)]$
- Finally, ask: *'How many different numbers can we make in this way using all four numbers, 4, 6, 7 and 8?'*

Part 2
- On the board, draw six 'bricks' arranged as shown.
- Ask three pupils for numbers less than 10 (to keep the arithmetic simple). Write each number in its own box in the bottom row of bricks.
- Show how to add two adjacent bricks and write that sum in the brick above them.
- Repeat this for the next layer and the last brick at the top.
- Ask whether it makes a difference where the starting numbers are put. Could 7, 3, 5, for example, be put in the order 3, 7, 5 and give the same answer? (No.)

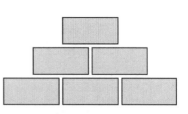

- Draw another set of bricks on the board. Ask if anyone can tell you what the top number will be. Wait for some pupils to calculate this.
- Then discuss Example 2 in Pupil Book 1.1. Ask how the missing number in the bottom layer might be found. Lead away from trial-and-improvement to an algebraic solution.
- Go through the algebraic solution.
- **Pupils can now do Exercise 14A from Pupil Book 1.1.**

Part 3

- Ask the class how many solutions there would be if only the top number were known. Suggest that the top number is 15. What could the next two numbers be? What could the bottom three numbers be?
- How would they find out how many different possible solutions gave 15 at the top?
- Remind pupils that negative numbers could be involved.

Answers

Exercise 14A

1	**a** 3	**b** 4	**c** 8	**d** 5	**e** 7	**f** 13	**g** 4	**h** 9
2	**a** 4	**b** 6	**c** 8	**d** 11	**e** 2	**f** 7	**g** 10	**h** 5
3	**a** 8	**b** 13	**c** 7	**d** 10	**e** 6	**f** 8	**g** 11	**h** 14
4	**a** 6	**b** 6	**c** 13	**d** 11	**e** 8	**f** 4	**g** 19	**h** 7
5	**a** 6	**b** 4	**c** 3	**d** 2				

6 **a** 6   **b** $b = 8$ and $c = 4$ **c** $d = 10$ and $e = 3$

7 **a** $a = 7$ and $b = 8$ **b** $c = 12$ and $d = 4$ **c** $e = 13$ and $f = 11$

8   12

9   12

10 £9.25

Challenge: Number triangles

A   **a** $a = 5$ and $b = 6$ and $c = 11$
     b $d = 2$ and $e = 11$ and $f = 9$
     c $h = 11$ and $j = 4$ and $k = 15$
     d $m = 8$ and $n = 5$ and $p = 12$

B $x = 3$ and $y = 7$ and $z = 5$

Lesson 14.2 Solving equations

Learning objectives

- To understand what an equation is
- To solve equations involving one operation

Links to other subjects

- **Design and technology** – to calculate materials for a given perimeter or area
- **Science** – to use speed, distance and time equations

Resources and homework

- Pupil Book 1.1, pages 274–279
- Homework Book 1, section 14.2
- Online homework 14.2, questions 1–10

Key words

- Equation
- solve

Problem solving and reasoning help

- The challenge activity at the end of Exercise 14B in the Pupil Book requires pupils to complete equations for different values of x. This should help to consolidate pupils' understanding of how the use of algebra generalises equations.

Common misconceptions and remediation

- Pupils often want to substitute numeral values into equations instead of solving them algebraically. Provide pupils with practice in writing equations in as many ways as possible.

Probing questions

- What are the important steps when solving an equation?
- What would you do first? Why?
- How would you continue to find the answer?

Part 1

- Ask if anyone knows the 13× multiplication table. Let a **more able** pupil show this.
- Explain that although they do not need to know the 13× table, it will help them to be able to multiply by larger numbers. For example, ask who can multiply 13 by 7 in their heads. Allow pupils 30 seconds to do this. See who has the correct answer (91). Ask that pupil to demonstrate how they worked it out. They probably multiplied 7 by 10 to get 70, then by 3 to get 21, and added the two to get 91.
- Allow pupils to talk about other methods they might have used. Show that there are quick ways of doing this type of multiplication mentally. Ask a few others:
    - 13 × 5 = 65   13 × 8 = 104   13 × 9 = 117
- Next, introduce other numbers such as 17.
- Ask: 17 × 6 (10 × 6 + 7 × 6 = 102), and then these:
    - 17 × 8 (136)   18 × 6 (108)   19 × 5 (95)
- Stress that it is important to try to calculate these mentally.
- You could give pupils six mental questions to answer at the back of their books, allowing 10 seconds to calculate each one.

Part 2

- An excellent start would be to demonstrate this first part with a pair of scales and some bags of marbles or coins. (But *do* practise this to make sure that the scales are sensitive enough.)
- Show a set of scales as illustrated. The left-hand pan has three bags. The right-hand pan has 15 marbles. The scales balance when the two sides are equal. Each bag holds the

same number of marbles. How many marbles are in one bag? At this point, introduce the '*What is it we want to know? Let's call it x.*' (It could be *m* or any other letter except *o*.)

- What do the scales show us? Both sides are equal. That is: Left-hand side = Right-hand side
- The left-hand side is 3*x*. (Discuss why.) The right-hand side is 15. So: $3x = 15$
- Explain this next stage carefully to pupils. Class discussion is invaluable for everyone to recognise that 3*x* means 3 times *x*, so we are looking at '*3 times what = 15*', leading to *x* = 5.
- Now discuss with the class equations such as: $x + 3 = 7$. Talk about simplifying the equation by subtracting the same number from both sides. It is important to start off with this next step written down (drop it later if you like) to get $x + 3 - 3 = 7 - 3$, leading to $x = 4$. Go over a few other examples, including the type $x - 4 = 9$, where we add to both sides.
- Work through Example 4 in Pupil Book 1.1, which shows pupils how to set out solutions.
- Now explain that you often have to solve algebraic equations in other areas of mathematics. Go over examples 5 and 6 in the Pupil Book.
- **Pupils can now do Exercise 14B from Pupil Book 1.1.**

Part 3

- Ask pupils to solve $8x = 4$. The likely answer is 2, but some pupils will give the correct answer of $\frac{1}{2}$. Emphasise the need to check answers. Use the answer of 2 to demonstrate how pupils can use what they know to show that this answer cannot be correct.
- Ask pupils to solve $x + 6 = 2$. The likely answer is 4, but some pupils will give the correct answer of –4. Encourage pupils to check if their answer makes sense. You may find it useful to use Cuisenaire rods to demonstrate to pupils, at this link: **http://nrich.maths.org/4348**.

Answers

Exercise 14B

1 **b** r = 11   **c** t = 24   **d** x = 12   **e** a = 3   **f** b = 6   **g** c = 8   **h** w = 17
2 **b** a = 13   **c** t = 17   **d** t = 10   **e** x = 21   **f** b = 25   **g** m = 36   **h** r = 50
3 **a** x = 3   **b** x = 9   **c** y = 12   **d** y = 3   **e** w = 5   **f** t = 7   **g** z = 3   **h** p = 5
4 **b i** w+14=23 **ii** w=9   **c i** u+18=30 **ii** u=12   **d i** v+19=33 **ii** v=14
   e i k+15=22 **ii** k=7   **f i** m+35=50 **ii** m=15
5 **b i** 4y = 36 **ii** y = 9   **c i** 6k = 72 **ii** k = 12   **d i** 5m = 60 **ii** m = 12
   e i 7n=49 **ii** n=7   **f i** 10t=200 **ii** t=20
6 **b i** y+78=180 **ii** y=102   **c i** a+130=180 **ii** a=50   **d i** t+106=180 **ii** t=74
   e i w+24=180 **ii** w=156   **f i** x+145=180 **ii** x=35
7 **b i** 5t=360 **ii** t=72   **c i** 6a=360 **ii** a=60   **d i** 8c=360 **ii** a=45
   e i 10m=360 **ii** m=36
8 **a i** 15+x=24 **ii** x=9   **b i** y+21=32 **ii** y=11   **c i** 14+k=39 **ii** k=25
9 **a i** 5t = 45 **ii** t = 9   **b i** 4x = 60 **ii** x = 15   **c i** 3d = 75 **ii** d = 25

Challenge: Making equations

A   **a** 2x=8   **b** x+1=5   **c** 2x+1=9   **d** 2(x+1)=10
B   **a** 2x=10   **b** x+1=6   **c** 2x+1=11   **d** 2(x+1)=12
C   **a** 2x=20   **b** x+1=11   **c** 2x+1=21   **d** 2(x+1)=22

Lesson 14.3 Solving more complex equations

Learning objectives

- To solve equations involving two operations

Links to other subjects

- **Design and technology** – to use conversion equations to convert between different units of measure.
- **Geography** – to convert between different units of temperature or distance

Resources and homework

- Pupil Book 1.1, pages 279–282
- Homework Book 1, section 14.3
- Online homework 14.3, questions 1–10

Key words

- inverse
- operation

Problem solving and reasoning help

- The challenge activity at the end of Exercise 14C develops confidence and fluency by using tables to solve equations.

Common misconceptions and remediation

- Pupils often want to substitute numerical values into equations instead of solving them algebraically. Give them with lots of practice in writing equations in as many ways as possible. Reinforce inverse relationships.

Probing questions

- How are these two equations different?
- Write your own single-step equation for a partner to solve. Now write a two-step equation for your partner to solve.
- $8 = 2q - 6$. How many solutions does this equation have? Give me other equations with the same solution. Why do they have the same solution? How do you know?

Part 1

- Write two different examples on the board, one a single-step problem, and one a two-step problem.
- Ask pupils to write an equation for each problem.
- Discuss what is the same, or what is different about the problems and which is easier or more difficult to solve and why.

Part 2

- In the last lesson we looked at solving single-step equations. The equations we need to solve often have more than one step.
- Show the class the equation $7x + 4 = 88$, and ask how they would solve it.
- Using pupils' suggestions, lead them through the strategy of:
- Subtract 4 from both sides: $7x + 4 - 4 = 88 - 4$ so $7x = 84$
- Divide both sides by 7: $7x \div 7 = 84 \div 7$ so $x = 12$
- Similarly, allow pupils to help you with the solution to $8x - 5 = 115$:
- Add 5 to both sides: $8x - 5 + 5 = 115 + 5$ so $8x = 120$
- Divide both sides by 8: $8x \div 8 = 120 \div 8$ so $x = 15$
- Conclude by asking the class to solve $19x + 41 = 288$:
- Subtract 41 from both sides: $19x + 41 - 41 = 288 - 41$ so $19x = 247$

- Divide both sides by 19: $19x \div 19 = 247 \div 19$ so $x = 13$
- You will need to tell the class that they may use their calculators – unless you wish to use this as a way of revising awkward divisions.
- **Pupils can now do Exercise 14C from Pupil Book 1.1.**

Part 3

- Discuss how to solve equations of the form:

$$\frac{x}{4} = 2$$

- The principle to make is that equations are 'undone' by using the appropriate inverse operation and doing the same thing to both sides.

Answers
Exercise 14C
1   **a** a = 4   **b** a = 8   **c** a = 14
2   **a** a = 5   **b** a = 9   **c** a = 16
3   **a** a = 4   **b** a = 6   **c** a = 7   **d** a = 4   **e** a = 7   **f** a = 12
4   **a** a = 4   **b** a = 7   **c** a = 12   **d** a = 4   **e** a = 9   **f** a = 18
5   **a** The perimeter is a+5+a+5.   **b** a = 8
6   **a** The perimeter is t+12+t+12.   **b** t=8
7   **a** Add the two sides and double it.   **b** m = 7
8   **a** 2x + 30 or 2(x + 15)   **b** 2x + 30 = 52 or 2(x + 15) = 52   **c** x = 11
9   **a** The perimeter is t+t+t+20.   **b** 3t + 20 = 62   **c** t = 14
10 **a** 3a + 5   **b** 3a + 5 = 38   **c** a = 11
11 **a** 4x + 15   **b** 4x + 15 = 51   **c** x = 9
Challenge: Using tables to solve equations
A   9
B   The bottom line is 9, 13, 17, 21, 25, 29, 33, 37.
C   **i** x = 8   **ii** x = 14   **iii** x = 18
D   **i** x = 5   **ii** x = 11   **iii** x = 17

Learning objectives

- To use algebra to set up and solve equations

Links to other subjects

- **Science** – to set up formulae to generalise experimental outcomes

Resources and homework

- Pupil Book 1.1, pages 283–285
- Homework Book 1, section 14.4
- Online homework 14.4, questions 1–10

Key words

- No new key words for this topic

Problem solving and reasoning help

- All the questions in Exercise 14D of the Pupil Book require pupils to decode the mathematics in a range of word problems based on real-life situations. Before pupils work on the exercise, discuss the examples as a class to identify key principles or strategies for identifying the mathematical question and resulting equation in each case. The challenge question explores a conversion relationship which is a very common use of equations in real life, for example, look at 'temperature' at this link: **http://nrich.maths.org/5608.**

Common misconceptions and remediation

- Pupils often struggle to decode the mathematics in real-life problems. Give them plenty of experience in setting up equations for simple familiar situations before moving on to less familiar, more complex situations.

Probing questions

- How do you go about constructing equations from information given in a problem?
- How do you check whether the equation works?

Part 1

- I went shopping the other day, and one of the shops had a half-price sale. Each price shown was to be halved.
- What was the sale price of items marked at: £1.40, £1.60, £1.50, £1.10, £1.70?
- Discuss with the class the strategies they used. For example, dealing first with the pence and halving them. Then halving the £1 to get 50p and adding half the pence.
- Move the prices on to £2.20, £2.40, £2.50, £2.30, £2.70.
- Discuss the strategy of halving these amounts: half the £2 plus half the pence.
- Move the prices on to larger amounts such as: £3.40, £4.10, £5.60, £6.30, £7.90.
- Talk about the different strategies pupils use to halve these amounts.
- If pupils are confident in handling these forms of money, introduce figures such as: £1.24, £2.56, £5.78.
- Do not introduce amounts with odd numbers of pence unless pupils suggest this, in which case you must discuss with them the rounding off options. Shops can either round down to the customers' benefit or round up to the shops' benefit.

Part 2

- Share with pupils that it is often very useful to set up an equation for a real-life problem. Revisit Part 1 of this lesson and ask pupils to try and write an equation to describe how they work out the sale price.
- Ask pupils how they could solve the equation to find the original price if they know the sale price. Make clear links to the strategies of halving and doubling, as already discussed.
- Work through Example 10 in Pupil Book 1.1, which shows pupils how to set up equations for some real-life problems.
- Give pupils time to discuss each example before and after working through them.
- Ask **more able** pupils to write some word problems using their equations.
- You could use matching exercises to give pupils practice.
- **Pupils can now do Exercise 14D from Pupil Book 1.1.**

Part 3

- Given a list of linear equations, ask pupils:
    - Which of these are easy to solve?
    - Which are difficult and why?
    - What strategies are important with the difficult equations?
- Can you write a word problem for any of these equations? Compare your problems with those of a partner. What is the same? What is different?
- **Pupils can now do Exercise 14D from Pupil Book 1.1.**

Answers

Exercise 14D

1 **a** 17t+4   **b** 17t+4=106   **c** t = 6
2 **a** 22j+3   **b** 22j+3=179   **c** j=8
3 **a** 34y+8=314   **b** y=9
4 **a** 2d+3   **b** 2d+3=59   **c** d=28
5 **a** 2(c+1)   **b** 2(c+1)=24   **c** c=11
6 **a** 2n+7=41 **b** n=17
7 **a** 3(g-5)=36   **b** g=17
8 **a** 2a+18=28 or 2(a+9)=28   **b** a=5
9 **a** 2x+30=72 or 2(x+15)=72 **b** x=21
10 **a** 4c+20=76   **b** c=14

Challenge: Changing temperatures

A **a** 104 °F   **b** 140 °F
B The bottom line is 32, 68, 104, 140, 176, 212.
C C = 30
D C = 50
E 90 °C

Review questions (Pupil Book pages 286–287)

- The review questions will help to determine pupils' abilities with regard to the material within Chapter 14.
- These questions also draw on the maths covered in earlier chapters of the book to encourage pupils to make links between different topics.
- The answers are on the next page.

Investigation – Number puzzles (Pupil Book pages 288–289)

- In this activity, pupils apply what they know to an abstract number problem. They need to identify and solve multi-step linear equations to solve the problem.
- All the information required to answer the questions is given but pupils will need to read it carefully.
- Depending on the group, a class discussion could be used to identify the steps required. Set up and solve one or two examples as a class before pupils work independently.
- Support **less able** pupils with guided group work. Work through some simpler examples of single-step equations together with these pupils before they work on the main activity.
- Extend **more able** pupils by asking them to design their own puzzles. You may want to work through the strategies they might need to use first.

Answers to Review questions

1   **a** $x = 8$ **b** $y = 18$ **c** $t = 18$ **d** $a = 14$ **e** $b = 17$ **f** $c = 11$
2   **a** $x = 3$ **b** $y = 13$ **c** $t = 30$ **d** $a = 7$ **e** $b = 15$ **f** $c = 4$
3   **a** volume $= 4 \times 2 \times x = 8x$ **b** $8x = 24$ **c** $x = 3$
4   **a** $x + 33$ **b** $x + 33 = 55$ **c** $x = 22$
5   **a** $t = 5$ **b** $r = 12$ **c** $z = 14$
6   **a** $m = 11$ **b** $p = 17$ **c** $z = 11$
7   **a** $2 \times 1 + 1 = 3$ **b** $2 \times 2 + 1 = 5$ **c** $2 \times 4 + 1 = 9$ **d** 15
    e i $2p + 1 = 33$ **ii** $p = 16$
8   **a** £77   **b** $25 + 13d = 207$ **c** $d = 14$ **d** 9 days
9   **a** $2t + 4 + 80$ **b** $t = 38$
10   **a** subtract 4 then multiply by 3   **b** 18

Answers to Investigation – Number puzzles

1   A = 6, B = 7, C = 9
2   A = 8, B = 11, C = 6
3   A = 3, B = 17, C = 15
4   A = 5, B = 13, C = 15
5   A = 12, B = 13, C = 7
6   A = 5, B = 3, C = 7
7   A = 4, B = 6, C = 7
8   A = 2, B = 16, C = 11, D = 9
9   A = 12, B = 7, C = 10, D = 6
10   A = 11, B = 10, C = 16, D = 14
11   A = 9.5, B = 2.5, C = 3.5, D = 6.5

Learning objectives

- How to read data from a pie chart
- How to use the median and range to compare sets of data
- How to carry out and interpret a statistical survey

Prior knowledge

- How to work out the median and range of a set of data
- How to draw tally charts
- By the end of KS2, pupils will have connected their work on angles, fractions and percentages to the interpretation of pie charts. They will have interpreted and drawn graphs relating two variables as part of their own enquiry and in other subjects. They will also know when it is appropriate to find the mean of a data set in simple, familiar situations.

Context

- Statistical data is everywhere in a modern society and to function in this society it is important to be able to analyse critically the data being presented. You could show this video clip (about fewer children dying as women give birth to fewer children) to demonstrate the power of statistics: **http://www.gapminder.org/videos/the-river-of-myths/**.

Discussion points

- For a given pie chart, make up three questions that you can answer using the information represented.

Associated Collins ICT resources

- Chapter 15 interactive activities on Collins Connect online platform
- *Weather measures* Wonder of Maths on Collins Connect online platform
- *Drawing pie charts using scaling* Worked solution on Collins Connect online platform

Curriculum references

Statistics

- Describe, interpret and compare observed distributions of a single variable through: appropriate graphical representation, and appropriate measures of central tendency and spread
- Construct and interpret appropriate tables, charts, and diagrams, including pie charts

Reason mathematically

- Explore what can and cannot be inferred in statistical and probabilistic settings, and begin to express their arguments formally

Solve problems

- Begin to model situations mathematically and express the results using a range of formal mathematical representations

Fast-track for classes following a 2-year scheme of work

- You could leave out Lesson 15.1 on pie charts.
- During Lesson 15.2, comparing data by median and range, you could focus on the activity at the end of Exercise 15B in the Pupil Book.
- Then move straight on to the application of skills to do with statistical surveys in Lesson 15.3.

Learning objective
- To read data from pie charts, where the data is given in simple sectors

Resources and homework
- Pupil Book 1.1, pages 291–295
- Intervention Book 3, pages 71–72
- Homework Book 1, section 15.1
- Online homework 15.1, questions 1–10

Links to other subjects
- **Geography** – to compare populations
- **Physical education** – to interpret data on sports participation

Key words
- pie chart
- sector

Problem solving and reasoning help
- **PS** question 9 in Exercise 15A of the Pupil Book, and the problem-solving activity at the end of the exercise give pupils the opportunity to apply their knowledge to decode slightly more complex questions. If pupils require support, let them complete question 9 as a group activity before working on the problem-solving activity on their own. Encourage pupils to discuss the similarities and differences of the two questions to help them see the generic structure of the questions and how this helps them to identify the mathematics they will need to use.

Common misconceptions and remediation
- Pupils sometimes struggle to transfer their understanding of angles, fractions and percentages to the interpretation of pie charts. Stress these links with careful use of correct mathematical language.

Probing questions
- Make up a statement or question for this pie chart using one or more of the following words:
    - fraction
    - percentage
    - proportion.

Part 1
- Write 20 on the board.
- Ask the class to give you (mentally) the percentage of 20, for a value that you will state. For example, if you say 5, pupils should reply 25%.
- Repeat with 4 (20%), 7 (35%), 3 (15%), 2 (10%), 8 (40%), 1 (5%), 13 (65%), 18 (90%).
- Now write 30 on the board.
- Repeat the above activity with 9 (30%), 12 (40%), 3 (10%), 15 (50%), 24 (80%).
- Repeat with other multiples of 10 such as 40, 50 and so on.
- This activity could also be done using fractions instead of, or as well as, percentages.

Part 2
- Talk about pie charts, for example: Sometimes we are presented with pie charts that show percentages. The simplest of these are split into 10 sections, with each section representing 10%, like the one I am about to draw:

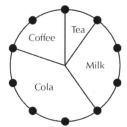

- Sketch the pie chart, which shows the favourite drinks of some Year 7 pupils. We see that:
    - Tea occupies one sector hence 10% have tea as their favourite.
    - Milk occupies three sectors hence 30% have milk as their favourite.
    - Cola occupies four sectors hence 40% have cola as their favourite.
    - Coffee occupies two sectors hence 20% have coffee as their favourite.
- **Pupils can now do Exercise 15A from Pupil Book 1.1.**

Part 3

- Review the method of looking at pie charts that have been drawn with 10 sectors and interpreting them in terms of percentages.
- Sketch the pie chart:

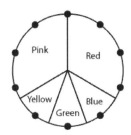

- Tell pupils that it shows the favourite colours of a group of pupils.
- Ask what percentage like: **a** red, **b** blue, and so on.

Answers

Exercise 15A

1	a 20	b 40	c 10	d 10	e 20	
2	a 30	b 20	c 10	d 10	e 30	
3	a 45	b 15	c 20	d 10	e 10	
4	a 4	b 4	c 8	d 24		
5	a 9	b 12	c 18	d 12	e 9	
6	a 8	b 12	c 20	d 16	e 24	
7	a 36	b 18	c 30	d 24	e 12	
8	a 98	b 7	c 35			
9	a 10	b 10	c 30	d 40	e 50	f 60

Problem solving: Journeys to school

A true for both

B true for neither

C true for neither

D true for class B

Learning objectives

- To use the median and range to compare data
- To make sensible decisions by comparing the median and range of two sets of data

Resources and homework

- Pupil Book 1.1, pages 296–299
- Intervention Book 3, pages 67–68
- Homework Book 1, section 15.2
- Online homework 15.2, questions 1–10

Links to other subjects

- **History** – to compare statistical measures of historical data

Key words

- data
- median
- range

Problem solving and reasoning help

- **MR** question 4 in Exercise 15B and the activity at the end of this exercise require pupils to compare the use of range and median when making decisions based on a set of data. PS question 5 requires pupils to think carefully about what they can and cannot assume from the information provided. Pupils should give reasons for their decisions. Any of the questions and/or the activity could be done as a class discussion or as part of guided group work.

Common misconceptions and remediation

- The non-technical use of the language of central tendency and spread in real life, including the media, often confuses pupils. Tackle this confusion by using clear examples.

Probing questions

- Make up a statement or question for this chart or graph using one or more of the following words:
  - o total
  - o range
  - o mode.

Part 1

- This activity will help you to check the prior knowledge within the group
- Write nine numbers on the board such as: 2, 4, 6, 3, 5, 6, 2, 8, 7.
- Ask the class if anyone can explain how to work out the median of these numbers. (5)
- Then ask them how to work out the range of these numbers. (6)
- Discuss the ways of doing this.

Part 2

- Say that you will now explore how to use statistical measures such as median and range, which will help them to make decisions in real life. Add that there is often more than one way to look at information.
- Write these two sets of numbers on the board. Explain that these are the number of netball goals scored by Ann and Bernice in the last nine matches.

| Ann | 3 | 5 | 5 | 3 | 4 | 6 | 3 | 3 | 5 |
| Bernice | 10 | 0 | 2 | 3 | 7 | 2 | 10 | 7 | 8 |

- Pupils should pick a girl for the local county team. Which girl would pupils pick and why?

- Pupils may have various reasons for picking one or the other. For example:
- Ann always scores; Bernice gets some high scores.
- Ask for a mathematical way of choosing. Lead pupils to the idea of using *median* and *range*.
- Median for Ann is 4 and her range is 4; median for Bernice is 7 and her range is 8.
- Given this information, who should they pick? Bernice, because her median is larger, or Ann, because her range is lower, so she is more consistent?
- **Pupils can now do Exercise 15B from Pupil Book 1.1.**

Part 3

- Review the reasons for making choices: high medians and consistency.
- Look at this data for the absence of 10 boys and 10 girls.

Boys	12	5	4	1	1	3	4	7	6	2
Girls	0	1	3	4	4	2	31	3	1	0

- Who has the worst record of absence? The boys have a median of 4 and a range of 11; the girls have a median of 2.5 and a range of 31. It appears that the girls have the worst record, but the data for both boys and for girls is affected by a large number.
- Discuss what can be done. One option is to eliminate the rogue values. Explain that in statistical terms these sorts of values are referred to as *outlier*s.

Answers

Exercise 15B
1   **a** 31   **b** 109   **c** 40   **d** 26   **e** Ali – more consistent and a higher median
2   **a** 3 min **b** 11 min **c** 5 min **d** 4 min
   e Bus A – apart from the once very late, it's usually not very late
3   **a** 12   **b** 6   **c** 13   **d** 13
   e A, although the median is slightly lower, it is more consistent
4   Josh, almost same median but more consistent
5   **a** Andrew is scoring more consistently about 17.
   Oliver is not consistent; he gets lows and highs.
   b No.
   c median increased from 17 to 20
   d more consistent – range down from 10 to 4

Lesson 15.3 Statistical surveys

Learning objectives
- To use charts and diagrams to interpret data

Resources and homework
- Pupil Book 1.1, pages 299–301
- Intervention Book 2, pages 76–79
- Intervention Workbook 3, pages 69–79
- Homework Book 1, section 15.3
- Online homework 15.3, questions 1–10

Links to other subjects
- **Geography** – to make data comparisons for different countries
- **Physical education** – to compare records for different athletes

Key words
- experiment
- questionnaire
- tally
- frequency
- statistical survey

Problem solving and reasoning help

- The questions in Exercise 15C of the Pupil Book are designed to prepare pupils for completing the activity at the end of the exercise, 'Do smaller people have smaller feet?' It would be helpful to explain that for some problems secondary sources may have to be used to collect the data, for example: newspapers, reference books, databases and the internet. Depending on the time available, the class could work on one problem, or pairs or groups could choose different problems. Ask pupils to present their findings to the rest of the group. Encourage the class to provide constructive feedback based on a set of success criteria (agreed on by all class members), which could include, for example:
  - clarity of presentation
  - statement of a clear hypothesis
  - use of data
  - use of graphical representations (Did pupils add to the clarity of the presentation?)
  - range of statistical measures used for comparison (Did pupils use a range?)
  - analysis and summary of findings.

Common misconceptions and remediation

- Pupils are often given lots of experience of drawing tables and charts but less experience of interpreting them in real-life situations. The data they are given often does not reflect the complexity of real-life data. To illustrate the true complexity of real-life data, you could find and use examples from a website such as 'Gapminder': **http://www.gapminder.org/**.

Probing questions

- Is this graphical representation useful in investigating this hypothesis? If not, why not? What would you change?
- When comparing a range of graphs representing the same data:
  - Which is the easiest to interpret? Why?
  - Which is most helpful in reflecting on the hypothesis? Why?

Part 1

- Write on the board: Young people do not read many books.
- Ask pupils how they would investigate this statement. Write the responses on the board.
- Discuss issues such as: samples, data collection sheets, questionnaires and diagrams, which pupils have worked with either earlier in this lesson or in KS2.

Part 2

- Tell pupils that after completing Exercise 15C they will carry out their own statistical survey. The activity involves collecting data and writing a statistical report, which will take time for most pupils and may cover more than one lesson. The activity is ideal to revise the Statistics work pupils have covered so far or in KS2, which you should recap before they start.
- Discuss different ways to collect and record data.
- Discuss the required sample size in order to validate or confirm the conclusions. A sample size of 30 or more is usually considered enough. For example, pupils could survey all pupils in their class or in their year group.
- When pupils have collected the data, they will need to analyse it. Then they should draw their conclusions, and state them at the end of the report. This may involve calculating statistical measures and/or drawing suitable diagrams. Pupils could calculate the median number, they could draw bar charts, or they could draw pie charts. In the report, pupils need to give reasons as to why they have used particular diagrams.
- Finally, pupils should write a conclusion based on all the evidence. Pupils should include references to any original hypotheses.
  If pupils struggle with completing all the steps independently, use whole class and/or small group discussion to check progress at regular intervals.
- **Pupils can now do Exercise 15C from Pupil Book 1.1.**

Part 3

- As pupils are completing their reports, ask them to explain the methods they have used. Ensure that they understand these terms: *sample size*, *hypothesis*, *data collection sheet*, *questionnaire*.
- Make a display of pupils' work in the classroom.

Answers

Exercise 15C
1 **a** frequencies are 12, 9, 5, 4
2 **a** frequencies are 9, 2, 4, 11, 3
3 **a** frequencies are 12, 15, 8, 22, 3
4 **b** No.
5 **a**

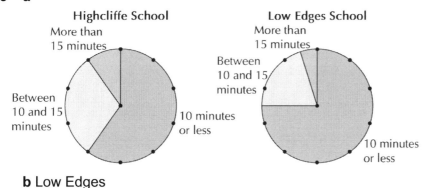

b Low Edges

Review questions
(Pupil Book pages 302–303)

- The review questions will help to determine pupils' abilities with regard to the material within Chapter 15.
- These questions also draw on the maths covered in earlier chapters of the book to encourage pupils to make links between different topics.
- The answers are on the next page.

Challenge – Dancing competition
(Pupil Book pages 304–305)

- This activity is designed to use both the interpretation and communication skills covered in this chapter in a familiar scenario.
- All the information required to answer the questions has been provided in the text, but pupils will need to analyse the data carefully. They need to make their own choices and decisions, and be able to justify them.
- A discussion about what they have learnt about conducting a statistical investigation may be appropriate, depending on the group.
- An important part of this activity is the role of audience and purpose for statistical data. Ask pupils some warm-up questions to get them thinking about this. Here are some examples:
    - What is the newspaper trying to achieve?
    - Who will read this article?
    - How will you appeal to this audience?
- You could also look for some real-life stories in the media to discuss with pupils.
- Pupils can now work on the questions in small groups.
- Ask pupils to develop this topic further by using the internet to research other news stories. **More able** pupils could consider how the stories might differ depending on the newspaper for which the article was being written.
- You could ask pupils to act as news presenter to read out their stories with the rest of the group asking questions. The class could give feedback based on a set of agreed success criteria similar to those used in Lesson 15.3 under the heading 'Problem solving and reasoning help'.

Answers to Review questions

1

2 **a** 15 **b** 20

3 **a** Rachel 4, Joe 5 **b** Rachel 3, Joe 2 **c** Rachel 4, Joe 4
    d Joe, range of only 2   **e** Rachel, scores less than Joe more often.

5 **a** no   **b**

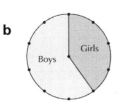

6 **a** £120   **b**   **c** Lindsey

7 **a** 5 **b** 15

Answers to Challenge – Dancing competition

1 Final column values are 23, 17, 22, 16 and 23.
2 David and Hanna – 19; James and Helena – 15; Joy and Chris – 19; Tom and Eve – 12; Bain and Kathy – 21
3 For example: Judges X and Z both have a range of 3, but Judge Y only has a range of 2.
4 pupils' own graphs/charts
5 Tom and Eve – they have the biggest range
6 David and Hanna – their score has increased by 2 every week. You would expect them to win with a score of 25.

16 3D shapes

Learning objectives

- The names of 3D shapes you need to know
- How to draw the net of a 3D shape
- How to construct a 3D shape
- The rule connecting the number of faces, edges and vertices for 3D shapes

Prior knowledge

- The names of some 3D shapes such as a cube, cuboid and pyramid
- By the end of KS2, pupils should be able to draw shapes and nets accurately using measuring tools and conventional markings and labels for lines and angles. Pupils should also be able to describe the properties of familiar shapes.

Context

- There are only five regular 3D shapes or (regular polyhedra) that can be made using the same regular polygon throughout. These were discovered by the ancient Greeks. They are: tetrahedron, cube, octahedron, dodecahedron and icosahedron.
- These shapes were also named the Platonic Solids, after the ancient Greek philosopher Plato, who speculated that these five solids were the shapes of the fundamental components of the physical universe.

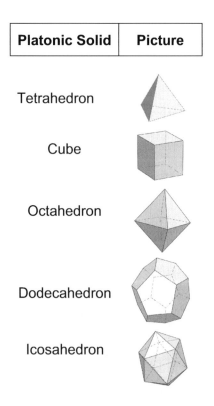

Platonic Solid	Picture
Tetrahedron	
Cube	
Octahedron	
Dodecahedron	
Icosahedron	

- We will look more closely at some of these shapes in this chapter.

Discussion points

- Can you describe a rectangle precisely, so that someone else can draw it?
- What mathematical words are important when describing a square or cube?

Associated Collins ICT resources

- Chapter 16 interactive activities on Collins Connect online platform
- *Sonobe cube* Wonder of Maths on Collins Connect online platform
- *Using nets to construct 3D shapes* Worked solution on Collins Connect online platform

Curriculum references

Develop fluency

- Use language and properties precisely to analyse 3D shapes

Reason mathematically

- Begin to reason deductively in geometry, number and algebra, including using geometrical constructions

Geometry and measures

- Use the properties of faces, surfaces, edges and vertices of cubes, cuboids, prisms, cylinders, pyramids, cones and spheres to solve problems in 3D

Fast-track for classes following a 2-year scheme of work

- Use discussion to check pupils' recall of terminology; then focus on the **MR** and **PS** questions in the exercises in each lesson, and on the challenge and practical activities at the end of Exercise 16A and Exercise 16B in the Pupil Book.

Lesson 16.1 3D shapes and nets

Learning objectives

- To know how to count the faces, vertices and edges on a 3D shape
- To draw nets for 3D shapes

Resources and homework

- Pupil Book 1.1, pages 307–309
- Intervention Workbook 1, pages 37–41
- Intervention Workbook 3, pages 50–51
- Homework Book 1, section 16.1
- Online homework 16.1, questions 1–10

Links to other subjects

- **Art** – to use the properties of 3D shapes to construct models and sculptures
- **Design and technology** – to produce 2D plans for 3D constructions

Key words

- 3D
- face
- square-based pyramid
- triangular prism
- edge
- net
- tetrahedron
- vertex
- vertices

Problem solving and reasoning help

- In Exercise 16A of the Pupil Book, questions 5 and 6 are **MR** and **PS**, respectively. Support pupils who struggle by modelling an example and/or providing concrete models.
- The challenge at the end of the exercise requires pupils to make all 11 nets for a cube. Encourage pupils to be methodical and to justify how they know they have them all.

Common misconceptions and remediation

- Problems can occur with the change of vocabulary between 2D and 3D, for example, sides become faces. Use visual images to support understanding and memory. The imprecise use of language in real life can also confuse pupils. Discuss examples of this. Also discuss the concept of subsets, for example, a cube is a regular cuboid. Identify this concept of subsets as being applicable across mathematics.

Probing questions

- Can you build a cuboid with 16 interlocking cubes?
- What about with 27 cubes? Explain your answer.

Part 1

- Ask the class how many mathematical names they know for 3D shapes or solids.
- Write them on the board or ask pupils to write them in their books. Stress the importance of correct spelling.
- Show the class everyday objects such as a book, a can, a ball, a dice, different-shaped boxes, pencils.
- Draw a table in which to write down the mathematical name for each object.

Part 2

- Explain that it is difficult to draw 3D shapes accurately on squared paper.
- Show the class how to draw a *cuboid* on the isometric grid, stressing that the columns of dots must be *vertical*.
- Show the class various 3D shapes. Explain the terms 'face', 'vertex' and 'edge'.
- Discuss why shapes like a cone and a sphere are different because of their curved faces.
- Define a prism: 3D shape that has the same 2D shape (cross-section) all the way through it.
- Explain the terms: triangular prism; hexagonal prism; that a cuboid is an example of a prism.

- **Pupils can now do Exercise 16A from Pupil Book 1.1.**

Part 3

- Ask the class to write down the mathematical names for all the 3D shapes they have met during the lesson.
- Ask the class why we use isometric paper.

Answers

Exercise 16A

1 **a** 16 **b** 15 **c** 14 **d** 14

2 **a** and **e**, **b** and **f**, **c** and **d**

3

3D shape	No of faces	No of vertices	No of edges
Cuboid	6	8	12
Square-based pyramid	5	5	8
Triangular prism	5	6	9
Tetrahedron	4	4	6

4 6, 8, 12

5 **a** False **b** True **c** True **d** False **e** False **f** True

6

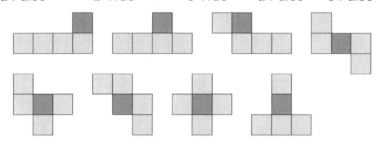

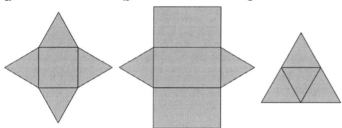

7 **a** **b** **c**

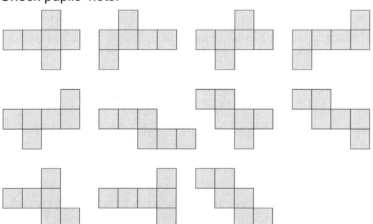

Challenge: Nets for a cube

Check pupils' nets.

Lesson 16.2 Using nets to construct 3D shapes

Learning objectives
- To construct 3D shapes from nets

Links to other subjects
- **Design and technology** – to use nets to construct packaging

Resources and homework
- Pupil Book 1.1, pages 310–312
- Homework Book 1, section 16.2
- Online homework 16.2, questions 1–10

Key words
- construct

Problem solving and reasoning help

- The practical activity at the end of Exercise 16B of the Pupil Book builds on the introduction to the lesson by asking pupils to choose suitable measurements to make the more complex 3D shapes from cards. Pupils will need to decide if they need to add tabs to the nets.

Common misconceptions and remediation

- Give **less able** pupils who may struggle with visualising the nets the opportunity to construct pre-prepared nets. Encourage pupils to suggest answers to questions such as 'Which faces will meet?' before actually constructing the model. Check pupils' suggestions once they have constructed the model. If they were wrong they need to reflect on why they were wrong and then try again. Pupils could do this in pairs, taking it in turns to ask questions.

Probing questions

- Start from a 2D representation of a 3D shape and ask:
  - How many faces will the 3D shape have? How do you know?
  - What will be opposite this face in the 3D shape? How do you know?
  - Which side will this side join to make an edge? How do you know?

Part 1

- Draw or put the name of a 3D shape on the board.
- List a set of properties on the board. Ask pupils to identify which property is NOT true for the given shape.
- Differentiate the activity based on the shapes and its properties.

Part 2

- This work may take more than one lesson. For the lesson, it is useful to have the following solids in class: a cube, a cuboid, a square-based pyramid, a tetrahedron, a triangular prism, a hexagonal prism, an octahedron, a dodecahedron, a cone, a cylinder, a sphere.
- The class will require squared paper, scissors and glue.
- Remind pupils of the activity at the end of Exercise 16A when they found the nets of a cube.
  - On the board, draw two possible nets for a cube, one correct and one incorrect.
  - Ask pupils which is correct and which is not. Encourage them to explain why, to help them visualise shapes.
- If pupils struggle you could model an example for them, emphasising the language you use to justify your explanations.
- Now show this net. Ask pupils to explain where the tabs need to go.

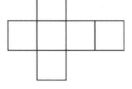

- **Less able** pupils may have difficulty drawing the nets. They could use commercially made plastic kits, or straws and modelling clay or Plasticine.
- Using a prepared net for a cube with tabs, show the class how to score the edges that must be folded. Then construct the cube.
- **Pupils can now do Exercise 16B from Pupil Book 1.1.**

Part 3

- Ask the class to write down the names and draw sketches of all the 3D shapes that they have constructed during these two lessons.
- Ask the class to explain how to draw the nets for various solids: for example, a square-based pyramid or a tetrahedron.

Answers
Exercise 16B
1 to 4 Check pupils' drawings.

5 For example:

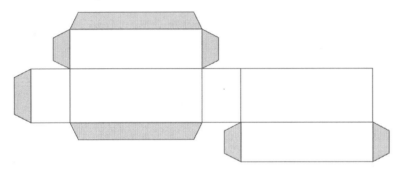

Practical activity: Making an octahedron
Before pupils construct the octahedron, check that the tabs are in the correct position.

Lesson 16.3 3D investigations

Learning objectives

- To work out the rule connecting faces, edges and vertices of 3D shapes
- To solve problems involving 3D shapes

Links to other subjects

- **Design and technology** – to use nets to construct packaging

Resources and homework

- Pupil Book 1.1, pages 313
- Homework Book 1, section 16.3

Key words

- Euler
- octahedron
- hexagonal prism
- pentagonal-based pyramid

Problem solving and reasoning help

- Pupils need to draw on the previous two lessons and be methodical in the way they approach these problems. A reading images approach may help pupils to get started. Place a copy of the problem in the centre of a large sheet of paper. Around this, pupils should write what they know or the key information from the problem. In the next layer they should write what mathematics they are going to use and/or how they are going to record information. Finally, in the outside layer they should solve the problem. This approach encourages pupils to think carefully about the steps involved in solving the problem instead of trying to find a solution immediately. This generic approach to problem solving can be used across mathematics.

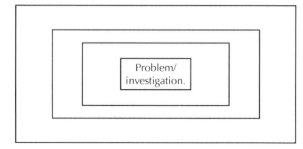

Problem/investigation.

Common misconceptions and remediation

- Pupils are often careless in the way they record information, especially when they are asked to be sure that they have found all possibilities. Model an example, working through each step and sharing your thoughts as you go. Be clear about how you are going to record information and how you will be sure that you have found all the possible solutions.

Probing questions

- Is it possible to slice a cube so that the face you see is: a rectangle; a triangle?
- Are there any other 2D shapes you could make by slicing a cube?
- Would it make any difference if you started with a cuboid?

Part 1

- This is a recap of work done by pupils in Lesson 16.1, which they will need later in this lesson. If necessary, remind pupils of the terminology of: faces, edges and vertices.
- Draw a cube on the board. Ask: How many faces, edges and vertices are there?
- Ask pupils to record their answers. Say that you will return to it at the end of this lesson.

Part 2

- Explain to the class that they will now apply what they have done on cubes to some slightly more complex, less familiar 3D shapes.
- Introduce them to Euler and show them the table on page 313 of the Pupil Book. As a class, discuss the rows that have been completed and complete one more row together.

- Allow the class to work independently for about 10 minutes and then to start sharing some thoughts as a class. Encourage discussion and sharing ideas. Pupils could explore the patterns they see in words before trying to write them algebraically.
- If pupils struggle to work independently, search for 'Euler's formula' or use a website similar to this one to help them: **http://www.mathsisfun.com/geometry/eulers-formula.html**.
- **Pupils can now do Exercise 16C from Pupil Book 1.1.**

Part 3

- The relationship pupils should have found between the number of faces (F), the number of vertices (F) and the number of edges (E) is: $F + V = E - 2$
- Ask: '*Does this rule agree with your answers in Part 1? If not, what did you do wrong?*' For a cube, another rule is: the number of edges is four times the number of faces divided by 2. Ask pupils to write a formula for this rule. Is this true? Can you explain why it makes sense? This diagram may help.
- Use grouping to support **less able** pupils or challenge **more able** pupils. Ask **more able** pupils to find a similar rule to connect the number of vertices to the number of edges. Or, talk pupils through this example and then let them try to find the similar rule for vertices.
- You could extend this to other 3D shapes.

Answers
Exercise 16C

1 a

3D shape	Number of faces	Number of edges	Number of vertices
Cube	6	12	8
Cuboid	6	12	8
Square-based pyramid	5	8	5
Tetrahedron	4	6	4
Triangular prism	5	9	6
Hexagonal prism	8	18	12
Octahedron	8	12	6
Pentagonal-based pyramid	6	10	6

b Number of faces + the number of vertices − the number of edges = 2

2 5 different cuboids (1 by 1 by 12, 1 by 2 by 6, 1 by 3 by 4, 2 by 2 by 3, 2 by 3 by 4)

Review questions (Pupil Book pages 314–315)

- The review questions will help to determine pupils' abilities with regard to the material within Chapter 16.
- These questions also draw on the maths covered in earlier chapters of the book to encourage pupils to make links between different topics.
- The answers follow.

Problem solving – Packing boxes (Pupil Book pages 316–317)

- Task 1 is a common type of problem used at GCSE so it is important that pupils can identify this type of problem.
- You could model the approach required using a small cardboard box and some multi-link cubes.
- Pupils often want to calculate total volume instead of visualising the problem. In this case, encourage pupils to visualise the problem in context with questions such as, '*What would you do in reality?*'
- Encourage pupils to explore how the same approach can be used to 3D packing problems in a range of contexts.
- Task 2 is a network problem. Model the approach for this type of problem with a simple network.
- Encourage **more able** pupils to design their own network problems for other pupils to solve.

Answers to Review questions

1 **a** and **b**, **c** and **g**, **e** and **h**

2 **a** C   **b** A and E   **c** B

3 7 faces, 10 vertices and 15 edges

4 **a**, **c** and **e**

5 **a** 1, 4, 10, 20

b

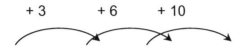

Number of cubes   1   4   10   20
in each tower

c the triangle numbers starting at 3

d 35

6 **a** Accurate net for an open box:

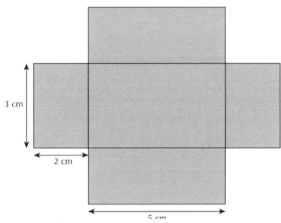

3 cm

2 cm

5 cm

b 47 cm²

7

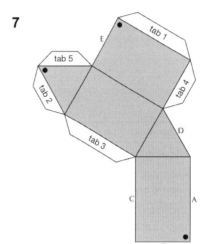

Answers to Problem solving – Packing boxes

1 65 miles

2 Note that routes could be given in reverse.

Route	Miles travelled	Total mileage
W → A → E → B → D → C → W	5 + 16 + 18 + 8 + 10 + 12	69
W → B → A → E → D → C → W	7 + 6 + 16 + 14 + 10 + 12	65
W → A → B → E → D → C → W	5 + 6 + 18 + 14 + 10 + 12	65
W → A → E → D → B → C → W	5 + 16 + 14 + 8 + 9 + 12	64
W → B → C → D → E → A → W	7 + 9 + 10 + 14 + 16 + 5	61

3 **a** W → B → C → D → E → A → W or
          W → A → E → D → C → B → W

   b 61 miles

4 **a** W → B → D → E → A → W or
          W → A → E → D → B → W

   b 50 miles

5 W → A → E → B → C → W or
      W → C → B → E → A → W

6 Just over 12 gallons

Learning objectives

- How to use ratio notation
- How to use ratios to compare quantities
- How to simplify ratios
- How to use ratios to find missing quantities
- The connection between ratios and fractions

Prior knowledge

- How to simplify fractions. In KS2, pupils will have divided numerators and denominators by common factors.
- How to find a fraction of a quantity. Pupils will be familiar with percentage notation.
- How to interpret bar charts and pie charts

Context

- Ratios are a very useful way to compare quantities without the distraction of the actual values. For example, saying that the diameter of Saturn is 10 times the diameter of the Earth (or the ratio is 10 : 1) provides an immediate mental image. This would not be as obvious just by quoting the diameters.
- Many pupils will have experience of riding a bicycle with gears. It may come as a surprise to them to learn that ratios are used to compare one gear with another. If you know the gear ratio, you know if it will be easy or difficult to pedal in that gear.

Discussion points

- Provide pupils with questions to activate prior knowledge and exercise mathematical 'fluency', that is, the ability to manipulate mathematical language and concepts and apply them in different contexts.

Associated Collins ICT resources

- Chapter 17 interactive activities on Collins Connect online platform
- *Zodiac map* Wonder of Maths on Collins Connect online platform
- *Lines of the form x + y = a* Worked solution on Collins Connect online platform
- Ratio and proportion tool on Collins Connect platform

Curriculum references

Reason mathematically

- Extend and formalise their knowledge of ratio and proportion in working with measures and geometry, and in formulating proportional relations algebraically

Solve problems

- Develop their use of formal mathematical knowledge to interpret and solve problems, including in financial mathematics

Fast-track for classes following a 2-year scheme of work

- Pupils will have worked with ratio in KS2, when comparing quantities and in problems involving unequal sharing. Pupils may have been introduced to the $a : b$ notation. If pupils can show understanding by answering one or more of the later questions in Exercise 17A of the Pupil Book, they can move on to simplifying ratios in Exercise 17B.
- Similarly, if pupils are confident about simple sharing problems, as provided in Exercise 17C, then they can move on to concentrate on the mixed questions in Exercise 17D.

Learning objectives
- To introduce ratio notation
- To use ratios to compare quantities

Resources and homework
- Pupil Book 1.1, pages 319–323
- Intervention Book 2, pages 43–45
- Homework Book 1, section 17.1
- Online homework 17.1, exercises 1–10

Links to other subjects
- **Science** – to compare quantities in experiments or compounds; to compare distances in astronomy
- **Geography** – to compare populations, areas, heights or other physical measures

Key words
- quantity
- ratio

Problem solving and reasoning help

- In the **PS** and **MR** questions in Exercise 17A in the Pupil Book, pupils are required to apply their understanding of ratio to some familiar but increasingly complex real-life situations.
- The investigation requires pupils to decode some quite complex information in less familiar situations. If necessary, go through Example 1 as a group, discussing how you identify the relevant information.

Common misconceptions and remediation

- Pupils sometimes have difficulty remembering how to pronounce 'ratio'. They may pronounce it as rat-i-o, with a 't' sound rather than with an 'sh' sound. Help pupils by saying the word often and asking them to use it. Point out that ratio is related to the word 'ration', and that sometimes spell checkers change 'ratio' to 'ration'.
- The order of the numbers in a ratio is important and relates to the order of the quantities being compared. Emphasise this by asking for the ratio the other way round and what it means when looking at examples.

Probing questions

- The ratio of two distances is 10 : 1. Do you know either of the distances? (No)
- Do you know if they are both a whole number of centimetres? (No)
- What do you know about the distances? (One distance is 10 times greater than the other distance.)

Part 1

- Write or place these numbers on the board, randomly scattered:
  15, 4, 27, 24, 9, 20, 45, 60, 8, 12.
- Ask pupils to arrange the numbers in two sets in any way they choose.
- Ask one or two pupils to give their sets, with reasons.
- Odd and even numbers is one obvious way. Try to find a pupil who has put: 4, 8, 9, 15, 20 in one group and 12, 24, 27, 45, 60 in the other. If no one has done this, do it yourself and ask pupils what is the logic behind your choice. (In these sets, the numbers in one set are three times the numbers in the other set.)
- Write these numbers on the board and ask pupils to divide them into two sets in a similar way: 2, 5, 10, 20, 25, 40, 50, 100, 200, 250.

- Here we are looking for: 2, 5, 20, 40, 50 and 10, 25, 100, 200, 250. Here, the multiple is 5.
- If pupils need extra multiplication practice, give them a number by which to multiply (such as 4 or 20) and then some quick-fire numbers to multiply by that. So if the number is 4, you might ask them to multiply by, for example: 5, 7, 20, 11 ….

Part 2

- Look at the numbers in the first set in Part 1. They can be paired as 4 and 12, 8 and 24 …. Explain that we would say: 'The ratio *for each pair is 1 to 3 or 1 : 3*'. Explain this notation. (Each time, the second number is three times the first.)
- Ask for some other pairs of numbers in the same ratio.
- **Less able** pupils may find a visual representation helpful. Draw two columns of equal width, one three times the height of the other. Say that the ratio of the heights is 1 : 3 and divide the second column into three parts to demonstrate this.
- Pupils should be able to say that the numbers in the second example in Part 1 give pairs in the ratio of 1 : 5. A visual representation would help **less able** pupils.
- Look at the example of the beads at the start of Lesson 17.1 in Pupil Book 1.1. The ratio of red beads to blue beads is 2 : 1. The ratio tells us is that there are two red beads for every blue bead. Explain that the ratio can be written the other way around, so that the ratio of blue to red beads is 1 : 2.
- **Pupils can now do Exercise 17A in Pupil Book 1.1.**

Part 3

- After completing the investigation at the end of Exercise 17A, ask pupils to share their findings. They should compare the ratios of the number of coins with the ratios of the values.
- If pupils have not done the investigation, ask individuals to draw a diagram to illustrate a particular ratio such as 1 : 6 or 5 : 2.

Answers

Exercise 17A
1 4 : 1
2 Drawing with the number of black beads 3 times the number of white beads
3 a 2   b 2 : 1
4 3
5 10 : 1
6 a 3   b 3
7 a 4   b 4 : 1
8 a 8   b 8 : 1   c 2 : 1
9 a 5 : 1   b 6 : 1   c 3   d 3 : 1
10 a 4 : 1   b 5 : 1
11 a i 8   ii 16   b 2   c 1 : 2
    d 2 : 1
12 a 3 : 1   b 4 : 1

13 a Mazda RX7
    b Peugeot to Mazda = 1 : 2 or Mazda to Peugeot = 2 : 1
    c Lexus LFA
    d Fiesta to Lexus = 1 : 3 or Lexus to Fiesta = 3 : 1
    e i 3 : 1   ii 4 : 1
14 a i 2 : 1   ii 3 : 1   iii 5 : 1
    b 20 million
Investigation: It's in the bag
A   a £20   b £10   c 2 : 1
B   a £10   b £1   c 10 : 1
C   £1 or £2 : 10p or 5p
D   £1 or £2 : 2p or 1p
E   a 100   b 50   c 2 : 1   d 2 : 1
F   a own choice   b Find the two ratios

Lesson 17.2 Simplifying ratios

Learning objective
- To write a ratio as simply as possible

Resources and homework
- Pupil Book 1.1, pages 323–328
- Homework Book 1, section 17.2
- Online homework 17.2, exercises 1–10

Links to other subjects
- **Science** – to compare the amounts of two elements in a chemical formula
- **Geography** – to compare the area of one country to the area of another, for example, comparing the size of other countries to the size of Wales

Key words
- fraction
- simplify

Problem solving and reasoning help
- The investigation at the end of Exercise 17B requires pupils to combine their understanding with other areas of mathematics, in this case algebra and sequences. This is very useful as ratio is a key concept underpinning work across the strands in mathematics.

Common misconceptions and remediation
- Pupils forget that if quantities being compared must be in the same units. The activity in Part 3, below, addresses this point clearly.
- Pupils can also be careless about which way around they write ratios.

Probing questions
- When you are given a ratio, how do you know if it is in its simplest form?
- Is the ratio 1 : 5 the same as the ratio 5 : 1?

Part 1
- Write some fractions on the board and ask pupils to write them in their simplest forms. Start with fractions that simplify to 1 in the numerator; progress to more complicated examples.
- Emphasise the fact that you want the simplest possible form. For example, the simplest form of $\frac{12}{20}$ is $\frac{3}{5}$, not $\frac{6}{10}$.
- Match the difficulty to the ability of your pupils. Ask individuals to give answers. For **more able** pupils, choose examples where the common factor is more or less obvious (such as 7), or where there are multiple factors.

Part 2
- Draw two lines, one line that is 24 cm long and one that is 40 cm long. Do not reveal the lengths yet.
- Ask pupils to estimate the ratios of the lengths. Do not comment on whether the suggestions are correct or not. If you get several suggestions, ask pupils to say which is best, and why.
- Now write the lengths on the lines and say that we could use these to write the ratio of the shorter length to the longer length as 24 : 40. Imagine each line marked in centimetre sections. There will be 24 on one line and 40 on the other.

- Say that we can simplify ratios in the same way that we simplify fractions – by dividing by a common factor.
- Ask pupils to simplify $\frac{24}{40}$ to its simplest form. The answer is $\frac{3}{5}$.
- In the same way, the ratio 24 : 40 simplifies to 3 : 5. Did anyone have this as their estimate?
- What does this mean? Divide the 24-cm line into three equal sections (8 cm each) and the 40-cm line into five equal sections (8 cm each). This visually represents the ratio.
- **Pupils can now do Exercise 17B from Pupil Book 1.1.**

Part 3

- At the end of the lesson, ask pupils to share their findings from the investigation at the end of the exercise. Check that pupils can a work out all the ratios required.

Answers
Exercise 17B
1 **a** 3 : 5   **b** 5 : 3
2 **a** 2 : 3   **b** 3 : 2
3 **a** 3 : 2   **b** 2 : 3
4 **a** 18   **b** 9 : 2   **c** 2 : 9
5 **a** 3   **b** 2 : 3   **c** 3 : 2
6 **a** 1 : 7   **b** 5 : 3
7 2 : 5
8 **a** 2 : 3   **b** 3 : 2   **c** 2 : 5   **d** 5 : 2
9 **a** 3 : 2   **b** 1 : 3   **c** 2 : 1
10 **a** 5 : 2   **b** 2 : 5
11 **a** 1 : 4   **b** 2 : 3
12 **a** 3 : 2   **b** 2 : 1
13 **a** 1 : 2   **b** 4 : 1   **c** 1 : 4   **d** 1 : 2
14 **a** 3 : 1   **b** 1 : 3   **c** 2 : 1   **d** 1 : 2
15 5 : 6
16 **a** 1 : 5   **b** 10 and 30   **c** 1 : 3
Investigation: Red and green
A 1 : 2 , 2 : 1 , 4 : 1
B own drawings
C 13 : 2 and 19 : 2

Lesson 17.3 Ratios and sharing

Learning objective
- To use ratios to find missing quantities

Resources and homework
- Pupil Book 1.1, pages 329–331
- Intervention Book 3, pages 43–44
- Homework Book 1, section 17.3
- Online homework 17.3, exercises 1–10

Links to other subjects
- **Science** – to compare quantities in different types of materials
- **Food technology** – to combine recipe ingredients in the correct quantities

Key words
- No new key words

Problem solving and reasoning help
- In **MR** question 6 of Exercise 17C in the Pupil Book, the crucial step is finding the fraction of the 20 people who are women. This is best achieved by changing the ratio to make the calculation easier.
- In the challenge at the end of the exercise, the link between carat and percentage of gold can be illustrated by a horizontal line with a scale from 0 to 24 carats at the top and 0 to 100% on the bottom. This way, pupils can see easily that 24 carats is 100% gold, 12 carats is 50% gold, 18 carats is 25% gold, and so on.

Common misconceptions and remediation
- Pupils sometimes get confused about the exact relationship between ratios and fractions. Emphasise the link between the ratio numbers and the numerators of the fractions, as outlined in the lesson plan.

Probing questions
- If the ratio of boys to girls in a class is 3 : 1 could there be exactly 30 children in the class?
- Could there be 25 boys? Why?

Part 1
- Pupils can work in pairs on this activity.
- Write £20 on the board. Ask pupils to find what fractions of this will be a whole number of pounds. If they need clarification, show that $\frac{1}{2}$ is £10, which is a whole number of pounds; $\frac{1}{3}$ is £3.33 with 1p left over, which is not a whole number.
- After a few minutes check answers.
- Check that pupils remember how to find a fraction:

  For example, $\frac{1}{5}$ of £20 = 20 ÷ 5 = £4; $\frac{3}{5}$ of £20 = 3 × £4 = £12

- **Less able** pupils may need more practice with finding fractions. If so, repeat the activity with £18 and/or £12.

Part 2

- Draw a 4 × 3 grid of 12 squares. Colour three of the squares. Ask: What fraction is coloured? What fraction is uncoloured? The answers should be one-quarter and three-quarters.
- In the example we have just done, the ratio of shaded to unshaded parts is 1 : 3. Make sure that pupils are happy with this.
- Repeat this activity but shade different numbers of squares each time. For example, 4 or 2, or 1 or 6. Each time, ask for the fraction shaded, the fraction unshaded and the ratio of the two. Pupils should see that the numerators of the fractions give the numbers in the ratio.
- Now work through Example 4 and Example 5 above Exercise 17C in the Pupil Book. In Example 4, £200 is divided into shares in a given ratio. This is done by using a visual image which can reinforce the link between fractions and ratios. In Example 5, one share is given and the total must be found. Again, fractions are used to tackle this problem.
- **Pupils can now do Exercise 17C from Pupil Book 1.1.**

Part 3

- Say that Eve has 20 apples to share with Adam. Can they share them in the ratio 2 : 1 and have an equal number each? What about sharing them in the ratio 2 : 3?
- What is the smallest number that can be divided equally in the ratio 2 : 1 or 2 : 3? (The answer is 15; the lowest whole number is divisible by both 3 and 5.)
- A question for **more able** pupils is to find the smallest number that can be divided equally in the ratio 2 : 1 or 2 : 5.

Answers

Exercise 17C

1	**a** 10	**b** 20
2	**a** 200	**b** 800
3	**a** £6	**b** £18
4	**a** 30	**b** 20
5	**a** 360	**b** 40
6	8	
7	24	
8	30	
9	24	
10	75 g	
11	400	
12	**a** 2 and 5 are the missing numbers.	**b** 35
13	20	

Challenge: All that glitters

A   **a** 3 : 1   **b** 18 carat

B   **a** 3 : 5   **b** 9 carat

C   **a** 6 g   **b** 3 g

      c There is twice as much gold in the 18 carat ring. The ratio of 18 carat to 9 carat is 2 : 1.

D   **a** a diagram showing $\frac{3}{4}$ gold   **b** a diagram showing $\frac{3}{8}$ gold

Lesson 17.4 Ratios and fractions

Learning objective
- To understand the connections between fractions and ratios

Links to other subjects
- **Science** – to find unknown quantities of substances
- **Geography** – to compare the resources of different countries

Resources and homework
- Pupil Book 1.1, pages 332–335
- Homework Book 1, section 17.4
- Online homework 17.4, exercises 1–10

Key words
- No new key words for this topic

Problem solving and reasoning help
- In **PS** question 8 of Exercise 17D of the Pupil Book encourages pupils to apply their understanding. The challenge at the end of the exercise is an extension of the investigation at the end of Exercise 17B.

Common misconceptions and remediation
- Pupils can make mistakes by not being clear about whether they know the whole or a part when working out missing values. Encourage pupils always to ask themselves if they know the whole or a part before they try to answer a question.

Probing questions
- Ann and Baz share some money in the ratio 3 : 2
- If you know the total amount, how can you work out what Ann has?
- If you know what Ann has, how can you work out what Baz has?
- If you know what Baz has, how can you work out what Ann has?

Part 1
- Write down the following sentences: '*Tim and Claire bake 60 biscuits in total. Tim bakes 24 of them.*'
- Ask pupils to work in pairs and find different ways to write this information. They can use fractions, percentages or ratios.
- After a few minutes take answers from selected pupils. Possible statements are:
  - Tim bakes $\frac{2}{5}$ and Claire bakes $\frac{3}{5}$.
  - Tim bakes 40% and Claire bakes 60%.
  - Tim and Claire bake biscuits in the ratio 2 : 3.
- Make sure that pupils can remember the equivalences between simple fractions and percentages. If not, ask more questions about this, for example, writing tenths, fifths or quarters as percentages.
- This should remind pupils of the work covered in the last lesson.

Part 2
- This lesson is about using the ideas about ratios that pupils have met so far in questions, in a realistic context.

- Tell pupils that the ratio of teachers to pupils in a school is 1 : 12 (or use your own figure if you know it, but round it to a whole number).
- Ask a volunteer to explain what this means. A possible answer is that there is one teacher for every 12 pupils.
- Ask questions that require pupils to use this information in different ways, for example:
  - If there are 30 teachers, how many pupils are there?
  - If there are 60 teachers, how many pupils are there?
  - If there are 1300 pupils and teachers, how many of each are there?
- Ask pupils to explain how they work out the answers each time and check that their reasoning is correct.
- **Pupils can now do Exercise 17D from Pupil Book 1.1.**

Part 3

- Pupils can work in pairs or small groups of three on this task.
- Ask pupils to produce a concise statement that will help them to remember the key points about ratios. This could be an example, a diagram or a sentence or two.
- Ask one or two groups to share what they have done with the rest of the class.
- As an extension, pupils could use these ideas to produce posters for a wall display.

Answers
Exercise 17D

1 a 1 : 3   b $\frac{1}{4}$ c $\frac{3}{4}$

2 a $\frac{1}{6}$ b $\frac{5}{6}$

3 a 1 : 2   b $\frac{2}{3}$

4 a The missing numbers are 3 and 2

   b $\frac{3}{5}$ c $\frac{2}{5}$

5 $\frac{4}{5}$

6 a 3 : 2   b $\frac{3}{5}$ c $\frac{2}{5}$

7 a 8 : 1   b $\frac{1}{9}$

8 a 1 : 2   b i $\frac{1}{3}$ ii $\frac{2}{3}$ c 1 : 3

   d i $\frac{1}{4}$ ii $\frac{3}{4}$

9 a 3 : 2   b $\frac{3}{5}$ c $\frac{2}{5}$

10 a $\frac{2}{3}$ b 1 : 2

11 a $\frac{1}{4}$ b 3 : 1

12 4 : 1

13 a $\frac{3}{4}$ b $\frac{1}{4}$

14 a 18 and 12   b 3 : 2   c i $\frac{3}{5}$ ii $\frac{2}{5}$

15 a 3 : 1   b $\frac{3}{4}$ c 2 : 1   d $\frac{2}{3}$

Challenge: Coloured patterns

A a 1 : 2   b $\frac{1}{3}$ c $\frac{2}{3}$

B own drawing

Review questions (Pupil Book pages 336–337)

- The review questions will help to determine pupils' abilities with regard to the material within Chapter 17.
- They also draw on the maths covered in earlier chapters of the book to encourage pupils to make links between different topics.
- The answers are on the next page.

Problem solving – Smoothie bar (Pupil Book pages 338–339)

- This activity is designed to reinforce the use of the techniques from this chapter in realistic contexts, asking questions that customers or shopkeepers may reasonably be expected to ask.
- The questions can be answered in any order as each section is independent.
- Different groups of pupils could take on the roles of shopkeeper or customer and devise similar questions for each other.
- Discuss strategies for increasing sales or for saving money.
- Pupils will find the information they need in various places on the double page spread of the Pupil Book. They will need to use the appropriate information in each question.
- Pupils should be familiar with grams and millilitres as measures of mass and capacity, respectively.
- The level of difficulty can be changed by adjusting the prices or the quantities.

Answers to Review questions

1 **a** 5 is the missing number   **b** 5 : 1
2 **a** 2 : 1   **b** 4 : 1
3 **a** 20   **b** 2 : 1   **c** 2 : 1   **d** 3 : 1   **e** 6 : 1
4 **a** 75%   **b** 3 is the missing number   **c** 3 : 1
5 **a** 2 : 1   **b** 3 : 1   **c** 3 : 2
6 **a** red, blue, blue, from the bottom up   **b** 1 : 2   **c** $\frac{1}{3}$ **d** $\frac{2}{3}$
7 **a** 6   **b** 2 : 1
8 **a** 2 : 1   **b** 2 × (8 + 4) = 24   **c** 3 : 1   **d** 6 : 1
9 **a** drawing
   b No, because the lengths are not in the same units. The correct ratio is 2 : 4 = 1 : 2.
10 **a** 4 : 1   **b** 2 : 1

Answers to Problem solving – Smoothie bar

1 **a** 50 g mango, 25 g strawberries, 50 g banana, 125 ml orange juice
   b 300 g mango, 150 g strawberries, 300 g banana, 750 ml orange juice
   c 50 g strawberries, 100 g banana, 50 g yogurt
   d 300 g strawberries, 600 g banana, 300 g yogurt
2 **a** 4 : 3   **b** 3 : 2   **c** size = 2 : 1, cost = 2 : 1   **d** 4 : 3 = 1.333 : 1 and 3 : 2 = 1.5 : 1.
The medium smoothie is only 1.333 times the size of the small smoothie, but 1.5 times the price so is not better value for money
3 **a** 2 : 1   **b** 1 : 1   **c** Yes, all quantities are halved so the ratios will be the same.
   d Yes, all quantities are doubled so the ratios will be the same.
4 **a** 300 g   **b** 3 : 1   **c** $\frac{1}{4}$ **d** $\frac{3}{4}$
5 Fruity Surprise : Tropical Fruit = 2 : 3
Fruity Surprise : Breakfast Boost = 1 : 3
Tropical Fruit : Breakfast Boost = 1 : 2
All these ratios can be reversed.

1 Using numbers

Learning checklist

I can show my understanding of how the number line extends to include negative numbers. ☐

I can carry out addition and subtraction involving negative numbers. ☐

I can use my understanding of negative numbers to solve simple real-life problems. ☐

Learning checklist

I can find the output for a single function machine when I know the input value. ☐

I can find the output for a double function machine when I know the input value. ☐
I can write down a sequence, given the first term and a term-to-term rule. ☐
I can give the term-to-term rule for a sequence. ☐
I know how to work out square numbers and triangular numbers. ☐

I can find any term in a sequence, given the first term and a term-to-term rule. ☐

3 Perimeter and area

Learning checklist

I can draw and measure lines.	☐
I can find the perimeter of a shape.	☐
I can find the area of a shape by counting squares.	☐
I can find the perimeter of a rectangle by using perimeter = 2 lengths + 2 widths.	☐
I can find the area of a rectangle by using area = length × width.	☐

4 Decimal numbers

Learning checklist

I can order decimals by size. ☐

I can add and subtract decimal numbers. ☐
I can multiply and divide decimal numbers by 10, 100 and 1000. ☐
I can estimate answers and check if an answer is about right. ☐
I can multiply and divide decimals by any whole number. ☐

5 Working with numbers

Learning checklist

I can round numbers to make sensible estimates. □

I know and can use square numbers up to 15×15. □

I can carry out calculations, knowing the correct order of operations. □
I can use written methods to carry out calculations involving multiplications and divisions. □
I can convert measurements. □

6 Statistics

Learning checklist

I can find the mode and range for a set of data. ☐
I can find the median for a set of data. ☐

I can compare two simple distributions. ☐
I can use a data collection form to collect data. ☐
I can group data, where appropriate, into equal class intervals. ☐

7 Algebra

Learning checklist

I can write simple algebraic expressions. ☐

I can substitute numbers into algebraic expressions, such as $2n + 3$. ☐
I can simplify algebraic expressions such as $2a + 5a$. ☐
I can substitute values into simple formulae. ☐
I can construct formulae to show connections between variables. ☐

8 Fractions

Learning checklist

I can find simple equivalent fractions.	☐
I can write fractions in their simplest form.	☐
I can add and subtract with the same denominators.	☐
I can add and subtract fractions with different denominators.	☐
I can convert between mixed numbers and improper fractions.	☐
I can add and subtract mixed numbers.	☐

9 Angles

Learning checklist

I can use points of a compass. ☐
I know the names for different types of angles. ☐

I know the names of the different types of triangles and quadrilaterals. ☐

I can draw and measure angles. ☐
I know that angles on a straight line add up to 180°. ☐
I know that angles at a point add up to 360°. ☐
I know the properties of simple 2D shapes. ☐
I can solve simple problems about triangles and quadrilaterals. ☐

10 Coordinates and graphs

Learning checklist

I can read coordinates. ☐

I can plot coordinates. ☐

I can work out and plot coordinates from a simple rule. ☐
I can recognise and draw lines such as $x = 3$ and $y = 1$. ☐
I can read values from conversion graphs. ☐

11 Percentages

Learning checklist

I can write percentages such as 75% or 20% as fractions. ☐

I can work out a fraction of a quantity. ☐

I can find percentages like 75% or 40% of a quantity by using fractions. ☐

I can write a percentage as a decimal. ☐

I can work out percentages of a quantity by changing the percentage to a decimal and by using a calculator. ☐

I know that to increase, or decrease, a quantity by a percentage you either add it to, or subtract it from, the original value. ☐

12 Probability

Learning checklist

I can use probability words to describe the chance of things happening. ☐

I can use a probability scale in words. ☐
I can use a probability scale marked from 0 to 1. ☐

I can use equally likely outcomes to calculate probabilities. ☐
I can calculate probability from experimental data. ☐
I understand the differences between theoretical and experimental probability. ☐

13 Symmetry

Learning checklist

I can draw lines of symmetry on 2D shapes. ☐

I can reflect 2D shapes in a mirror line. ☐

I can find the order of rotational symmetry of a 2D shape. ☐
I know how to make a tessellation from 2D shapes. ☐

14 Equations

Learning checklist

I can solve simple equations that involve one operation. ☐

I can solve simple equations that involve two operations. ☐
I can set up and solve an equation for a simple real-life problem. ☐

15 Interpreting data

Learning checklist

I can read data from tally charts and create bar charts. ☐
I can use the median and range to compare data. ☐

I can read data from pie charts marked into ten sectors. ☐
I can use charts and diagrams to interpret data. ☐

16 3D shapes

Learning checklist

I can make 3D shapes using cubes. ☐
I know the mathematical words for various 3D shapes.. ☐

I can count the faces, vertices and edges on a 3D shape. ☐

I can draw nets for 3D shapes. ☐
I can use nets to construct 3D shapes. ☐

17 Ratio

Learning checklist

I can use ratio notation. ☐

I know how to use ratios to compare quantities. ☐
I know how to write a ratio as simply as possible. ☐
I know how to share a quantity in a given ratio. ☐
I know how to write a fraction if I am given a ratio. ☐

The following scheme of work provides a suggestion for how Pupil Book 1.1 can be taught over the course of one year, as part of a 3-year Key Stage 3 course.

Please note that you can recombine the test questions provided on Collins Connect to create new tests if your frequency of assessment differs from that below, or if you wish to combine content from different chapters in your own half-term tests.

This scheme of work is provided in editable Word and Excel format on the CD-ROM accompanying this Teacher Pack.

Chapter	Lesson	No. of hours	Learning objective	Comments/ suggestions
Half-term / Term 1				
1 Using numbers	1.1 The calendar	1	• To read and use calendars	Tables and charts appear all over in real life. It is important that pupils become confident in their ability to extract and use information from tables and charts in increasingly unfamiliar and complex situations.
	1.2 The 12-hour and 24-hour clocks	1	• To read and use 12-hour and 24-hour clocks • To convert between the 12-hour and 24-hour systems	
	1.3 Managing money	2	• To work out everyday money problems	Money problems have to be dealt with daily in real life and pupils need to realise how important their ability to interpret these problems and identify the mathematics involved is to their future financial wellbeing. This chapter provides plenty of financial skills (FS) questions for practice.
	1.4 Positive and negative numbers	1	• To use a number line to order positive and negative whole numbers • To solve problems involving negative temperatures	
	1.5 Adding negative numbers	1	• To carry out additions and subtractions involving negative numbers • To use a number line to calculate with negative numbers	Pupils often confuse the operation of addition and subtraction of negative numbers as numbers on a number line, especially as the sign is the same for both. Encourage pupils to visualise the number line when making calculations.
	1.6 Subtracting negative numbers	1	• To carry out subtractions involving negative numbers	
	Problem solving – Where in the UK?	1		This activity is designed to use both the mathematical reasoning and problem-solving outcomes covered in this chapter in a series of real-life problems.
2 Sequences	2.1 Function machines	1	• To use function machines to generate inputs and outputs	The ability to generalise is crucial in a complex modern society. Being able to identify and generate number sequences is the first step towards progressing from the
	2.2 Sequences and rules	2	• To recognise, describe and write down sequences that are based on a simple rule	

	2.3 Finding terms in patterns	1	• To find missing terms in a sequence	particular to the general in mathematics.
	2.4 The square numbers	1	• To introduce the sequence of square numbers	
	2.5 The triangular numbers	1	• To introduce the sequence of triangular numbers	
	Mathematical reasoning – Valencia Planetarium	1		This is an opportunity to apply what pupils have learnt to a less familiar problem.
3 Perimeter and area	3.1 Length and perimeter	1	• To measure and draw lines • To work out the perimeter of a shape	Measurement, perimeter and area are used widely in many jobs and professions, from farming to astronomy. Encourage pupils to talk to family and relatives to see if anyone uses these skills in their work or to explore specific jobs on the internet. A good example is the building industry, which is totally dependent on workers being able to measure lengths and calculate areas.
	3.2 Area	1	• To work out the area of a shape by counting squares	
	3.3 Perimeter and area of rectangles	1	• To work out the perimeter of a rectangle • To work out the area of a rectangle	
				Pupils could also talk to family and relatives about how they might use area and perimeter in projects such as laying carpets and flooring, and decorating, to estimate how much carpet, flooring or wallpaper is needed.
	Problem solving – Design a bedroom	1		This activity is designed to show pupils an everyday situation that involves area and perimeter. Pupils are given practice in using their measuring, mathematical reasoning and problem-solving skills.
Chapter 1–3 assessment on Collins Connect				
Half-term				
Half-term / Term 2				
4 Decimal numbers	4.1 Multiplying and dividing by 10, 100 and 1000	1	• To multiply and divide decimal numbers by 10, 100 and 1000	Pupils will be aware of decimals all around them, and should know that the decimal is used to separate: pounds from pence in prices; kilograms from grams in weights;
	4.2 Ordering decimals	1	• To order decimal numbers according to size	

	4.3 Estimates	2	• To estimate calculations in order to spot possible errors	kilometres from metres in distances. Make sure they are aware of the impact of incorrect conversions. When solving money problems, pupils need to draw on their financial skills abilities.
	4.4 Adding and subtracting decimals	1	• To add and subtract decimal numbers	
	4.5 Multiplying and dividing decimals	1	• To be able to multiply and divide decimal numbers by any whole number	The zeros in decimals may cause confusion, for example, when comparing and ordering decimals. Provide pupils with plenty of practice in giving values to each digit.
				When asked to estimate an answer, pupils often think that the full calculation will be better. Pupils may also be unable to see how to simplify a calculation in order to complete it mentally. Provide plenty of practice.
	Financial skills – Shopping for leisure	1		This activity is designed to apply the skills learnt in this chapter to a multi-step problem. The context may be familiar but pupils are unlikely to have engaged with it themselves.
5 Working with numbers	5.1 Square numbers	1	• To recognise and use square numbers up to 225 (15 × 15)	The objectives in this chapter are probably some of the most widely-used objectives in terms of real-life application. It is important for pupils to build on their mental methods when developing written methods, so that they understand why they are doing this, and are not just applying a set of rules that they do not understand.
	5.2 Rounding	1	• To round numbers to the nearest whole number, 10, 100 or 1000	
	5.3 Order of operations	1	• To use the conventions of BIDMAS to carry out calculations	
	5.4 Long and short multiplication	2	• To choose a written method for multiplying two numbers together • To use written methods to carry out multiplications accurately	Remind pupils that these objectives will be very useful in building confidence and fluency in applying their financial skills in the questions and in real life.
	5.5 Long and short division	2	• To choose a written method for dividing one number by another • To use written methods to carry out divisions accurately	

	5.6 Calculations with measure-ments	1	• To convert between common metric units • To use measurements in calculations • To recognise and use appropriate metric units	
	Problem solving – What is your carbon footprint?	2		This activity is designed to use the skills covered in this and earlier 'number' chapters to give a real-life context to mathematics.
6 Statistics	6.1 Mode, median and range	1	• To understand the meaning of mode, median and range	Pupils need to think about how we use statistics to model populations where it is difficult or in many cases impossible to gather all the population information.
	6.2 Reading data from tables and charts	1	• To read data from tables and charts	
	6.3 Using a tally chart	1	• To create and use a tally chart	
	6.Using data	1	• To understand how to use data	Pupils also need to consider how they could present this information.
	6.5 Grouped frequency	2	• To understand and use grouped frequency	
	6.6 Data collection	2	• To gain a greater understanding of data collection	
	Challenge – Trains in Europe	1		This activity is designed to use both the mathematical reasoning and problem solving outcomes covered in this chapter se in a situation that is familiar to pupils. Ask pupils to summarise what they have learnt in the chapter, as they will use much of this material to complete the activity.
Chapter 4–6 assessment on Collins Connect				

<table>
<tr><td colspan="5" align="center">Holidays</td></tr>
</table>

Half-term / Term 3

7 Algebra	7.1 Expressions and substitution	1	• To use algebra to write simple expressions • To substitute numbers into expressions to work out their value	In algebra, pupils often struggle to recognise that letters represent variables and that the answer can vary depending on the situation. Provide lots of opportunities for pupils to see this in action in familiar contexts such *as 'Think of a number'* word problems.
	7.2 Simplifying expressions	2	• To learn the rules for simplifying expressions	
	7.3 Using formulae	2	• To use formulae	

	7.4 Writing formulae	1	• To write formulae	To avoid serious confusion when multiplying brackets, make sure pupils understand that letter symbols used in algebra stand for unknown numbers or variables and *not* labels. For example, '5b cannot mean '5 bananas.
	Problem solving –Winter sports	1		A common response to algebra is to ask how it can be used. This activity provides one of the everyday uses of algebra in terms of using a formula to work out costs.
8 Fractions	8.1 Equivalent fractions	1	• To find simple equivalent fractions • To write fractions in their simplest form	Pupils are encouraged to think about and explore the fact that fractions as we know them did not exist in Europe until the 17th century. At first, fractions were not even thought of as numbers in their own right, simply as a means of comparing whole numbers with one another. When working with fractions, pupils are often aware of the role of the denominator when finding equivalent fractions but may fail to understand the role of the numerator. Working with visual images may help.
	8.2 Comparing fractions	1	• To compare and order two fractions	
	8.3 Adding and subtracting fractions	2	• To add and subtract fractions with the same denominator • To add and subtract fractions with different denominators	
	8.4 Mixed numbers and improper fractions	1	• To convert mixed numbers to improper fractions • To convert improper fractions to mixed numbers	
	8.5 Calculations with mixed numbers	1	• To add and subtract simple mixed numbers with the same denominator • To add and subtract simple mixed numbers with different denominators	
	Challenge – Fractional dissection	1		This activity explores partitioning in a familiar context, which is an important concept in understanding fractions. The tasks involve splitting a shape into unequal parts, which will help pupils' understanding of the part–whole relationship between the numerator and denominator in fractions.

9 Angles	9.1 Using the compass to give directions	1	• To use a compass to give directions	In the real world, geometry is everywhere, for example, in buildings, planes, cars and maps, homes. Without an understanding of angles and their properties none of these structures would stay together. Show examples to the class.
	9.2 Measuring angles	1	• To know the different types of angles • To use a protractor to measure an angle	
	9.3 Drawing angles	1	• To use a protractor to draw an angle	Another use of angles in real life is how we find our way around the world. Without a basic understanding of angles in terms of a measure of rotation we would not reach our destination.
	9.4 Calculating angles	1	• To calculate angles at a point • To calculate angles on a line • To calculate opposite angles	
	9.5 Properties of triangles and quadrilaterals	2	• To understand the properties of parallel, intersecting and perpendicular lines • To understand and use the properties of triangles • To understand and use the properties of quadrilaterals	Pupils often do not appreciate the need for accuracy when measuring and drawing angles. Make sure that pupils are given plenty of practice in using a protractor accurately.
	Investigation – Snooker tables	1		This activity encourages pupils to think about how angles can affect a possibly familiar real-life situation – the way one plays the game of snooker. Pupils may find it interesting to see how much mathematical calculation is involved in playing a good game.
Chapter 7–9 assessment on Collins Connect				
Half-term				
Half-term / Term 4				
10 Coordinates and graphs	10.1 Coordinates and graphs	1	• To understand and use coordinates to locate points	The use of graphs to represent data is probably one of the most common uses of mathematics in the modern world. Pupils may be surrounded to such an extent by visual representations of data in the media, and become so used to it, that they no longer notice it. The
	10.2 From mappings to graphs	1	• To work out coordinates from a rule • To draw a graph for a simple rule	
	10.3 Naming graphs	1	• To recognise and draw line graphs of fixed values	

	10.4 Graphs from the real world	1	• To learn how graphs can be used to represent real-life situations • To draw and use real-life graphs	following website provides some interesting insights into the use of data in a modern society: **http://www.gapminder.org**
	Challenge – Global warming	2		This activity is designed to apply pupils' learning in a real-life topical situation.
11 Percentages	11.1 Fractions and percentages	1	• To understand what a percentage is • To understand the equivalence between some simple fractions and percentages	Percentages are everywhere in real life. From bargains in the shops to taxes on payslips. It is important for pupils to be comfortable with calculating percentages if they are going to be functional in a modern society.
	11.2 Fractions of a quantity	1	• To find a fraction of a quantity	
	11.3 Percentages of a quantity	1	• To find a percentage of a quantity	
	11.4 Percentages with a calculator	1	• To write a percentage as a decimal • To use a calculator to find a percentage of a quantity	
	11.5 Percentage increases and decreases	2	• To work out the result of a simple percentage change	
	Financial skills – Income tax	2		This activity is designed to use both the mathematical and transferable process skills covered in this chapter in a very important real-life context, which may be completely unfamiliar to pupils.
12 Probability	12.1 Probability words	1	• To learn and use words about probability	Probability is an area of mathematics that pupils often find interesting but may be contrary to what seems right.
	12.2 Probability scales	1	• To learn about and use probability scales from 0 to 1 • To work out probabilities based on equally likely outcomes	
	12.3 Experimental probability	2	• To learn about and understand experimental probability • To understand the difference between theoretical probability and experimental probability	

	Financial skills – School Easter Fayre	1		This activity combines pupils' understanding of experimental and theoretical probability and applies it in a real-life context.
Chapter 10–12 assessment on Collins Connect				
Holidays				
Half-term / Term 5				
13 Symmetry	13.1 Line symmetry	1	• To recognise shapes that have reflective symmetry • To draw lines of symmetry on a shape	Symmetry is everywhere around us, both natural and human-made. Symmetry is probably one of the easier topics for pupils to see links to the real world, although some links may not be as obvious as others. This chapter provides many real-life examples, and each lesson has links to a number of these.
	13.2 Rotational symmetry	1	• To recognise shapes that have rotational symmetry • To find the order of rotational symmetry for a shape	
	13.3 Reflections	1	• To understand how to reflect a shape • To use a coordinate grid to reflect shapes	
	13. 4 Tessellations	1	• To understand how to tessellate shapes	
	Activity – Landmark spotting	1		This activity is designed to show pupils some of the aspects of symmetry used in the real world, by examining the line symmetry of six famous landmarks.
14 Equations	14.1 Finding unknown numbers	1	• To find missing numbers in simple calculations	The history of algebra goes back to ancient Egypt and Babylon. However, it is not just an ancient topic. Most of our modern society is dependent on the use of algebra. For more information search the internet for: 'mathematician Andrew Wiles' or 'Fermat's last theorem'.
	14.2 Solving equations	1	• To understand what an equation is • To solve equations involving one operation	
	14.3 Solving more complex equations	1	• To solve equations involving two operations	
	14.4 Setting up and solving equations	2	• To use algebra to set up and solve equations	
	Challenge – Number puzzles	1		In this activity pupils apply what they know to an abstract number problem. They need to identify and solve multi-step linear equations to solve the problem.

15 Interpreting data	15.1 Pie charts	1	• To read data from pie charts, where the data is given in simple sectors	Statistical data is everywhere in a modern society and to function in this society it is important to be able to critically analyse the data being presented.
	15.2 Comparing data by median and range	1	• To use the median and range to compare data • To make sensible decisions by comparing the median and range of two sets of data	
	15.3 Statistical surveys	2	• To use charts and diagrams to interpret data	
	Challenge – Dancing competition	1		This activity is designed to use both the interpretation and communication skills covered in this chapter in a familiar scenario.

Chapter 13–15 assessment on Collins Connect

Half-term

Half-term / Term 6

16 3D shapes	16.1 3D shapes and nets	1	• To know how to count the faces, vertices and edges on a 3D shape • To draw nets for 3D shapes	There are only five regular 3D shapes or (regular polyhedra) that can be made using the same regular polygon throughout. Problems can occur with the change of vocabulary between 2D and 3D, for example, sides become faces. Use visual images to support understanding and memory. The imprecise use of language in real life can also confuse pupils. Discuss examples of this. Also discuss the concept of subsets, for example, a cube is a regular cuboid. Identify this concept of subsets as being applicable across mathematics.
	16.2 Using nets to construct 3D shapes	1	• To construct 3D shapes from nets	
	16.3 3D investigations	2	• To work out the rule connecting faces, edges and vertices of 3D shapes • To solve problems involving 3D shapes	
	Problem solving – Delivering packages	1		This is a common type of problem used at GCSE so it is important that pupils can identify this type of problem.
17 Ratio	17.1 Introduction to ratios	1	• To introduce ratio notation • To use ratios to compare quantities	Ratios are a very useful way to compare quantities without the distraction of the actual values. For example, saying that the diameter of Saturn is 10
	17.2 Simplifying ratios	1	• To write a ratio as simply as possible	

	17.3 Ratios and sharing	1	• To use ratios to find missing quantities	times the diameter of the Earth (or the ratio is 10 : 1) provides an immediate mental image. This would not be as obvious just by quoting the diameters.
	17.4 Ratios and fractions	1	• To understand the connection between fractions and ratios	
	Problem solving –Smoothie bar	1		This problem-solving activity is designed to reinforce the use of ratios by putting ratios in a realistic context.
Chapter 16–17 assessment on Collins Connect				

The following scheme of work provides a suggestion for how Pupil Book 1.1 can be taught over the course of one year, as part of a 2-year Key Stage 3 course.

Please note that you can recombine the test questions provided on Collins Connect to create new tests if your frequency of assessment differs from that below, or if you wish to combine content from different chapters in your own half-term tests.

This scheme of work is provided in editable Word and Excel format on the CD-ROM accompanying this Teacher Pack.

Chapter	Lesson	No. of hours	Learning objective	Comments/ suggestions
Half-term / Term 1				
1 Using numbers	1.1 The calendar	1	• To read and use calendars	If pupils are familiar with the material in lessons 1.1 and 1.2 from KS2, they can leave out Exercise 1A and 1B, and jump straight to the PS questions at the end of each exercise.
	1.2 The 12-hour and 24-hour clocks		• To read and use 12-hour and 24-hour clocks • To convert between the 12-hour and 24-hour systems	
	1.3 Managing money		• To work out everyday money problems	Ensure that pupils understand all the rules that they are applying throughout the chapter.
	1.4 Positive and negative numbers	1	• To use a number line to order positive and negative whole numbers • To solve problems involving negative temperatures	
	1.5 Adding negative numbers	1	• To carry out additions and subtractions involving negative numbers • To use a number line to calculate with negative numbers	
	1.6 Subtracting negative numbers		• To carry out subtractions involving negative numbers	
	Problem solving – Where in the UK?	1		This activity is designed to use both the mathematical reasoning and problem-solving outcomes covered in this chapter in a series of real-life problems.
2 Sequences	2.1 Function machines	1	• To use function machines to generate inputs and outputs	For more able pupils, put greater emphasis on inverse functions.

	2.2 Sequences and rules	1	• To recognise, describe and write down sequences that are based on a simple rule	Make sure pupils realise that there is a range of types of sequences, and that within this range, specific examples often follow specific patterns. Provide opportunities for pupils to become fluent in identifying types of sequences.
	2.3 Finding terms in patterns	1	• To find missing terms in a sequence	
	2.4 The square numbers	1	• To introduce the sequence of square numbers	
	2.5 The triangular numbers		• To introduce the sequence of triangular numbers	Increase the emphasis on being able to explain and justify the patterns spotted, using the structure of the problem. This will start to make the link between pattern spotting and mathematical proof.
	Mathematical reasoning – Valencia Planetarium	1		This is an opportunity to apply what pupils have learnt to a less familiar problem.
3 Perimeter, area and volume	3.1 Length and perimeter	1	• To measure and draw lines to work out the perimeter of a shape	Leave out Exercises 3.1 and 3.2 in the Pupil Book if you are happy that the class is familiar with this material from KS2.
	3.2 Area		• To work out the area of a shape by counting squares	
	3.3 Perimeter and area of rectangles	1	• To work out the perimeter and area of a compound shape	Most pupils will have met the basic concepts in this chapter. If they can demonstrate that they are confident and fluent with these basic concepts they can move on to the activity, challenge or investigation questions at the end of each exercise.
	3.4 Volume of cubes and cuboids	1	• To work out the perimeter of a rectangle • To work out the area of a rectangle	
	Problem solving – Design a bedroom	1		This activity is designed to show pupils an everyday situation that involves area and perimeter.
Chapters 1–3 assessment on Collins Connect				
4 Decimal numbers	4.1 Multiplying and dividing by 10, 100 and 1000		• To multiply and divide decimal numbers by 10, 100 and 1000	You could leave out Lesson 4.1 if you are confident that your class is familiar with this material from KS2.
	4.2 Ordering decimals	1	• To order decimal numbers according to size	Most pupils will have met the basic concepts in this chapter, although

	4.3 Estimates	1	• To estimate calculations in order to spot possible errors	they may not have applied them to decimals. If pupils can demonstrate their ability to transfer this understanding efficiently, they can move on to the activities in the boxes at the end of each exercise in this chapter of the Pupil Book.
	4.4 Adding and subtracting decimals	1	• To add and subtract decimal numbers	
	4.5 Multiplying and dividing decimals		• To be able to multiply and divide decimal numbers by any whole number	
	Financial skills – Shopping for leisure	1		This activity is designed to apply the skills learnt in this chapter to a multi-step problem. The context may be familiar but pupils are unlikely to have engaged with it themselves.

Half-term				
Half-term / Term 2				
5 Working with numbers	5.1 Square numbers	1	• To recognise and use square numbers up to 225 (15 × 15)	Pupils will have considered written methods for working with numbers in KS2. After a brief recap of methods, pupils should concentrate on the MR and PS questions in Exercise 5D and Exercise 5E of lessons 5.4 and 5.5.
	5.2 Rounding	1	• To round numbers to the nearest whole number, 10, 100 or 1000	
	5.3 Order of operations	1	• To use the conventions of BIDMAS to carry out calculations	
	5.4 Long and short multiplication	1	• To choose a written method for multiplying two numbers together • To use written methods to carry out multiplications accurately	
	5.5 Long and short division	1	• To choose a written method for dividing one number by another • To use written methods to carry out divisions accurately	
	5.6 Calculations with measurements	1	• To convert between common metric units • To use measurements in calculations • To recognise and use appropriate metric units	

	Problem solving – What is your carbon footprint?	1			This activity is designed to use the skills covered in this and earlier 'number' chapters to give a real-life context to mathematics.
6 Statistics	6.1 Mode, median and range	1	• To understand the meaning of mode, median and range	If your pupils are confident with measures of central tendency and range (covered in KS2), you could leave out Lesson 6.1. Provide a brief recap and move on to the later lessons where you will need to encourage pupils to interrogate data and make choices and decisions about the statistical measures they use.
	6.2 Reading data from tables and charts		• To read data from tables and charts	
	6.3 Statistical diagrams		• To be able to read and interpret different statistical diagrams	
	6.4 Collecting and using data	1	• To create and use a tally chart	
	6.5 Grouped frequency	1	• To understand and use grouped frequencies	
	6.6 Data collection	1	• To develop greater understanding of data collection	
	Challenge – Trains in Europe	1			This activity is designed to use both the mathematical reasoning and problem solving outcomes covered in this chapter se in a situation that is familiar to pupils. This activity encourages pupils to think about statistics in train travel – a form of travel with which many pupils may be familiar Ask pupils to summarise what they have learnt in the chapter, as they will use much of this material to complete the activity.
Chapter 4–6 assessment on Collins Connect					
7 Using algebra	7.1 Expressions and substitution	1	• To use algebra to write simple expressions • To substitute numbers into expressions to work out their value	More able pupils could skip every other question in the Pupil Book exercises of this chapter if they grasp the material quickly. However, it would be unwise to miss large chunks, as much of this material will be unfamiliar to the majority of pupils.
	7.2 Simplifying expressions	1	• To learn the rules for simplifying expressions	
	7.3 Using formulae	1	• To use formulae	
	7.4 Writing formulae	1	• To write formulae	

	Problem solving – Winter sports	1		A common response to algebra is to ask how it can be used. This activity provides one of the everyday uses of algebra in terms of using a formula to work out costs.
8 Fractions	8.1 Equivalent fractions	1	• To find simple equivalent fractions • To write fractions in their simplest form	By the end of KS2, pupils will have compared and ordered fractions and identified simple equivalent fractions. If they can demonstrate confidence and fluency with the KS2 content they could move straight to applying their understanding to the problem solving and mathematical reasoning questions in each exercise in the Pupil Book of this chapter. Check pupils' understanding by using one or two simple examples and/or the probing questions.
	8.2 Comparing fractions	1	• To compare and order two fractions	
	8.3 Add and subtracting fractions	1	• To add and subtract fractions with the same denominator • To add and subtract fractions with different denominators	
	8.4 Mixed numbers and improper fractions	1	• To convert mixed numbers to improper fractions • To convert improper fractions to mixed numbers	
	8.5 Calculations with mixed numbers		• To add and subtract simple mixed numbers with the same denominator • To add and subtract simple mixed numbers with different denominators	More able pupils could leave out Exercise 8A and Exercise 8B and move on to Exercise 8C.
	Challenge – Fractional dissection	1		This activity explores partitioning in a familiar context, which is an important concept in understanding fractions. The tasks involve splitting a shape into unequal parts, which will help pupils' understanding of the part–whole relationship between the numerator and denominator in fractions.
Chapter 7–9 assessment on Collins Connect				
Holidays				
Half-term / Term 3				
9 Angles	9.1 Using the compass to give directions	1	• To use a compass to give directions	Pupils following a two-year scheme of work will most likely be proficient

	9.2 Measuring angles	1	• To know the different types of angles • To use a protractor to measure an angle	at using a compass. If this is the case, then leave out Lesson 9.1 and start with Lesson 9.2.
	9.3 Drawing angles	1	• To use a protractor to draw an angle	
	9.4 Calculating angles	1	• To calculate angles at a point • To calculate angles on a line • To calculate opposite angles	
	9.5 Properties of triangles and quadrilaterals	1	• To understand the properties of parallel, intersecting and perpendicular lines • To understand and use the properties of triangles • To understand and use the properties of quadrilaterals	
	Investigation – Snooker tables	1		This activity encourages pupils to think about how angles can affect a possibly familiar real-life situation – the way one plays the game of snooker. Pupils may find it interesting to see how much mathematical calculation is involved in playing a good game.
10 Coordinates and graphs	10.1 Coordinates and graphs	1	• To understand and use coordinates to locate points	If your class is confident at working with coordinates, they could move straight on to questions 7 and 8 and the investigation at the end of Exercise 10A in the Pupil Book, which is intended to be used as consolidating work from KS2.
	10.2 From mappings to graphs	1	• To work out coordinates from a rule • To draw a graph for a simple rule	
	10.3 Naming graphs	1	• To recognise and draw line graphs with fixed values	
	10.6 Graphs form the real world	1	• To learn how graphs can be used to represent real-life situations • To draw and use real-life graphs	
	Challenge – Global warming	2		This activity is designed to apply pupils learning in a real-life topical situation.

11 Percentages	11.1 Fractions and percentages	2	• To understand what a percentage is • To understand the equivalence between some simple fractions and percentages	Work through some of the examples in in the first three lessons as a class. Then work on the investigations or challenge questions at the end of each exercise, either as a class or pupils could work independently. Then move straight on to Lesson 11.4.
	11.2 Fractions of a quantity		• To find a fraction of a quantity	
	11.3 Percentages of a quantity		• To find a percentage of a quantity	
	11.4 Percentages with a calculator		• To write a percentage as a decimal • To use a calculator to find a percentage of a quantity	
	11.5 Percentage increases and decreases		• To work out the result of a simple percentage change	
	Financial skills – Income tax	2		This activity is designed to use both the mathematical and transferable process skills covered in this chapter in a very important real-life context that may be completely unfamiliar to pupils.
12 Probability	12.1 Probability words	1	• To learn and use words about probability	You could briefly recap probability scales and equally likely outcomes using some of the examples in the Pupil Book if necessary. Check pupils' understanding using some of the probing questions. Provided pupils seem confident they could then move straight on to Lesson 12.3 on experimental probability.
	12.2 Probability scales		• To learn about and use probability scales from 0 to 1 • To work out probabilities based on equally likely outcomes	
	12.3 Experimental probability		• To learn about and understand experimental probability • To understand the difference between theoretical probability and experimental probability	
	Financial skills – School Easter Fayre	1		This activity combines pupils' understanding of experimental and theoretical probability and applies it in a real life context.
Chapter 10–12 assessment on Collins Connect				
Half-term				

13 Symmetry	13.1 Line symmetry	1	• To recognise shapes that have reflective symmetry • To draw lines of symmetry on a shape	Many concepts in this chapter will be familiar to pupils from KS2. If pupils can demonstrate confidence with these basic concepts they can focus on working through the exercises and doing the activities after each exercise. Encourage pupils to explore the suggested links to real-life contexts.
	13.2 Rotational symmetry	1	• To recognise shapes that have rotational symmetry • To find the order of rotational symmetry for a shape	
	13.3 Reflections	1	• To understand how to reflect a shape • To use a coordinate grid to reflect shapes	
	13. 4 Tessellations	1	• To understand how to tessellate shapes	
	Activity – Landmark spotting	1		This activity is designed to show pupils some of the aspects of symmetry used in the real world, by examining the line symmetry of six famous landmarks
14 Equations	14.1 Finding unknown numbers	1	• To find missing numbers in simple calculations	Recap 'Finding unknown numbers' in Lesson 14.1 and run through 'Solving equations' in Lesson 14.2, before moving on to Lesson 14.3 and Lesson 14.4.
	14.2 Solving equations		• To understand what an equation is • To solve equations involving one operation	
	14.3 Solving more complex equations		• To solve equations involving two operations	
	14.4 Setting up and solving equations	1	• To use algebra to set up and solve equations	
	Challenge – Number puzzles	1		In this activity pupils apply what they know to an abstract number problem. They need to identify and solve multi-step linear equations to solve the problem.
15 Interpreting data	15.1 Pie charts	1	• To read data from pie charts, where the data is given in simple sectors	You could leave out Lesson 15.1 on pie charts. During Lesson 15.2

	15.2 Comparing data by median and range		• To use the median and range to compare data • To make sensible decisions by comparing the median and range of two sets of data	During Lesson 15.2, comparing data by median and range, you could focus on the activity at the end of Exercise 15B in the Pupil Book.
	15.3 Statistical surveys	1	• To use charts and diagrams to interpret data	Then move straight on to the application of skills to do with statistical surveys in Lesson 15.3.
	Challenge – Dancing competition	1		This activity is designed to use both the interpretation and communication skills covered in this chapter
Chapter 13–15 assessment on Collins Connect				
16 3D shapes	16.1 3D shapes and nets	1	• To know how to count the faces, vertices and edges on a 3D shape' • To draw nets for 3D shapes	Use discussion to check recall of terminology then focus on the MR and PS questions in the exercises in each lesson, and on the challenge and practical activities at the end of Exercise 16A and Exercise 16B in the Pupil Book.
	16.2 Using nets to construct 3D shapes		• To construct 3D shapes from nets	
	16.3 3D investigations	1	• To work out the rule connecting faces, edges and vertices of 3D shapes • To solve problems involving 3D shapes	
	Problem solving – Delivering packages	1		This is a common type of problem used at GCSE so it is important that pupils can identify this type of problem.
Holidays				
Half-term / Term 5				
17 Ratio	17.1 Introduction to ratios	1	• To introduce ratio notation • To use ratios to compare quantities	Pupils will have worked with ratio in KS2, when comparing quantities and in problems involving unequal sharing. Pupils may have been introduced to the $a : b$ notation. If pupils can show understanding by answering one or more
	17.2 Simplifying ratios		• To write a ratio as simply as possible	
	17.3 Ratios and sharing	1	• To use ratios to find missing quantities	

| | 17.4 Ratios and fractions | 1 | • To understand the connection between fractions and ratios | of the later questions in Exercise 17A of the Pupil Book, they can move on to simplifying ratios in Exercise 17B.

Similarly, if pupils are confident about simple sharing problems, as provided in Exercise 17C, then they can move on to concentrate on the mixed questions in Exercise 17D. |
| | Problem solving – Smoothie bar | 1 | | This problem-solving activity is designed to reinforce the use of ratios by putting ratios in a realistic context. |

Chapter 16–17 assessment on Collins Connect
Work continues with Pupil Book 2.2

Half-term

Half-term / Term 6
Work continues with Pupil Book 2.2